Private Collections: A Culinary Treasure

Private Collections:
A Culinary Treasure

Edited by Janet E. C. Wurtzburger
in collaboration with Mac K. Griswold

THE WOMEN'S COMMITTEE OF
THE WALTERS ART GALLERY

Frontispiece: Pu-tai Ho-shang in an ormolu bower, festooned with flowers of Vincennes porcelain. The Chinese *blanc-de-chine* figure was thus lavishly mounted to satisfy the French passion for Chinoiserie in the mid-18th century. The gilt-bronze (ormolu) mounts of the figure bear the tax mark of the crowned "C" used between 1745 and 1749. The entire group was probably assembled under the direction of one of the *marchands-merciers,* perhaps Lazare-Duvaux who had a strong impact on the taste of Paris.

First printing, October 1973
Second printing, March 1974
Third printing, November 1974
Fourth printing, August 1976
Fifth printing, August 1979
Sixth printing, June 1982

Copyright © 1973 by The Walters Art Gallery, Baltimore, Maryland
Library of Congress Catalog Card Number: 73-85611
Designed by Klaus Gemming, New Haven, Connecticut
Composed by P&M Typesetting, Inc., Waterbury, Connecticut
Printed by The Meriden Gravure Company, Meriden, Connecticut
Bound by A. Horowitz & Son, Clifton, New Jersey

CONTENTS

List of Illustrations 7

Introduction by James Beard 9

Preface by Richard H. Randall, Jr. 11

Foreword by J.E.C.W. 13

Appetizers & First Courses 15

Soups 35

Meat 48

Poultry 79

Fish 99

Eggs & Cheese 127

Vegetables 135

Rice, Pasta & Beans 154

Salads 164

Desserts 169

Breads 213

Cookies 224

A Note on Wine by Philip M. Wagner 232

Menus 234

Index 240

An English centerpiece or ornament made as a pot-pourri jar in the form of a dovecote. Derby porcelain, about 1760.

ILLUSTRATIONS

- 2 Frontispiece: Pu-tai Ho-shang, Chinese porcelain, French mount, mid-18th century
- 6 Pot-pourri Jar, English (Derby), ca. 1760
- 12 Diana on a Stag, German (Augsburg), ca. 1610
- 19 *Still Life* by Léon Bonvin (French, 1834–1866)
- 29 *Politics in the Oysterhouse,* by Richard Caton Woodville (American, 1825–1855)
- 33 Cup of Augustus the Strong, German (Dresden), ca. 1720
- 38 "In the Kitchen" from *The Art of Cookery,* London, 1747
- 43 "Pot Luck," woodcut from *Tacuini Sanitatis,* Strassburg, 1531
- 47 Rhyton, Sasanian, 6th century A.D.
- 51 Knife and Fork, German, 18th century
- 58 *Preparing the Evening Meal,* by A. J. Miller (American, 1810–1874)
- 62 *The Fruits of the Earth,* by Francesco Bassano (Italian, 1549–1592)
- 67 Sauceboat, English (Worcester), 18th century
- 75 The Prodigal Son (detail of a tapestry), Flemish, about 1500
- 78 Wine Strainer, Roman, 1st century A.D.
- 83 Aquamanile, German, early 15th century
- 94 Serving Implements, German, 16th century
- 97 Ivory Mirror Case, French, 14th century
- 117 Pottery Dish, Greek, 4th century B.C.
- 121 Madonna and Child, by Giorgio Schiavone (Italian, ca. 1436–1504)
- 126 A Toast, illustration by Grandville (French, 1803–1847)
- 140 Wall Painting, Egyptian, Middle Kingdom

150 Manhattan—1609, drawing by William H. Drake for *Knickerbocker's History of New York*, 1886
153 Traveling Case, French, 18th century
156 Clay Jug, Roman, 1st century A.D.
162 *Kovsh*, Russian, 18th century
167 Mortar and Pestle, German, 17th century
168 Still-life detail, Dutch, 17th century
173 Faience Dish, French, ca. 1570–80
186 "A Feast for a King," from the *Schatzbehalter*, Nuremberg, 1491
192 Chocolate Cup and Saucer, French (Vincennes), 18th century
201 Dessert Pots, French (Sceaux-Penthièvre), 18th century
203 Stained-glass Roundel, English, 15th century
206 Marginal Figure from a Gospels, Armenian, 1455
226 "V'la l'coco," by Gavarni (French, 1804–1866)
231 Chocolate Pot, French, 18th century
233 Bride's Cup, German (Munich), ca. 1640
237 "Ordre et Marche du Cortège," illustration by Grandville (French, 1803–1847)
238 Drollery, pen drawing from a Psalter, English, 14th century, Ms. 79

Calligraphic designs, engravings from a writing book printed in Lisbon in 1719: 1,239

Metalcuts from a Book of Hours printed by Pigouchet in Paris in 1498: 5, 98

Woodcuts from *Hortus Sanitatis*, printed at Mainz by Jacob Meydenbach, 1451: 26, 49, 64, 77, 107, 113, 130, 133, 134, 149, 163, 182, 209, 218, 222

INTRODUCTION

There are three reasons I am very pleased to do an introduction to the Walters Art Gallery cookbook, *Private Collections* — and all of them are of great importance to me.

First of all, the Walters Art Gallery has had a long history of interest in food. It has sponsored a series of benefit demonstrations over the years that brought such famous names as Michael Field, Muriel Downes, Philip Brown, Malvina Kinard and others, including myself, to help raise funds for the Gallery. I look back with great nostalgia to the various and sundry happenings on those occasions when it was my privilege to do demonstrations. One was impressed with the zest people had for both the fund raising and the Gallery itself and to see people pay $1.00 a bite for the dishes we had prepared, enjoying it with great alacrity and fine appetite on a warm feeling. They were delightful days.

Secondly, I have always had a burning curiosity about Americana as related to American cooking — which means to me books published by charitable organizations, galleries, ladies' aid societies, sisterhoods, schools and other organizations over a period of more than a century. Some of them indeed are collectors' items. The Webfoot Cookbook which was published in 1883 by the Ladies' Circle of the First Presbyterian Church in Portland, Oregon brings a price of $100.00 if one can be found. Such books are the history of American regional food. I feel certain this volume will be a shining star in the galaxy of Americana. It represents the best food in its community. It has been carefully edited, carefully tested and had loving care. It comes forth as a most important and gracious example of fine American cookery from one of our richest food regions.

Thirdly, I am happy to be a part of this project because it was created and produced by someone I feel is highly qualified to bring such a book to completion and whose love for this project and for good cooking is intense. Janet Wurtzburger's vision and her untiring toil, together with the Women's Committee, to bring this collection of delectables to fruition is labor in a great cause. I am sure collectors in 2073 will be seeking out *Private Collections* and will be grateful, as I am, to Janet Wurtzburger for having made her dream a reality.

James A. Beard

PREFACE

The treasure house of the Walters Art Gallery was a princely gift to the citizens of Baltimore by Henry Walters in 1931. It contains a range of material from ancient Egypt to royal Easter eggs made by Fabergé for the Russian Czars, and illustrates the entire history of world art—East and West.

To say what is famous in the collection, or in any museum, is subject to change at the next moment with the tastes of men. There was a day when "The Attack at Dawn" by de Neuville and Gérôme's "Duel After the Masquerade" were the most famous works in the Walters. Today one is more likely to think of Manet's "At the Café." There are the porcelains of China for certain tastes and their cousins from Sèvres for others. One could argue if Pontormo's portrait of Maria Salviati and Cosimo de' Medici was more impressive than Hugo van der Goes' "Donor in Prayer", and in another mind both paintings might be surpassed by the statue of the Besançon Madonna or the stained-glass windows of Saint-Germain-des-Prés.

The appeal of works of art depends on time, light, mood, and company—just like the selection of a good recipe.

Richard H. Randall, Jr., Director

A wine-pitcher automaton with Diana and cupid riding on a stag. The base contains a clockwork mechanism to propel the wine from guest to guest. It was fashioned of silver with gilt details by Jacob Miller of Augsburg, about 1610.

FOREWORD

Eleven years ago when the Walters Art Gallery decided to form a Women's Committee it seemed a delightful and unexpected idea to broaden the Gallery's scope by offering a new twist—classes in the art of cooking. Naturally, these were not to be of the thick-white-sauce variety.

With never a second thought this institution, which had long welcomed scholars from here and abroad to study its vast collections, enticed a new group of students—this time by presenting the finest available authors and teachers of *haute cuisine* from James Beard in America to Muriel Downes in England. Once a year, for the better part of a week, talk of food swirls around the Gallery like butter in a pan; every member of the staff can discuss the relative merits of a *beurre manié* and egg yolks as thickeners for a sauce.

The logical next step in this course of events was to offer a cookbook—one which would reflect the maturing knowledge and interest in the culinary arts of the Walters' friends. A postal card was sent to all the Members of the Gallery asking them to share their most cherished recipes for a book to be named *Private Collections*. In response more than a thousand recipes poured in, reflecting a variety of life styles: the grand manner for which Old Baltimore is famous, and the simple, do-it-yourself manner of the present. Some of the best of these recipes have been omitted, but only due to lack of space or their similarity to others.

By larding this book with pictures from the rich fare of the Walters collection it is hoped that it will portray handsomely the enduring interest in the art of cooking throughout the ages and that *Private Collections* can take its place among the other volumes for which The Walters Art Gallery is so justly famous.

The Trustees and the Women's Committee wish to thank the contributors for their generous response and especially that small group of dedicated friends who helped with the research and testing of these interesting recipes.

J. E. C. W.

APPETIZERS & FIRST COURSES

Almonds, Glazed and Salted

300°

2 pounds almonds, blanched
1 egg white
Coarse salt

With your fingers, coat the almonds with the unbeaten egg white, being sure only that they are sticky but not too wet. Immediately roll them in coarse salt (Kosher salt does well for this) and put them on a lightly buttered baking sheet to bake until just brown enough to please you.

Mrs. Lawrence Bachman

Pickled Antipasto

24 servings

1-1/2 cups catsup
1-1/2 cups chili sauce
1-1/2 cups water
3/4 cup olive oil
3/4 cup tarragon vinegar
3/4 cup lemon juice
3 cloves garlic, mashed
3 tablespoons brown sugar
1-1/2 tablespoons Worcestershire sauce
1-1/2 tablespoons horseradish
1 teaspoon salt
Dash of cayenne
1 head cauliflower, cut in flowerets
1 pound small white onions, peeled
6 medium carrots, peeled and cut in quarters
4 stalks celery, sliced diagonally in 2-to-3-inch pieces
2 large cans whole string beans
2 pounds small mushrooms
3 packages frozen artichoke hearts, thawed
2 jars pepperoncini, drained
3 cans flat anchovy fillets
3 cups stuffed green olives
1 bunch parsley, chopped

Combine in a large saucepan the catsup, chili sauce, water, oil, vinegar, and lemon juice. Season with garlic, brown sugar, Worcestershire sauce, horseradish, salt, and cayenne. Bring the mixture to a boil and simmer for 5 minutes. Add to the sauce the cauliflowerets, onions, carrots, celery; simmer 5 minutes; add the beans, mushrooms, artichokes, and pepperoncini and simmer for another 5 minutes. The vegetables should be crisp and barely cooked. Remove the mixture from the heat; add the anchovies, olives, and chopped parsley. Refrigerate for 24 to 48 hours. Serve in a large glass bowl; eat with toothpicks.

Miss Rita St. Clair

Little Drums of Chicken Wings

350°

8 chicken wings
1 egg
1/4 cup milk
Salt and pepper
1 cup Italian flavored bread crumbs
1/2 cup flour
1 teaspoon barbecue spice
1/2 teaspoon pepper

Separate the large "drums" from the tip and center of the wings. (The spare parts may be used for chicken broth.) Beat the egg with the milk, add salt and pepper to taste. Mix the dry ingredients in a shallow dish. Dip the chicken pieces first in the egg mixture and then in the crumbs. Arrange them in a baking dish and bake until golden brown. Serve with cocktails.
Mrs. Calvin Eldred Young

Dilled Green Beans

Makes 4 pints

2 pounds small tender green beans
1 teaspoon red pepper
4 cloves garlic
3 large heads dill
2 cups water
1/4 cup salt
1 pint vinegar

Stem the green beans and pack them uniformly in 4 hot sterilized pint jars. To each pint add 1/4 teaspoon red pepper, 1 clove garlic, and 1/2 – 3/4 head of dill. Heat together the water, salt, and vinegar. Bring to a boil. Pour over the beans. Seal at once.

Chill thoroughly and serve in a bowl for a supper relish or as an hors d'oeuvre.
Mrs. A. Stanley Brager, Jr.

Almond Chutney Spread

2 tablespoons butter
1 cup chopped almonds
Tabasco sauce
3 tablespoons Major Grey's chutney, chopped

Melt the butter in a frying pan over low heat and slowly brown the chopped almonds. Add 2 or 3 drops of Tabasco sauce to the chopped chutney and mix thoroughly with the nuts. Serve the spread on slices of melba toast made from icebox rye bread.
Frank D'Amanda

Guacamole Avocado Dip

2 ripe avocados
2 hard-cooked eggs
3 small peeled tomatoes
6 stuffed olives
1 small onion
Tart French dressing
Chili pepper or chili powder

Put the avocados, eggs, tomatoes, olives, and onion in the jar of a blender, thinning them with a tart French dressing. Season with fresh chili pepper or, failing that, chili powder. Add salt to taste.

This is preferably made soon before serving. If Guacamole must be made in advance, cover it closely with a plastic wrap to prevent darkening.
Mrs. Henry T. Rowell

Brussels Sprouts

Brussels sprouts
Roquefort cheese
Cream cheese

Parboil Brussels sprouts only until tender-crisp. Cool quickly in ice water. Drain and stuff with a mixture of Roquefort and cream cheese to use with cocktails.
Mrs. Robert A. Milch

Marinated Vegetables

A SIMPLER VERSION OF
PICKLED ANTIPASTO

12 small white onions, peeled
1 small cauliflower in flowerets
1 pound small mushrooms
2 green peppers in 1/2-inch strips
18 black olives
1 cup olive oil
1-1/2 cups wine vinegar
2 teaspoons salt
3/4 teaspoon freshly ground pepper
4 tablespoons sugar
1 clove garlic, minced

Toss together the vegetables and olives. Bring the oil, vinegar, and seasoning to a boil, then cool and pour over the vegetables. Marinate in the refrigerator overnight. Drain well and serve with cocktails or as a first course with toast fingers.

Mrs. Morton Baum

Chicken Bits for Cocktails

3 whole boned chicken breasts, cut in bite-size pieces
1/2 teaspoon salt
1/8 teaspoon pepper
1/2 teaspoon granulated sugar
1/2 teaspoon ground rosemary
1/4 teaspoon ground ginger
2 tablespoons olive oil
1 tablespoon soy sauce
Butter

Mix the salt, pepper, sugar, rosemary, ginger, olive oil, and soy sauce in a bowl. Stir in the chicken bits so that they are all covered with the marinade. Cover with a piece of aluminum foil and leave in the refrigerator overnight. Drain the bits, fry them in butter and serve hot as an appetizer.

Frank D'Amanda

Eggplant Caponata

2 pounds eggplant
1/2 cup olive oil
3 large green peppers, seeded and chopped
3 onions, chopped
2 cups pitted green olives
3 large tomatoes, peeled, seeded, and coarsely chopped
2 tablespoons sugar
1/4 cup water
1/2 cup vinegar
Sour cream
Lemon slices
Toast

Cut the unpeeled eggplant into small cubes. Sauté it in the olive oil over high heat for about 15 minutes, turning it often. Add the green peppers, the onions, and the olives. Reduce heat and cook the mixture for 10 minutes. Near the end of the time add the tomatoes. Stir the sugar into the water, add the vinegar, and pour it all into the eggplant mixture. Taste for seasoning and chill well before serving.

As an hors d'oeuvre serve it with sour cream, sliced lemon, and Melba toast. It may also be used as a relish for cold sliced meat.

Mrs. S. Page Nelson, Jr.

Baked Cheese Balls

400°

5-ounce jar of any soft cheese spread or grated cheese
3 tablespoons butter
3/4 cup flour
1/2 teaspoon salt
1/4 teaspoon paprika

Cream all the ingredients together and refrigerate for several hours or overnight. Form into balls and bake for 10 minutes.

Mrs. Mary F. Barada

Cheese Bouchées

425° / 40 appetizers

1 package (3 ounces) cream cheese
1/4 pound sharp Cheddar cheese
4 tablespoons butter
1/2 teaspoon prepared yellow mustard
1/2 teaspoon Worcestershire sauce
Shake of cayenne pepper
2 egg whites, stiffly beaten
10 slices of white bread

In a heavy pan over very low heat, combine the cream cheese, Cheddar, and butter; melt and stir until smooth. Add the mustard, Worcestershire sauce, and cayenne pepper. Cool slightly. Fold in the egg whites. Remove the crusts from the bread and cut each slice into 4 squares. With a spoon or 2 forks dip the bread into the cheese mixture; cover all sides. Place on a buttered cookie sheet. Set low under broiler (or in a 425° oven) until puffy.
Mrs. David Watson, Mrs. Arthur Wilkoff

Crab Dip

3 large packages (8 ounces) cream cheese
1 pound fresh crab meat or 2 cans crab meat
1/2 cup mayonnaise
2 tablespoons prepared mustard
1 tablespoon powdered sugar
1 teaspoon onion juice
Salt and pepper to taste
1/2 cup sherry

Combine all the ingredients but the sherry in the top of a double boiler and heat until creamy. Add sherry to taste; half a cup is not too much, depending on whether it is to be served from a chafing dish or as a dip, when the mixture should be slightly thicker.
Mrs. Robert Berney,
Mrs. Frances Gorman,
Mrs. Curran W. Harvey

Deep-Fried Cheese Balls

3 egg whites
2 cups grated sharp cheese
Salt
Red pepper
Cracker crumbs
Deep fat for frying

Beat the egg whites stiffly. Add the grated sharp cheese and blend until smooth, then add salt and red pepper to taste. Make into small bite-size balls, roll in freshly rolled fine cracker crumbs, and fry in deep fat until brown. Serve hot.
Mrs. Keith McBee

Crab Lorenzo

50 pieces

4 egg yolks
1/2 cup lemon juice
1/4 teaspoon white pepper
1/2 teaspoon salt
1 cup melted butter
1 pound crab meat
1/3 cup chopped mushrooms
1 jigger sherry
3 teaspoons chopped green onions
50 small squares of toasted buttered bread
Parmesan cheese
Paprika

Make a hollandaise of the beaten egg yolks, lemon juice, pepper, salt, and melted butter. When it is thick, remove it from the fire before adding the crab meat, mushrooms, sherry, and onion. Put a teaspoon of this mixture on the buttered toast squares, sprinkle with Parmesan cheese and a dash of paprika. Heat in the broiler until well browned.
Mrs. Marvin B. Perry

Still life of cruets and vegetables, painted in watercolor by Léon Bonvin in 1863. Bonvin was a favorite of William Walters, who bought still-life paintings which were usually flower subjects.

Curried Clam Dip

4 tablespoons butter
1 teaspoon curry or more, to taste
1/2 clove garlic, crushed
4 tablespoons flour
2 cans (7-1/2 ounces) minced clams

Melt the butter and add the curry powder and garlic. Stir in the flour and add the juice from the drained clams and some bottled clam juice if a runnier dip is wanted. Cook this until it is thick and smooth, then add the drained clams. Serve warm with potato chips or crackers.

Mrs. Curran Harvey

Hot Canapé Rolls

400°

2 loaves thinly sliced bread
1 pound fresh crab meat, chicken, or tuna
1/4 cup mayonnaise
1/2 cup finely chopped onion (optional)
1 teaspoon Worcestershire sauce
1 pound cream cheese
1/4 pound butter, melted

Trim the crusts from the bread slices and roll each slice with a rolling pin until it is as flat as a wafer. Mix all the ingredients but the butter to make a well seasoned salad. Spread the flattened bread with the mixture, roll the top third onto the lower third and secure with toothpicks. (If the crab meat, chicken, or tuna are minced, you will have no trouble in rolling the bread.) Saturate each roll with the melted butter, dust some curry powder on a few of them and cut the rolls into three before either freezing them or browning them for ten minutes in a hot oven.

Mrs. Charles Liddle, Miss Ruth Fitzell

Hummus

1 cup cooked chick peas
Juice of 1 or more lemons
2 crushed garlic cloves
Salt and pepper to taste
1/2 cup sesame tahini
1/2 cup sesame, safflower, or olive oil

Put all the ingredients in the blender beginning with about 1/4 cup of the oil. Blend at high speed and then slowly add more oil until the purée is barely thick enough to hold its shape. Serve liberally covered with chopped parsley. More lemon juice and salt may be needed. The result should be a spicy mixture which can be used as a cocktail dip.

The sesame tahini is available in health food stores. Hummus is an Arab dish served with Arab or Syrian bread.

Mrs. Richard Jackson

Knockwurst in Chafing Dish

4 knockwurst
2 full teaspoons brown sugar
1/2 teaspoon freshly ground pepper
1/2 teaspoon oregano
1/4 teaspoon dry mustard
1 4 cup chili sauce
1/4 teaspoon salt
2 teaspoons soy sauce
1/2 teaspoon rosemary
1/8 cup catsup

Heat knockwurst; skin and then slice. Mix all the other ingredients together, heat over low flame, add knockwurst rounds, and stir until well coated. Serve in a chafing dish with toothpicks.

Mrs. Alfred Himmelrich,
Mrs. Louis Kramer

Mushroom Caviar

1/2 medium onion, minced
1 tablespoon butter
1/4 pound fresh mushrooms, chopped fine
1 tablespoon lemon juice
1/2 teaspoon Worcestershire sauce
Mayonnaise (enough to bind mixture)
Salt and fresh ground pepper

Sauté the onion in butter until golden. Add the mushrooms and sauté for 5 minutes, stirring lightly to mix well. Add lemon juice and Worcestershire sauce, mix again, and remove from the stove. Cool. Add enough mayonnaise to bind and then mound on a serving plate. Chill well and serve with Melba toast or any bland cracker. This keeps well in the refrigerator.
Mrs. Thomas Wright

Cheese-Stuffed Mushrooms

400°

36 large mushrooms
1 onion
Butter
Salt
Pepper
1 cup grated sharp cheese

Clean and separate caps from stems, chop the stems. Sauté onion, finely chopped, in butter until tender. Add the stems and sauté for 2 minutes. Add salt and pepper to taste. Stir in grated cheese and remove from the heat. Sauté the caps briefly in additional butter and stuff with the stem mixture. Top with grated cheese and bake for 10 minutes.
Mrs. F. Barton Harvey, Jr.

Raw Filled Mushrooms

3 dozen fresh medium-sized mushrooms
Juice of 1/4 lemon
1/2 teaspoon salt
1/2 teaspoon Accent
1/4 teaspoon Beau Monde seasoning
1 teaspoon Worcestershire sauce
1 tablespoon homemade mayonnaise
1/4 teaspoon celery salt

Wipe the mushrooms and stems well, but do not wash them. Remove the stems by pulling them out, and with the addition of 3 to 4 whole mushroons chop the stems finely with a sharp knife. Mix the chopped stems with all the ingredients listed and fill the mushrooms with this. Chill and serve as an hors d'oeuvre.
Mrs. Stanford Z. Rothschild

Stuffed Mushrooms

350° / 3 servings

12 mushrooms about the size of a half dollar
Salt and pepper
A little minced garlic
Chopped almonds
Bread crumbs, freshly made
8 teaspoons olive oil

Remove the stems from mushrooms and place the caps, hollow side up, in a shallow pan. Sprinkle with salt, pepper, and a bit of garlic; fill about 1/3 full with chopped almonds and fill the remaining 2/3 with bread crumbs. Make a slight depression in the crumbs (so oil won't run out) and carefully put in 2/3 teaspoon oil. Bake for 10 minutes, then brown lightly under a broiler.
Frank D'Amanda

Marinated Olives

1 jar (9 ounces) large green olives
1/4 cup red wine vinegar
1/4 cup salad oil
1/4 teaspoon crushed red pepper
1 clove garlic, minced
1/4 cup chopped onion
1 teaspoon oregano

Turn olives and liquid into a quart jar with a tight-fitting lid. Add the rest of the ingredients. Shake well and vigorously, every so often. Refrigerate for several days or weeks.

Mrs. Curtan W. Harvey

Angels on Horseback, English Style

375°

24 shucked oysters
12 slices of bacon, cut in half
Freshly ground black pepper

Sprinkle the oysters with pepper. Wrap a half slice of bacon around each and fasten with a toothpick. Arrange on a rack in a pan and bake for 10 minutes, or until bacon is browned and crisp. Serve hot for hors d'oeuvre. *Mrs. Charles T. Albert*

Chicken Liver Pâté

1 pound chicken livers
3 tablespoons minced shallots
4 tablespoons butter or more
1 tablespoon chopped parsley
1 teaspoon thyme
1 teaspoon sage (optional)
1/3 cup Madeira or Cognac or both
Salt
Pepper
Nutmeg
3/4 cup lightly whipped cream (optional)
Clarified butter

Cook the chicken livers and the shallots in the butter, using more butter if needed. Do not overcook the livers; they should remain pink. Add the parsley, thyme, and sage and cook just until the parsley has wilted. Flame with the Cognac or add the Madeira and deglaze the pan, or do both procedures in succession. Now, either chop the livers finely or put them into the blender, depending on your preference in texture. Add salt, pepper, and nutmeg, and if a very light pâté is wanted, fold in the whipped cream, though it can be omitted. Taste to be sure the pâté is not too bland; more wine can be added. Pack in crocks and put clarified butter on top.

Mrs. Robert D. Dripps, Mrs. Ronald Diana

Olive Cheese Puffs

400°

1/4 pound grated sharp cheese
1/4 pound soft butter
1/2 cup sifted flour
1/2 teaspoon paprika
1/4 teaspoon salt
24 medium stuffed olives

Mix the cheese and butter. Add all the other ingredients except the olives. Pat a teaspoon of dough securely around each olive. Place in a dish, cover completely, and refrigerate for 5 hours or overnight. Place the puffs on a cookie sheet, leaving space between them, and bake for 10 to 15 minutes, until golden brown. Serve warm.

Unbaked puffs will keep for 2 weeks in the refrigerator.

Mrs. Robert Berney, Mrs. Joseph D. Brown

Taramasalata or Pâté of Cod's Roe

1 jar (4 ounces) smoked cod's roe
1 cup fresh white bread crumbs
1 shallot, finely chopped
1/2 clove garlic, minced
Juice of 1 lemon
1/2 cup olive oil
Chopped parsley
Green or black olives
Hot toast fingers

This is traditionally made in a mortar, but anyone with a blender or even a mixer can save time and trouble with the same result.

Put the roe in a blender; add the bread crumbs which have been dipped in water and squeezed dry; add the shallot, a bit of garlic, and the lemon juice. Then, as in making mayonnaise, add the oil by degrees, mixing all the while. Serve in a salad bowl, liberally sprinkled with parsley, with the olives as garnish. Lemon slices may be added, too, and hot toast should be on hand to eat with it.

Mrs. John F. C. White

Pâté in Jelly

10 servings
This should be prepared a day ahead.

1-1/2 pounds smoked goose liver (or good liverwurst or Sell's Liver Paté)
1/2 pound cream cheese
1/2 cup Madeira
1 tablespoon brandy
1 envelope plain gelatin
1-1/2 cans (10-1/2 ounces) consommé

Work the liver and cream cheese into a smooth paste, adding half of the Madeira and all the brandy. Heat the consommé and dissolve the gelatin, which has been softened in the rest of the Madeira. Set the consommé to cool. Pour about 3/4 inch of consommé into a mold and place in ice-making unit of refrigerator. When the consommé has set, remove the mold from the refrigerator and with a knife, carefully place the pâté into the mold, leaving space between the pâté and the sides of the mold. Pour the rest of the consommé around and over the pâté and chill, but do not freeze. Unmold to serve.

Do not fail to butter the mold lightly but well, and be sure your goose liver is not of the salty variety. The quantity given above fits into a standard-size ice-cube tray.

Mrs. Charles Eisman, Mrs. Bradford Jacobs, Mrs. S. Page Nelson, Jr., Mrs. Frank Weller

An English Pâté

2 or 3 slices of sugar-cured bacon
1 clove garlic, finely chopped
A bit of brown sugar
1/4 pound chicken livers or duck or goose livers or any combination of good liver
Butter
Some red wine
Whole peppercorns
Bouquet of herbs—basil, thyme, bay leaves
1 whole onion
A small truffle with its juice, if available
2 ounces sweet butter
1/4 glass brandy, Grand Marnier, curaçao, or port
1 egg yolk and/or a bit of cream (optional)

This inexact recipe is easy to follow once one understands that it is a smooth pâté with bits of crisp bacon stirred through it. The flavor can vary with the extent of one's wine cellar; the onion and truffles are whims of the cook.

Cut the bacon in small bits with a floured kitchen scissor. Fry it until crisp and crackly with a finely chopped clove of garlic and a small amount of brown sugar. Set it aside to drain well.

In a covered pan, stew about 1/4 pound of livers, again the cook's choice, in butter and red wine, with a few peppercorns, the bouquet of herbs, the whole onion, and the truffle with its juice. Cook, covered, until the livers are well done, which should be in about 10 minutes. Remove the herbs and onion. Sieve or put through a food mill. Add about 2 ounces of sweet butter to arrive at the desired consistency, remembering that the butter will help keep the pâté firm. Add the bacon bits and the liquor. If a richer pâté is wanted, a beaten yolk of egg and/or a bit of cream will do it.

Mrs. Alan Campbell

Peanut Butter, Cocktail Style

1 Pullman loaf sliced bread
1 12-ounce jar creamy peanut butter
1/3 cup peanut oil
1 tablespoon sugar

Cut the crusts off the bread, then cut the bread in sticks, perhaps 4 to each slice. Put the sticks on a cookie sheet with the crusts of bread too, and dry them out in the oven set at a low temperature. Roll the crusts into crumbs.

In a skillet, (a teflon one if possible, for the ingredients may stick slightly), heat the peanut butter, oil, and sugar together. Then, using a fork, swirl the dry sticks of bread in the warm peanut butter until well coated on all sides. Roll them in the crumbs, set them on a cookie sheet, and allow them to dry out. These may be frozen.

Mrs. George F. Roll

Peperonata

4 to 6 servings
Olive oil
1/2 can Italian peeled tomatoes
6 green peppers
2 cups olive oil

Cover the bottom of a frying pan with a little olive oil. (The 2 cups are for the pepper frying). Add the tomatoes and cook down over a slow fire, stirring frequently, for at least 3-1/2 hours. The tomatoes should look dark red and glossy. Halve the peppers, remove the stalks and seeds, and slice in inch strips. Fry them in the 2 cups of oil until they are brownish and soft, turning occasionally. Remove from the oil and salt them generously. Combine the peppers and tomatoes and serve warm with Italian bread. This can be served with drinks or as a first course.

Frank D'Amanda

Russian Piroshki

MUSHROOM PASTIES

350°

Cream Cheese Pastry

1 cup butter
1 package (8 ounces) cream cheese
1/2 teaspoon salt
2 cups sifted all-purpose flour

Allow the butter and cream cheese to come to room temperature, add the salt and mix it thoroughly in a mixer. Work in the flour with your fingers, roll it into a ball, wrap in waxed paper, and chill overnight or at least several hours.

Mushroom Filling

1/2 pound fresh mushrooms
2 tablespoons butter
1/2 cup very finely chopped onion
1/2 teaspoon salt
Dash nutmeg
1 teaspoon lemon juice
2 teaspoons flour

1 cup sour cream
1 teaspoon dried dill

Trim the mushrooms, chop finely, heat the butter, and add both onion and mushrooms. Cook 4 minutes. Add the seasoning, the lemon juice, and the flour and mix together. Remove from the heat; add the sour cream and dill. Roll the pastry in 2 sections to keep it cool. Roll it out on a floured board, and cut it into 2-1/2-inch circles. Put a teaspoon of filling in the center of each. Fold over and seal the half circles with the tines of a fork. Chill or freeze. Bake for 25 minutes.

Mrs. Walter G. Lohr, John Pluckett

Spinach and Rice Hors d'Oeuvre

350°

1 package frozen chopped spinach
1/2 pound ricotta cheese
4 large eggs
3 cups cooked rice
1 cup Parmesan cheese, grated
Pepper
Olive oil
Dry, finely grated bread crumbs

Cook the spinach, drain well, and then squeeze out all the moisture again. Put the ricotta cheese through a ricer. Have ready 3 eggs beaten well. Combine in a large bowl the spinach, rice, ricotta, Parmesan cheese, seasoning, and beaten eggs.

Oil a 9-inch square pan, sprinkle with the crumbs, and shake them over the bottom and sides. Put the spinach mixture evenly into the pan, beat the fourth egg, and with a pastry brush coat the top of the food with the beaten egg. Bake until firm, about 30 minutes. Run a spatula around the edges to loosen it, cut into small squares.

This can be served warm and it can be frozen.

Mrs. Ernest Freudenheim

Ever-Ready Individual Pizzas

350° / 32 pizzas

16 English muffins
Butter
2 large onions
2-1/2 pounds ground chuck
Crushed red peppers
Garlic
Salt and pepper
Parmesan cheese

Split, toast, and butter the muffins. Sauté thinly diced onions with the ground chuck, then add the seasonings. Spoon the mixture onto the muffins. Cover generously with Parmesan cheese and bake to the desired degree of doneness. These can be frozen and heated from their frozen state.

Mrs. L. Wilson Davis

Potato-Skin Hors d'Oeuvre

450°

Cut baked-potato skins in strips, butter and salt them, and bake in a hot oven until crisp.

Use the potato insides for mashed potatoes or potato cakes.

Mrs. Peter Dane

Gravlaks

PICKLED SALMON

4 pounds fresh salmon, center cut
2 bunches fresh dill
1/2 cup salt
2 ounces sugar
1/4 teaspoon allspice
1 tablespoon vinegar

Bone the salmon and cut it into 2 fillets. Chop the dill and divide it into 2 equal parts. Put half of the dill into the bottom of an enamel or ovenware dish large enough to place the fillets side by side. With the skin side down, lay the salmon on top of the dill. Mix the salt, sugar, and allspice together and dust over the salmon. Sprinkle the vinegar and the remaining dill over this and cover with wax paper or plastic wrap. Press with a heavy weight and place in the refrigerator for 24 to 36 hours.

Drain the salmon, reserving the liquid. Transfer the salmon fillets to a board and with a very sharp knife slice them thinly at an angle. Serve the salmon with the following mustard sauce. (The salmon will keep refrigerated for 1 week.)

Mustard Sauce for Gravlaks

**3/4 cup mayonnaise
6 tablespoons Düsseldorf mustard
2 tablespoons salmon liquid
2 tablespoons chopped dill**

In a bowl, combine the mayonnaise, mustard, and reserved liquid from the salmon and beat the mixture thoroughly. Stir in the chopped dill and pour the sauce into a sauceboat.

Mrs. Stanford Z. Rothschild

Broiled Scallops

4 to 6 servings as an hors d'oeuvre

**1/2 pound breaded scallops
1/4 cup dry vermouth
1/4 cup olive oil
1/4 teaspoon finely chopped garlic
1/4 teaspoon salt
1 tablespoon minced parsley**

Marinate the scallops in a marinade made of the other ingredients for several hours. When ready to serve, place the scallops with the marinade in a shallow pan. Put under a pre-heated broiler 2 inches from the heat. Broil 5 to 6 minutes.

Frank D'Amanda

Artichoke First Courses

Artichoke bottoms make a tasty first course filled with one of the following fillings:

1. **Egg salad topped with caviar**
2. **Cold poached egg topped with caviar and tarragon-flavored homemade mayonnaise.**
3. **Cold puréed peas, broccoli, or spinach topped with hollandaise sauce**
4. **Crab, chicken, or shrimp salad topped with capers**
5. **Duxelles with sauce Béarnaise**
6. **Fresh lobster salad topped with homemade mayonnaise, sliced hard-boiled eggs, and watercress.**

Serve on a bed of Bibb lettuce. The most important ingredient is your own imagination. Use generously.

Mrs. Irwin Nudelman

Artichoke Hearts in Aspic

4 servings

12 canned artichoke hearts
4 hard-cooked eggs, riced and deviled
2 packages lemon gelatin
1-1/2 cups boiling water
1-1/2 cups cold water
1/2 teaspoon pepper
6 tablespoons vinegar
4 teaspoons grated onion
1 teaspoon salt

Use enough artichoke hearts to fill a 4-cup ring mold and enough riced deviled egg to stuff them. This is inexact for the size of the artichoke hearts differs. Rice the eggs, reserving 2 of the whites to be sliced as decoration. Mix the riced eggs with mayonnaise, vinegar, and seasoning to taste.

Make an aspic of the gelatin by dissolving it in the boiling water and then adding the cold water and other ingredients. Allow it to cool, then pour a little into the ring mold and let it set. Put the stuffed artichoke hearts upside down on this layer of aspic, using the sliced rings of the whites along the sides. Add a little more gelatin and when that has set, pour in the rest; chill until it too, has set and then unmold.

Lettuce is attractive served around the ring and a bowl of homemade mayonnaise should be in the center.
Miss Avonia Read

Avocado with Vermouth

Avocado
Vermouth
Crisp bacon

A Mexican first course of avocado cubes, tossed with vermouth and served in a footed glass. Crisp bacon is strewn on top at serving time.

Seviche in Avocados

5 to 6 servings

1 pound fresh white fish (flounder, sole, pompano, etc.)
3/4 cup lime juice
1 teaspoon salt
Pepper to taste
3 canned green chilies, chopped
2 tomatoes, skinned and chopped
1 large onion, chopped
2 tablespoons capers
4 tablespoons French olive oil
2 tablespoons dry white wine
2 teaspoons oregano
Cumin to taste
3-4 avocados

Slice the fish into 3/4-inch pieces, pour the lime juice over it; then mix all the other ingredients, except the avocados, and cover the fish with the mixture. Marinate at least overnight. Right before serving, slice the avocados in half, and put several tablespoons of the fish mixture into each avocado half.
Mrs. Jerrie Cherry

Broccoli or Cauliflower with Green Mayonnaise

3 servings

1-1/2 cups broccoli or cauliflower flowerets
1 whole egg
1 cup oil
1 tablespoon lemon juice or leftover wine
1/2 teaspoon sea salt
1/2 cup chopped spinach, sorrel, watercress, and scallions combined
Pinches of basil, chervil, tarragon, or parsley
Slivered almonds
Butter

Boil the cauliflower or broccoli for about 6 minutes, taking care to maintain their firmness. (This is easily accomplished by peeling and slitting the stems.) Refresh in cold water and drain.

Prepare a mayonnaise by putting the whole egg into the blender, and gradually adding, while the machine is going, the oil, then the salt, lemon juice, and dry mustard. Pack a cup half full with a mixture of the spinach, sorrel, watercress, and scallions in any proportion, add pinches of the herbs, and boil them uncovered in a little water only for 30 to 40 seconds. Drain them through a sieve, pressing out all the water. (A potato ricer is excellent for this feat.) Add the dried purée to the finished mayonnaise.

To serve the vegetable, pour this green mayonnaise over it, and garnish with slivered almonds which have been browned in burnt butter. This is a well-liked first course.

Mrs. Frank Griffith Dawson

Carrot Salad

4 servings

1 pound carrots, peeled and thinly sliced
2-3 cloves garlic, minced
1/3 cup vinegar
2/3 cup oil
Cumin
Chopped chili peppers (optional)
Chopped parsley
Coriander

Cover the carrots with water, add a few cloves of garlic, and boil them until they are tender, then drain. While they are still hot, season with the vinegar and oil. Add the powdered cumin and, if you wish, some chopped very hot peppers. Chill overnight. Serve with chopped parsley and a dash of coriander. Pass Melba toast with it as a first course.

Mrs. Douglas N. Sharretts

Carrot Pancakes

6 servings

Pancakes:

5 large carrots, peeled and grated
2 eggs
2 tablespoons flour
Salt and pepper
1/4 cup chopped nuts (optional)
2 tablespoons butter or cooking oil for frying

Mix all the ingredients but the butter or frying oil well. Heat the oil and fry the pancakes in small portions on both sides until brown. Drain if necessary on paper towels.

Sauce:

2 onions, sliced or chopped
2 ribs celery, finely chopped
1 green pepper, seeded and chopped
1-1/2 cups peeled, seeded, and chopped fresh tomatoes or drained canned tomatoes
1/4 cup tomato paste
1/4 cup brown sugar
Salt and pepper

Sauté the onions, celery, and green pepper in butter or oil until barely tender. Add the remaining ingredients and simmer for 10 minutes. Then simmer the pancakes in this, covered, for 10 minutes more. Serve this to carrot addicts as a first course. The pancakes and sauce can be made ahead of time and frozen separately.

Mrs. Frank T. Gray

Facing page: *Politics in the Oysterhouse* was painted by Richard Caton Woodville of Baltimore, in 1848. It is among his many genre scenes and was painted for the architect J. H. B. Latrobe.

Clams and Blini

8 servings

1/2 cup dry vermouth
1/2 cup clam juice
2 tablespoons butter
2 tablespoons flour
1/4 teaspoon salt and pepper
1 cup clam juice
1/3 cup heavy cream
1 can (7-1/2 ounces) minced clams, drained
Chives
2 teaspoons tarragon
2 egg yolks
2 tablespoons cream

Clams

Combine the dry vermouth and 1/2 cup of clam juice and reduce until it is but 3 to 4 tablespoonfuls. Meanwhile, melt the butter, add the flour, salt, and pepper, and when they are well blended add 1 cup of clam juice, plus the 3 or 4 tablespoonfuls of reduced liquid. Cook, stirring, for 2 minutes. Add the heavy cream, then the well drained clams, the chives, and the chopped tarragon. At the last moment bind the mixture by stirring into it the egg yolks blended with 2 tablespoonfuls of cream and returning it all to the fire briefly to thicken over low heat. Have ready 8 blini. (The recipe below is easy and quick.) Top each hot blini with its portion of the clam mixture and serve.

Blini

1 cup buckwheat pancake mix
1 cup sour milk or yoghurt
1 tablespoon butter
2 eggs, separated

Put all but the egg whites into a blender, blend for half a minute and allow the mixture to stay at room temperature at least 30 minutes. When ready to use, beat the whites stiffly and fold into the batter. Cook in a lightly greased skillet or on a griddle until lightly browned, turning only once. Keep warm in a very slow oven until all the blini are ready to serve. *Mrs. Irwin Nudelman*

Ham and Crab Meat, Rolled

425°

Ham, in thin slices
3 tablespoons crab meat for each slice of ham
Butter
Lemon juice
Cream
Chopped parsley

Heat the ham briefly in the butter and lemon juice. Heat the crab meat in another pan with a little butter and cream. Put the crab meat on the ham and roll it up like a pancake. Squeeze some lemon juice over the rolls and heat thoroughly in a hot oven. Sprinkle some parsley over them at serving time. Use 1 or 2 for a first course; accompanied by a vegetable or salad this will do for a summer luncheon. *Mrs. Alan Wurtzburger*

Ham Blender Aspic

6 servings

1 envelope gelatin
1-1/2 cups beef stock
1 tablespoon vinegar
1 small white onion, peeled
1/2 green pepper, seeded
1/4 small head cabbage, cut in chunks
6 black pitted olives
2/3 cup mayonnaise
1 tablespoon hot prepared mustard
1-1/2 cups diced ham

Soften the gelatin in 1/4 cup of the beef stock. Heat the remaining beef stock to the boiling point and whirl in a blender with the softened gelatin and the vinegar. Add the onion, green pepper, cabbage, and black olives and blend until finely chopped. Add the mayonnaise and mustard and pour the mixture over the diced ham in a bowl. Mix and spoon the mixture into a 6-cup mold or 6 cups. Chill until firm. *Mrs. James Grieves*

Fresh Peach Filled with Ham Mousse

6 servings

1 pound cooked ham
1/3 cup homemade mayonnaise
Cayenne
Pepper and salt to taste
1/3 cup sweet butter, softened
2 teaspoons medium-dry port wine
6 large fresh ripe peaches, peeled

Put the ham through the finest blade of a meat grinder. Place it in a mixing bowl. Beat the mayonnaise, cayenne, pepper, salt, butter, and port very slowly into the ham to make a fine mousse. Chill for about 1 hour.

Pit the peaches by placing a knife in the stem end of each peach and cutting around the pit. Stuff this cavity with the ham mousse. Serve in chilled coupe glasses lined with Bibb lettuce leaves and top with fresh watercress. Pass homemade herbed breadsticks with this for a summer luncheon or a first course before a light dinner.

Mrs. Irwin Nudelman

Herring Ring

4 to 6 servings

1 large jar Bismarck herring
1 large can tuna fish
1/2 pound sweet butter
1 tablespoon lemon juice
A little onion
1 jar stuffed olives

Put a ring of sliced olives in the bottom of a small ring mold. Grind herring in a meat grinder with the tuna fish and the remaining olives. Cream the butter well, add the seasonings, and mix with the ground herring and tuna. Place in the refrigerator until very firm.

Unmold, surround with lettuce, quartered tomatoes, artichoke bottoms, halved hard-cooked eggs, or better still, riced hard-cooked egg moistened with mayonnaise into which has been mixed a jar of caviar. Serve with a dressing made up of 1 cup homemade mayonnaise, 1/3 cup chili sauce, and chopped green pepper and pimiento in pleasing proportions. *Mrs. E. J. Garson*

Melon and Shrimp with Crème Fraîche

6 servings

3 melons (cantaloupes or other small melons)
Small shrimp, peeled and deveined
Crème fraîche (see note)
Catsup
Tabasco sauce

This inexact combination is necessary because both melon and shrimp vary in size. However, use enough shrimp to pile up attractively in the melon halves. Cook the shrimp only until firm, toss them with crème fraîche or lightly salted whipped cream or sour cream, to which you have added catsup and Tabasco sauce to taste. Fill the melons, add a little grated lemon rind, and serve well chilled.

Crème Fraîche

As crème fraîche is only available in France, a very reasonable and simple facsimile is made by adding 2 tablespoons of a commercial culture such as yoghurt, buttermilk, or sour cream to 1 pint of heavy whipping cream (as high as possible in butterfat content). Put this in a bowl or wide-mouthed jar in an oven which is warmed by a pilot light, or anywhere else you may find a constant 100° temperature. Let it remain at this temperature all day or night. Stir it, then put it in the refrigerator for 48 hours. This will keep several weeks, but it is so good with berries too that it may well be used up by everyone who opens the refrigerator.

Mrs. Frank Holm, Frank Perls

Mushrooms under Glass

In memory of my mother's Victorian table

Mushrooms
Butter
Sliced white bread
Salt
Pepper
Lemon juice
Chopped parsley
Heavy cream

Individual baking dishes with bell-shaped domes that fit over them are necessary for this recipe.

Toast the bread and, using one of the glass domes, cut each slice into a round. Wipe the baking dishes with butter and butter the rounds of toast, placing a slice in each baking dish. Remove the stems from mushrooms, wipe, and clean the caps. Use small and medium-size caps whole, but cut large caps into quarters. Arrange in a pyramid on top of each round of toast. Sprinkle with salt and pepper. Add 1/2 tablespoon of lemon juice to each dish. Pour about 1/6 cup of heavy cream over each serving. Cover with glass domes and bake about 1/2 hour. Remove glass domes as dishes are served. The delicate aroma of the mushrooms rising to one's nostrils as the dome is removed is enticing.

Mrs. Clarence D. Long

Pain de Laitue

A LIGHT FIRST COURSE

425°

1-1/2 pounds lettuce (Bibb, Boston or leaf)
1-1/2 cups chicken broth
1 cup thick white sauce, well seasoned
3 large eggs, beaten
Butter
Salt and white pepper to taste
Spicy tomato sauce

Simmer the lettuce 12 minutes in the chicken broth, drain, and squeeze in a potato ricer to get it very dry. Chop the lettuce coarsely and simmer in the white sauce for 5 minutes longer. Cool to lukewarm, stir in the beaten eggs and a bit of butter. Season to taste. Bake for 50 minutes in a buttered charlotte mold, set in a pan of hot water. Unmold and mask with the tomato sauce.

Edward L. Brewster

Prize Open Sandwich

2 large (2-1/2 inches in diameter) fresh closed mushrooms per person
Oil for sautéing
Salt and pepper
Madeira or Marsala wine
A mousse of foie gras or any delicately flavored liver paste
Paprika
1 slice of bread per person
Watercress
Raw carrot

Wipe the mushrooms and remove the stems carefully by cutting, not pulling, them out, so that the mushrooms will not collapse in cooking. To keep

Ceremonial cup of gold, enamel and agate made for Augustus the Strong, King of Saxony and Poland about 1720. It is the creation of the court goldsmith, Johann Melchior Dinglinger, who was later to design porcelain groups to be made at the Meissen factory of the same monarch.

the juiciness in, sauté them in oil, stem side down first, then outside down. Add salt, pepper, Madeira or Marsala, and cook the mushrooms until they are tender; cool them. With a fluted pastry tip and bag, pipe the mousse into the caps in a spiral. Dust with paprika in the grooves. Have the bread ready, crusts off and buttered. Carpet it with watercress, arrange the mushroom roses on top, and sprinkle with a few strands of raw carrot.

This recipe won first prize in a Norwegian food contest: a 2-week trip to Norway for 2 people.

Lady Penrose

Sardine Paste

1 can skinless and boneless sardines
1/2 pound Philadelphia cream cheese
1/2 tube anchovy or sardellen paste
1 small bunch of mint, finely chopped
Juice of half a lemon

Mix all the ingredients together and chill them in a greased bowl for several hours. (A double recipe fills a 10-inch fish mold.) Unmold and serve with deviled eggs and thin rye toast.

Mrs. Arthur Korach

Hawaiian Delight

12 servings

1 pint cherry tomatoes
2 large cucumbers, peeled and cubed
2 ripe avocados, peeled and cut in large pieces
6 green peppers, seeded and cut in thick pieces
6 cans water chestnuts, sliced
3 pounds chicken livers, sautéed
3 pounds cooked shrimp, peeled and deveined
Watercress

Sauce:

4 cups mayonnaise
1 cup sour cream
1 cup prepared grated horseradish, drained
1 teaspoon MSG
6 teaspoons dry mustard
2 tablespoons lemon juice
1 teaspoon salt

  Put all the salad ingredients on a large flat platter in a decorative manner. Beat the sauce well, and rather than mix everything together, which would spoil the effect, serve it in a separate bowl. Be sure everything is well chilled and that you have plenty of watercress to make it even more attractive.

Mrs. Arthur Wilkoff

Tomatoes with Smoked Salmon and Cucumber

8 servings

8 ripe tomatoes
1/2 pound sliced smoked salmon
2 large cucumbers
3/4 teaspoon salt
1 cup sour cream
1/4 teaspoon coarse-ground pepper
1 tablespoon drained capers
4 scallions, minced (tops too)
1 teaspoon or more minced fresh dill, or 1/2 teaspoon dried
3 tablespoons tarragon vinegar

  Peel the tomatoes, cut off the tops, scoop out the insides and turn the tomatoes upside down on paper towels to drain. Chill them. Cut the salmon into 1/2-inch squares. Peel the cucumbers, cut them into quarters, remove the seeds, and cut the firm portions into 1/2-inch pieces; salt them for 1/2 hour and drain. Mix the salmon and cucumber with the remaining ingredients. Chill for several hours. Fill the tomato cups with the salmon and cucumber mixture and garnish with additional dill.

Mrs. Jon Alan Wurtzburger

Tomato Surprise

4 servings

4 large ripe tomatoes, peeled
1/4 onion, grated
Salt and pepper
1/4 cup mayonnaise, homemade
2 teaspoons curry powder

  Chop the tomatoes, mix well with the onion, add the salt and pepper to taste, and pour into a refrigerator freezer tray. Freeze just to a mush, about 1/2 hour, and serve as a first course in chilled sherbet glasses, topped with curried mayonnaise which has been allowed to mellow in the refrigerator.

Herbert Powell

SOUPS

New England Bouillabaisse

6 servings

Heads and spines of fish
4 cloves garlic
2 onions (1 sliced, 1 chopped)
Bouquet garni of 1/2 teaspoon thyme, 1/2 teaspoon
 allspice, 3 bay leaves
2 tablespoons olive oil
6 fillets of red snapper
6 fillets of flounder or grouper
Salt, pepper, and cayenne
Juice of 1 lemon
1/2 bottle dry white wine
6 fresh tomatoes, peeled, seeded, and chopped, or
 2-1/2 cups canned tomatoes
1/4 teaspoon saffron

Make a fish stock of the bones and heads of the fish by simmering them until flavorful in water to cover with the garlic, the sliced onion, and the bouquet garni. Boil it down to about 1-1/2 cups and set it aside after straining it.

In olive oil, sauté the chopped onion until limp. Put the fillets on top, cover the pan and let steam for 10 minutes, turning once. Remove the fish and to the pan juices add the wine, fish stock, and tomatoes. Bring this to a boil; add the fillets and poach them for 5 minutes. Put the saffron in a small bowl with some of the stock and let it steep a few minutes. Put the fish on a serving dish; add the saffron to the tomato wine sauce and pour this over the fish.

Mrs. Sven Peuleché

Crab Soup

2 pounds plate or shin beef
1/2 pound bacon, coarsely chopped
6 steamed crabs
2 packages frozen mixed vegetables
1 package frozen corn
1 package frozen peas
1/2 green pepper, chopped
1 onion, chopped
2 cups canned tomatoes
3 potatoes, peeled and diced
1 small head cabbage, chopped
Salt and pepper
Celery seed
Bay leaf
Thyme
1 tablespoon Old Bay Seasoning
1 pound crab meat
2 cups cooked noodles

Put the meat, cut in 2-inch cubes, with the crabs, chopped in large pieces into a large pot. Cover with

36 SOUPS

4 quarts of water and cook until the meat is done. Strain the soup, then add the vegetables and seasoning and cook until flavorful. Add the cooked noodles and fresh crab meat and simmer only until heated through.
Mrs. Perry Bolton

Charleston Crab Soup

6 servings

1 pint milk
1/4 teaspoon ground mace
2 small pieces of lemon peel, finely chopped
1/2 stick butter
1 small onion, finely chopped
1 pound white crab meat, picked over
1 pint cream
1/4 cup cracker crumbs
Salt and pepper
2 tablespoons sherry

Put the milk, mace, and lemon peel in the top of a double boiler and heat over simmering water for a few minutes. Melt the butter in a small skillet and sauté the chopped onion for a minute or two. Add the onion and the melted butter, the crab meat, and the cream to the milk and heat for 15 minutes more. Thicken with cracker crumbs, correct the seasoning, and let it all stand for several minutes to develop flavor. Add the sherry just before serving.
Mrs. John Eager

Creole Crab Soup

6 servings

1/2 cup onion rings
1/4 cup chopped green pepper
2 tablespoons butter
2 tablespoons flour
1-3/4 teaspoons salt
1/4 teaspoon pepper
1/2 teaspoon thyme
Dash Tabasco sauce
1 cup (7-1/2 ounces) crab meat, or more
1 cup (8-ounce can) okra with liquid
2-1/2 cups (1-pound 3-ounce can) tomatoes with juice
2 cups milk

Sauté the onion and green pepper in the butter until tender; blend in the flour, salt, pepper, thyme, and Tabasco sauce to form a smooth paste. Stir in the crab meat, okra, and tomatoes; heat to boiling. Reduce the heat, cover, and simmer 20 to 25 minutes.* Gradually stir in the milk; cook a few minutes over medium heat, stirring occasionally, until heated through. Serve immediately. This is a thick soup, good for a main course at lunch or a first course at dinner. It is also very good served in mugs at a party on a cold night.

*This can be stored for several days in the refrigerator at this stage. Milk should be added just before serving.
Miss Sue McCoy

Cream of Broccoli Soup

6 servings

1 medium onion, sliced
1 medium carrot, sliced
1 stalk of celery with leaves
1 clove garlic
1/2 cup water
2 cups cooked broccoli, coarsely chopped
1 teaspoon salt
Generous pinch of cayenne pepper
1/2 cup cooked macaroni
1 cup chicken stock
1/4 cup cream (optional)
Sour cream (optional)

Simmer the onion, carrot, celery, and garlic in 1/2 cup water for 10 minutes. Transfer to a blender, add the chopped cooked broccoli, salt, cayenne pepper and macaroni. Cover and blend at high speed, then remove cover and with the motor running add the stock and perhaps the cream. Chill well and serve with sour cream if cream was not added in the original production. *Miss Grace Hatchett*

New Jersey Bean Soup

8 to 10 servings

1 ham bone with plenty of ham on it
2 quarts water
1 onion, chopped
4 potatoes, diced
1 pound dry lima beans, soaked overnight and drained
1 can tomatoes
1/2 teaspoon leaf thyme
1/2 cup diced celery (optional)
Chopped parsley

Simmer all ingredients except the parsley in a large heavy pot for about 4 hours or until the ham is ready to fall off the bone. Remove the ham bone, cut the meat into small pieces, and return the meat to the soup. Season to taste and serve sprinkled with chopped parsley.
Mrs. P. William Filby, Miss Janet Gross

An Authentic Borscht

6 servings

15 medium-sized beets
2 pounds short ribs of beef
1 onion, sliced finely
Salt and pepper
Strained juice of 3 lemons
1/2 cup sugar
Sour cream
6 boiled potatoes (optional)

Peel the beets and grate them over a pot so as to keep all the juice. Add the beef, sliced onion, salt, and pepper. Cover just barely with water and cook slowly about 2 hours. Add lemon juice or sugar, depending on your taste. Serve in soup plates with pieces of meat, and a dollop of sour cream floating on top. Hot boiled and peeled potatoes, quartered or sliced, may be added at the last minute.
Miss Alice Newman

Cream of Curry Soup

4 servings

1-1/4 cups rich chicken stock
1 cup cream
1/2 teaspoon curry powder
1 tablespoon finely minced parsley
1/4 teaspoon salt
2 eggs
1/2 cup sauterne
Slivered almonds

Heat the stock and cream, adding the curry powder, mixed first with a little of the stock, parsley, and salt. Mix well, but remove from the heat as it reaches the boiling point. Beat the eggs slightly and into them stir half of the hot mixture, returning this all to the soup, stirring constantly. Add the sauterne and return to the fire for 2 minutes. Do not boil. Serve at once topped with slivered almonds.
Mrs. Charles Bang

Brown Flour Soup

4 servings

2 cups diced raw potatoes
1/2 cup scallions, chopped
1 teaspoon salt
1-1/2 tablespoons butter
2 tablespoons flour
2 cups milk
Salt and pepper
Hard-boiled eggs

In a large saucepan place the diced raw potatoes and chopped scallions. Add enough water to cover and about 1 teaspoon salt. Boil gently until the potatoes are done (about 25 minutes). Meanwhile, in a small saucepan melt the butter, add the flour and, stirring constantly, cook until the flour is dark brown. Cool slightly and add enough milk to make a smooth paste. Add the rest of the milk to the potatoes and heat to a simmer, then stir in the browned flour, salt, and pepper to taste. Garnish with chopped hard-boiled egg.

Edward L. Brewster

Chilled Cantaloupe Soup

4 servings

1 3-pound ripe cantaloupe
1/4 cup sugar
1/2 cup dry sherry
1 tablespoon lime juice

In a blender combine the cantaloupe meat and the rest of the ingredients. Blend until smooth. Refrigerate, covered, until very cold.

Mrs. John E. Savage

New Jersey Clam Chowder

6 servings

1/2 pound salt pork
Marrow bone
2-1/2 cups canned tomatoes
1 pound peas, shelled
1 pound lima beans, shelled
4 potatoes, peeled and cut up
1/2 bunch celery, cut up
1 cup canned corn or 2 ears fresh corn, off the cob
1/2 pound string beans, trimmed and cut up
1 onion, chopped
1 quart clams
1/2 teaspoon thyme
Chopped parsley
Salt and pepper

Cut the salt pork into small pieces and fry until crisp. Put it in a large pot with the marrow bone, 2 quarts of water, and all the vegetables but the parsley. Steam the clams open, chop them, and add the broth to the pot. Add thyme and simmer about 5 to 6 hours. One hour before serving, add the clams and the finely chopped parsley. Season to taste.

Mrs. P. William Filby

Clam Soup

6 servings

2 cups clam broth or bottled clam juice
1 cup chicken broth
3 egg yolks
1/4 cup dry white wine or French vermouth
1 or 2 tablespoons heavy cream
1 tablespoon minced parsley

Mix the clam and chicken broths and bring to a boil. Beat the egg yolks with the vermouth or wine and beat in 1 cup of the broth. Pour this mixture into the remaining broth, whisking over low heat 1 minute. Add the cream if you like a thicker soup. Season to taste with salt and pepper (bottled clam juice is salty) and sprinkle with parsley.

Mrs. Benjamin Griswold, IV

Carrot Vichysoisse

4 servings

2 tablespoons butter
2 bunches scallions, sliced
2 cups seasoned chicken broth
2 cups cooked carrots
1/2 teaspoon salt
1/8 teaspoon pepper
1 tablespoon chopped chives or minced parsley
1/2 cup light cream

Melt the butter in a small saucepan. Add the sliced scallions and let them cook over moderate heat about 5 minutes. Add a cup of chicken broth, bring to a boil. Cover and simmer over low heat 15 minutes longer. Pour the scallions and the broth into an electric blender. Add the remaining cup of broth, carrots, and seasonings. Cover the container and blend until the contents are smooth, about 1 minute. Add cream and chill thoroughly. Top with chives or minced parsley. This may also be served hot.

Mrs. Arthur Stern

Cucumber Soup

6 servings

2 tablespoons chopped scallions (or onions or shallots)
2 tablespoons butter
2 8-inch cucumbers, peeled and chopped
1 tablespoon wine vinegar
1 quart chicken stock
1 tablespoon farina or cream of wheat
Salt
Fresh or dried tarragon or dill
1/2 cup sour cream or fresh cream
Cucumber slices
Chopped parsley

Cook the chopped scallions, onions, or shallots in 2 tablespoons butter until soft. Add the chopped cucumbers and the wine vinegar. Add the stock, farina or cream of wheat, and salt to taste; then add the tarragon or dill. Let it simmer 20 minutes until the cucumbers are soft. Put the soup into a blender and purée. Add the cream, beat well with a whisk, and taste for seasoning. Pour into bowls, decorate with cucumber slices and freshly chopped parsley. Serve hot or cold.

Mrs. Morton Baum, Mrs. Jerome Kidder

Garlic Soup

2 servings

1 tablespoon butter
12 cloves fresh garlic
4 cups water
Salt and pepper
2 eggs
2 tablespoons vinegar
Thin slices of dry French bread

Melt the butter in a heavy skillet. Peel the garlic cloves and cut them crosswise into slices 3/8 of an inch thick. Sauté the garlic, being careful not to let it turn brown, which causes it to be bitter. Add the water, salt, and pepper to taste. Simmer until the garlic is cooked. Separate the eggs and add the whites to the soup, stirring rapidly until they are cooked. Remove from the heat. Mix the vinegar and yolks and stir them into the soup. Return the soup to heat it but do not let it boil. Top with French bread slices.

This soup is popular around Bordeaux where the wine growers like it as a late snack. Surprisingly, the garlic is not overpowering.

Mrs. Harry E. Foster

Gazpacho
A REASONABLE FACSIMILE

6 servings

Run through the blender the following in any convenient order. It will require 2 or 3 loads.
5 large red ripe local tomatoes, peeled and seeded
1 large cucumber, peeled and seeded
1 small green pepper, seeded
1 fair-sized piece of the cucumber skin
1 large red onion, peeled
1 large clove of garlic (more if you like), peeled
2 slices of stale bread (not USA cardboard kind), softened in water
2/3 cup olive oil (Spanish, if you have it)
1/4 cup red wine vinegar
1 4-ounce jar pimiento
Salt to taste
Pepper to taste
MSG to taste

Dump all into a large bowl and add tomato juice to make 2 quarts. A little red food coloring helps the looks. Mix all thoroughly and then chill. Traditionally, chopped cucumber, green pepper, onions, and croutons are served separately to garnish the soup.

Edward L. Brewster

Canadian Goose Soup

1 goose carcass (see recipe for Joe's Goose)
Essence from roasting pan
1 large onion
4-5 sprigs of parsley
3 stalks of celery, leaves and all
1 small turnip
Salt and pepper
1/2 cup barley
1 cup celery, chopped fine
1/4 cup minced onion
Kitchen Bouquet
Pepper sherry (see below)

Simmer the carcass, and the essence from the pan in which the goose was roasted, in water to cover, with the onion, parsley, celery stalks, and turnip for 4 or 5 hours. Remove the carcass and pick off any pieces of meat (to use later in the dish). Season the broth to taste with salt and pepper and chill it to be able to remove all the grease.

To each quart of broth add 1/2 cup barley, 1 cup chopped celery, and 1/4 cup minced onion and simmer for 1 to 1-1/2 hours. Add a little Kitchen Bouquet for color. Right before serving, add diced pieces of the goose meat and at the table float some pepper sherry on top of the soup.

Homemade Pepper Sherry

Dried red pepper
Sherry

Add dried red pepper to a decanter of sherry and hold for several weeks.   *Mrs. Joseph B. Browne*

Blender Minestrone

8 servings

4 slices of bacon, cut fine
1 bunch leeks, chopped
1 large onion, chopped

3 cloves garlic, mashed
1/4 head of cabbage, shredded
1 can tomatoes
1 box frozen peas
1 bunch carrots, chopped
3 medium-sized turnips, chopped
1 tablespoon oregano
Salt and pepper
2 tablespoons sweet basil
1 quart of stock or consommé

Fry the bacon and add the leeks, onion, and garlic, cooking them until they are soft but not brown. Add the remainder of the ingredients and cook until done. Then put it all in a blender just to chop it a bit as you do not want it too smooth. Serve with Parmesan cheese on top, and toasted French bread.
Mrs. Robert Adler

Oyster Bisque

8 servings

**1-1/2 pints oysters
2 8-ounce bottles clam juice
1-1/2 cups white wine
2 stalks celery, sliced
2 medium onions, sliced
2 carrots, sliced
3 slices lemon
2 teaspoons dried parsley
1 pinch thyme
1 bay leaf
1/4 teaspoon nutmeg
2 teaspoons salt
1/2 teaspoon whole peppercorns
1/3 cup lightly salted butter
1/3 cup flour
2 eggs
3 cups light cream
1/4 cup sherry (Harvey's Bristol Cream, preferably)
Dash of cayenne pepper
2 tablespoons finely chopped fresh parsley**

Chop the oysters, saving all of the oyster liquor. Place the oysters and liquor in an enamel saucepan. Add the clam juice, white wine, celery, onions, carrots, lemon slices, herbs, nutmeg, salt, and peppercorns. Bring to a boil, reduce the heat and simmer gently uncovered for 45 minutes. Strain first through a fine sieve, then cheesecloth. Measure this stock and if necessary add enough water to make 5 cups.

Melt butter in a large enamel saucepan. Add flour and stir until smooth. Gradually, stir in the oyster stock and cook, stirring constantly, until the mixture thickens. With a fork, beat the eggs with 1/2 cup of the cream. Stir about 1 cup of the hot bisque into the egg-cream mixture, then gradually stir this mixture back into the bisque. Add the remaining cream and heat thoroughly. DO NOT BOIL. Before serving, stir in the sherry and a dash of cayenne. Serve in a soup tureen, sprinkled with finely chopped fresh parsley.

You may add an additional pint of fresh oysters, which have been poached in their liquor, and white wine. In effect, you may create an oyster stew from this basic recipe. Served with a salad and beaten biscuits, this is a lovely Sunday brunch.
Mrs. Irwin J. Nudelman

Oyster Stew

4 servings

**1/4 pound bacon or pork belly (or salt pork, pre-boiled)
1 quart scalded milk
2-3 large potatoes
Pinch thyme
Large bay leaf
2 tablespoons chopped parsley
1 pint oysters with their liquid
3 tablespoons butter
Salt and pepper to taste**

Dice the bacon or pork belly quite fine and try it out in a skillet over moderate heat. Remove the fried bacon or pork and add milk to the frying pan to scald it. Remove from the heat. Peel and boil the potatoes in salted water. Drain and mash them in a soup kettle, adding the hot milk gradually. Add the thyme, bay leaf, and parsley and bring up to a boil, but do not allow it to boil or it will curdle. Remove the bay leaf. Add the oysters and their liquid, and butter, salt, and pepper to taste. Serve with hot toasted bread or unsalted crackers.

Mrs. Douglas Warner Jr.

Purée of Oysters in Soup

4 servings

1 cup clam juice
1 teaspoon dried green onions
2/3 cup oyster liquor
3/4 cup puréed peas
2/3 cup raw oysters
2 tablespoons butter
1/4 cup dry white wine
1/2 teaspoon salt
1/4 teaspoon white pepper
Light cream
4 tablespoons whipped cream
1 tablespoon chopped parsley

Put the clam juice, onion, oyster liquor, and puréed peas in a heavy pot and heat thoroughly. Add the oysters, butter, wine, salt, and pepper. Heat just to cook the oysters through, put it all in a blender to become perfectly smooth, then pour it all into a large-mouthed jar to chill overnight. Thin it out with a little light cream and season to taste. At serving time, if it is to be served cold, put a dab of lightly salted whipped cream on each cup and a dusting of parsley. If it is to be hot, run the bowls, topped with the whipped cream, under the broiler to let the cream brown slightly.

Mrs. Robert A. Milch

Onion Soup Chablis

6 servings

1 pound white onions, sliced very thin
1/4 pound butter
3 cups chicken broth
1 cup Chablis
1 teaspoon salt
Pepper
2 cups medium cream
Swiss cheese, freshly grated

Sauté the onions in butter until soft and transparent but not brown. Add the chicken broth and simmer until the mixture is reduced to about half. Add the Chablis, salt, and pepper. Bring to a boil and simmer about 2 minutes. Stir in the cream, heat, and serve garnished liberally with Swiss cheese.

Miss Avonia Read

Cold Aspen Soup

20 servings

3 cups diced onion
5 tablespoons butter
3 bunches watercress (no stems)
4 canned peeled chilies, rinsed of seeds
3 cups milk
1 teaspoon salt
3 cloves garlic, crushed (approximately 1 heaping teaspoon)
6 cups sour cream
1 tablespoon lemon juice
Minced chives

Cook the onions in butter until barely tender. Add the watercress, chilies, milk, salt, and crushed garlic. Bring to just under a boil, then whirl smooth in a blender. Stir in the sour cream, adding more salt if required. Adjust the lemon juice after tasting. Chill. Serve in cups or glass mugs; sprinkle with fresh chives.

Miss Rita St. Clair

Thabeget.　　Suffrixa.　　Suffrixa salsa.　　Assum sup carb.　　Assum in ueru.

A Pot Luck Supper — *Thabeget* (sweet and sour meat), *Suffrixa* (stew), *Suffrixa Salsa* (salt stew), *Assum super carbones* (charcoal broiled), *Assum in verum* (roast on a spit). Woodcut from *Tacuini Sanitatis*, Strassburg, 1531

Cream of Chilled Pea Soup

16 servings

1 cup chopped onion
2 tablespoons butter
6 packages frozen peas
2 teaspoons dried chervil
2-1/2 cups beef consommé
8 cups of water
1 teaspoon freshly ground pepper
3 teaspoons salt
12 mint leaves, cut fine
4 cups light cream
1 cup chilled white wine or champagne
Sprigs of mint for garnish

    Sauté the chopped onion in the butter until it is limp but not colored. Add peas, chervil, consommé, water, pepper, and salt. Simmer this uncovered until the peas are barely done, then purée it in a blender. Strain it after whirling in the blender. Add the mint leaves. Chill this very well and before serving stir in the cream and wine. Garnish with sprigs of mint.

Mrs. Peter Dane, Mrs. Louis B. Kohn

Cream of Curried Pea Soup

6 servings

1 cup shelled fresh peas
1 small carrot, sliced
1 stalk celery with leaves, sliced
1 teaspoon salt
1 medium potato, sliced
1 medium onion, sliced
1 clove garlic
1 teaspoon curry powder
2 cups chicken stock
3/4 cup heavy cream

    Place the vegetables, seasonings, and 1 cup stock in a saucepan and bring to a boil. Cover, reduce the heat and simmer for 15 minutes. Transfer to the container of an electric blender. Cover and turn the motor on high. Remove the cover, and with the motor running, pour in the remaining stock and 1/2 cup of the cream. Chill. Before serving, whip the remaining 1/4 cup of cream to use as a garnish on top of each serving.

Herbert Powell

Potage Printanier

4 to 5 servings

2 carrots
1 turnip
2 celery ribs
1 piece cabbage
1 tomato
2 leeks
1-2 nuts of butter
2 potatoes
Chopped parsley
Salt and pepper

Cut every vegetable but the potatoes on a mandolin or, failing one of those admirable gadgets, slice them by hand, not too thinly. Dice the potatoes. Color them all in butter in a pot large enough to hold 6 cups of water as well. Add salt and pepper, chopped parsley, and 6 cups of water. Cook for 3/4 of an hour with the lid only partially on. At serving time you may add some hot cooked string beans, some more butter, and some sour cream, putting these in the bottom of a serving tureen before adding the contents of the soup pot.

Edward L. Brewster, Mrs. Alan Wurtzburger

Spinach Soup

4 servings

1 package frozen chopped spinach, cooked and drained
4 chicken bouillon cubes
3 cups light cream
1/4 cup dry vermouth
1 teaspoon grated lemon rind
1/2 teaspoon ground mace
2 hard-cooked eggs, chopped
Whipped cream for garnish

Reduce the cooked spinach to a purée in the blender, adding a little of the cream which makes it easier to achieve. Scald the rest of the cream and dissolve the chicken bouillon cubes in it. Off the stove add the vermouth, lemon rind, mace, and the puréed spinach. Chill it well, and serve with a tablespoon of the chopped egg, a blob of lightly salted whipped cream, and a speck of horseradish.

It is not necessary to use frozen spinach; the fresh is better but less convenient. If sorrel is to be found, by all means add some to the spinach before it is cooked. In that case, omit the vermouth.

Mrs. Benjamin Griswold, IV, Mrs. Allan Wetzler

Sopa con Gambas à la Mama Isabel

SOUP WITH SHRIMP

4 servings

1 pound shrimp, or more
4 medium onions, peeled and quartered
4 medium potatoes, peeled and quartered
4 large tomatoes or 2-1/2 cups canned tomatoes
1 large bay leaf
Generous pinch of saffron
Pepper
Salt
1 handful of blanched almonds, chopped
4 cloves garlic, chopped
Olive oil
White wine
Sherry

Clean raw shrimp well and cook until just pink. Strain, reserving the liquid. Put the onions, potatoes, and tomatoes in water to cover, with bay leaf, saffron, and pepper and salt to taste. Stir and cook gently until well done, then purée in a food mill. Return to the saucepan and thin to the desired consistency with reserved shrimp water. Keep warm. Sauté chopped almonds and chopped garlic in a small amount of olive oil until lightly browned. Place in a mortar and grind to a coarse paste with a pestle. Add to the soup and rinse the mortar with the remaining hot shrimp water. Add several tablespoons of white wine, all the shrimp, and stir until the soup is thoroughly hot.

Serve in heated soup plates. Have a bottle of good sherry on the table, and let each guest add sherry to his soup according to individual taste. Serve with hot French bread and tossed green salad.
Mrs. Sven Peuleché

Shrimp Consommé

4 servings

1 pound shrimp
2 cans (10 ounces) beef consommé
1 large slice onion
3 tablespoons chili sauce
4 tablespoons red wine
1 teaspoon parsley, chopped
1/2 teaspoon thyme
1/2 teaspoon salt
1/2 teaspoon pepper, freshly ground
A few drops red food coloring
2 tablespoons heavy cream

Wash and clean the shrimp, reserving the shells. Heat the consommé with the onion and the shells, and simmer until the consommé takes on a definite shrimp flavor. Strain the consommé, and add all the other ingredients except the shrimp and the cream. Simmer this again until flavorful. Bring the soup to the boil, turn the heat down, add the shrimp, which have been chopped coarsely, and simmer until the shrimp are done, a very few minutes. Just before serving, stir in the cream, and alter the seasoning to taste.

This can be served cold, too, in which case a little more cream may be added and some additional chopped parsley.
Miss Grace Hatchett

Butternut Squash Soup

6 servings

3 cups of butternut squash
4 cups chicken bouillon
2-1/2 onions, peeled and halved
3 or 4 whole cloves to taste
1 teaspoon curry powder
1/2 pint heavy cream
Chopped parsley

Seed, peel, and cut in small pieces the butternut squash, then cook it in the bouillon with the onions and cloves until tender. Remove the cloves and put the soup in the blender. Dissolve the curry powder in a little of the cream and put it and the rest of the cream in the blender too. Blend well. Serve hot or cold, with a dusting of chopped parsley over it.

Pumpkin can be substituted in this recipe. Some people prefer sherry to curry as flavoring.
Mrs. LeBaron S. Willard, Jr.

Tomato Dill Soup

6 servings

3 large tomatoes
1 medium onion, sliced
1 small clove garlic
1 teaspoon salt
1/4 teaspoon freshly ground black pepper
1 tablespoon tomato paste
1/4 cup cold water
1/2 cup cooked macaroni
1 cup chicken stock
3/4 cup cream
2 sprigs fresh dill

Peel and slice the tomatoes and place in a saucepan, add the onion, garlic, salt, pepper, tomato paste, and water, cover and simmer 12 to 15 minutes. Transfer to the container of an electric blender.

Add the macaroni, cover, and turn the motor on high. Uncover and, with the motor running, add the chicken stock and the cream. Chill and serve garnished with chopped fresh dill and chopped tomato.
Herbert Powell

Turkey Soup

AS A ONE-DISH MEAL

8 servings

Turkey carcass
2 bay leaves
Salt and pepper
Generous pinches of thyme, marjoram, and basil
4 tablespoons butter
3 tablespoons flour
1/4 cup uncooked rice
1/2 cup finely chopped parsley
1/2 cup chopped celery
Turkey meat, gravy, and dressing
2 cups fresh small mushrooms
1 pound chestnuts
3 tablespoons Madeira

Remove as much meat as possible from the carcass to use later. Break up the carcass and put it in a large pot along with bay leaves, salt, pepper, thyme, marjoram, and basil. Cover with water (at least 2-3 quarts) and simmer for 3 to 4 hours. Remove the bones and sieve the liquid. This is the stock. Chill to remove all the fat.

Melt 2 tablespoons of the butter in saucepan and stir in the flour until smooth. Add the stock gradually (you should have 1-1/2 to 2 quarts) and boil. Add thoroughly washed uncooked rice, chopped parsley, celery, additional salt and pepper to taste and cook until rice is done, 25 to 30 minutes.

Prepare the chestnuts by making an incision on the flat side, covering them with boiling water, and letting them simmer from 15 to 25 minutes. Drain and remove the shells, and if the chestnuts are not tender, cover them with boiling water or consommé and cook until sufficiently soft to put through a purée strainer. Sauté in the remaining 2 tablespoons of butter the mushrooms (left whole if small or sliced in two, if too large), and then add them to the stock along with the chestnut purée, the diced turkey meat, and any leftover gravy and turkey dressing. Simmer gently and then just before serving add 3 tablespoons of Madeira.

This is such a filling dish that only a salad and sherbet or fruit are needed to complete the meal.
Mrs. Luther C. Dilatush

Soup Andaluçian

6 servings

1 whole chicken
2 medium carrots
1 large onion
2 stalks celery with leaves
1 handful of parsley
Salt
Pepper
Juice of a lemon
Pinch of saffron (optional)
Chicken bouillon granules, if needed
1 20-ounce can chick peas
2 cups cooked rice (amount is variable)
White wine or sherry to taste

Peel and chop the carrots and onion; chop the celery. Place the chicken in a pot with enough water to cover, add the carrots, onion, celery, parsley, salt, pepper, and lemon juice. Simmer until the chicken is tender, then remove from the pot. Pick all the meat off the chicken, returning bones and skin to the stock. Simmer the stock for at least 1 hour, or until it has a good chicken flavor. Add a pinch of saffron if desired, and chicken bouillon granules if the stock requires more flavor. Add the chicken meat, cut to desired size, drained chick peas, and rice. Add white wine or sherry to taste (about 1/2 cup) and sample the soup to correct the seasonings.

A generous serving of this soup, with a green salad and hot French bread, is a bountiful meal.
Mrs. Sven Peuleché

Zuppa di Pesce

5 or 6 servings

1 tablespoon butter
3 tablespoons olive oil
3 sliced onions
1 minced garlic clove
1 pound fillet of haddock, cut up
1 pint tomato juice
1 bay leaf
1 dozen clams in shell
1 pound scallops
1 10-ounce package frozen cleaned shrimp or 1 pound fresh shrimp
1 green pepper, cubed
2 tablespoons minced parsley
Salt
Pepper
Pinch of saffron

Place the butter, oil, onions, and garlic in a deep heavy aluminum pot and cook until golden. Add the haddock, tomato juice, and bay leaf; cover and simmer 20 minutes. While this is cooking, scrub the clams, put them in a covered pot with no water and steam until the shells open. Stew the scallops in 1/2 cup of water until the edges curl. Remove the clams from the shells and cut off the tough muscles. Add the clams, scallops, shrimps, and broths in which they cooked to the haddock. Add the diced green pepper, minced parsley, and other seasonings to taste, and reheat.

If there is any left over, putting it through a blender with additional tomato juice makes a delicious seafood bisque. Some of these fish may be omitted, which would be a pity, but any combination of more than two makes a delicious stew.
Mrs. Henry T. Rowell, Mrs. Sven Peuleché

A silver drinking vessel (*rhyton*) in the shape of a horse's head. While this is Sasanian, 6th century A.D., animal-shaped cups have occurred in almost every culture and were particularly popular in Greece and Rome. Wedgwood revived them in the 18th century.

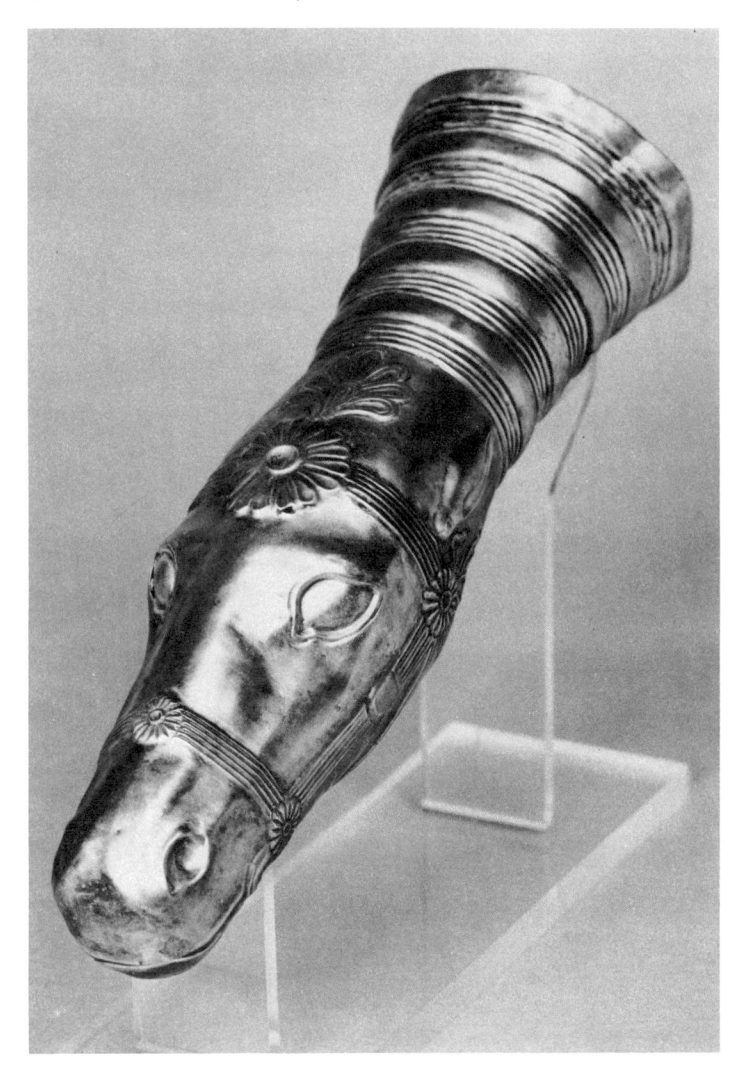

MEAT

Russian Meat Balls

350° / 4 servings

1 pound ground round
1/2 cup uncooked rice
3 tablespoons chopped onion
1 teaspoon salt
1/4 teaspoon pepper
1 can condensed tomato soup
2 cups water

Combine the beef, rice, onion, salt, and pepper. Mix well and form into small balls. Put in a casserole and add tomato soup and water, mixed together, cover and bake for 40 minutes, then remove the cover and brown well.

Mrs. Theodore Dankmeyer

Steak Tartare

8 servings

3 pounds ground sirloin
1 can (No. 202) anchovies, chopped fine
4 beaten eggs
1 bottle (2-1/4 ounces) capers, drained
1-1/2 teaspoons salt
1-1/2 teaspoons pepper
1/2 cup fine ground nuts
1-1/2 teaspoons Colman's mustard
1 cup chopped chives, basil, and parsley, mixed
1-1/2 teaspoons lemon juice
1-1/2 teaspoons olive oil
6 lemon peels (thin), finely chopped

Mix the meat, anchovies, eggs, capers, salt and pepper, nuts, mustard, and 2/3 cup of the herbs. Add the lemon juice and the olive oil, to taste. Chill for 1 hour. Form into balls and roll in the lemon peel and the remaining herbs mixed together.

Percival C. Keith

Roast Beef Vinaigrette

8 servings

3 tablespoons red wine vinegar
9 tablespoons olive oil
1/2 teaspoon freshly ground pepper
1 teaspoon salt
1 teaspoon Dijon mustard
2 tablespoons finely chopped capers
1/2 teaspoon finely chopped garlic
2 tablespoons finely chopped parsley
8 slices cooked roast beef or 3 cups cubed cooked beef
1/2 cup onion rings
Sliced tomatoes

Hard-boiled eggs
Cold cooked vegetables (optional)

    Make a vinaigrette sauce of the vinegar, oil, pepper, salt, mustard, capers, garlic, and parsley. Trim all fat and gristle from the beef and spread slices or cubes in a glass dish. Scatter very thinly sliced onion rings over this and pour in the dressing. Marinate at least several hours at room temperature, turning the meat and onions from time to time.

    To serve, arrange the meat neatly on a platter and scatter the onion rings on top. Sprinkle generously with chopped parsley. Decorate with tomatoes, hard-boiled eggs, and cold vegetables. Hot French bread is an excellent accompaniment. Leftover rare roast beef is best but pot-roasted meat is more traditional.   *Mrs. Thomas E. Allen, Jr.*

Individual Meat Loaves

350° / 4 servings

Meat Loaf

1 pound ground lean beef
1 egg, lightly beaten
4 tablespoons fine bread crumbs
1 tablespoon minced parsley
1/4 cup water
2 tablespoons chopped onion
2 tablespoons horseradish
1 teaspoon salt
1/2 teaspoon Accent
1/8 teaspoon pepper

Sauce

3 tablespoons catsup
1/2 cup chili sauce
1 teaspoon Worcestershire sauce
1/2 teaspoon dry mustard
Dash of Tabasco

    Combine all of the ingredients for the meat loaves, mix well, and shape into four oblong loaves. Place these in a greased shallow casserole, not touching. Combine the sauce ingredients and spread over the tops and sides of the loaves. Bake for 45 minutes, basting two or three times with the drippings which accumulate.
  Mrs. Jon Alan Wurtzburger

Edible Hamburgers

3 to 4 servings

1 pound lean ground beef
1 teaspoon chili powder
1/4 cup buttermilk
Salt to taste
2 tablespoons butter
1 tablespoon olive oil

Mix first 4 ingredients together lightly; don't pack it down. Form into 4 thick patties (about 1 inch thick). Heat butter and olive oil in a heavy frying pan until very hot. Put in the patties and quickly cover with a screen splatter guard. Cook about 2 minutes. Turn and cook the other side about 2 minutes. Turn again and cook the first side for another 2 minutes. Turn once more and do the second side for a final 2 minutes. Remove immediately and serve on dry toast. Keep the pan *very* hot throughout the cooking. They should be well-browned on the outside and pink and light inside.
Edward L. Brewster

Hamburger Stroganoff

375° / 5 servings

1/4 cup butter
1/2 cup minced onion
1/2 lb mushrooms, chopped
1/2 pound ground chuck
1 tablespoon flour
1 can (8 ounces) tomato sauce
1/4 cup Burgundy
1 can (10-1/2 ounces) bouillon
1 teaspoon salt
1/4 teaspoon pepper
1 cup sour cream
8 ounces medium noodles
Parmesan cheese

In hot butter, sauté the onion and mushrooms for 5 minutes. Add the beef, stirring until browned. Remove from the heat, stir in the flour, tomato sauce, wine, bouillon, salt, and pepper. Put back on the stove and simmer 10 minutes, stirring occasionally. Blend in the sour cream off the heat. Cook the noodles as directed on the package. Layer noodles and meat sauce in a 2-quart casserole. Sprinkle the top of the casserole liberally with grated Parmesan cheese and bake 30 minutes.
Mrs. Bertram Bernheim, Jr.

Stifado

GREEK STEW

6 servings

3 pounds lean beef stew meat, cut in 1-1/2-inch cubes
Salt and freshly ground pepper
1/2 cup butter
2-1/2 pounds small onions, peeled
1 can (6 ounces) tomato paste
1/3 cup red table wine
2 tablespoons red wine vinegar
1 tablespoon brown sugar
1 clove garlic, mashed
1 bay leaf
1 small stick cinnamon
1/2 teaspoon whole cloves
1/4 teaspoon ground cumin
2 tablespoons currants or raisins (optional)

Season the meat with salt and pepper. Melt the butter in a heavy kettle with a cover. Add the meat and coat it with butter, but do not brown. Arrange the onions over the meat. Mix the tomato paste, wine, vinegar, sugar, and garlic; pour over the meat and onions. Add bay leaf, cinnamon, cloves, cumin, and currants. Cover the onions with a plate to keep them from disintegrating; then cover the kettle and simmer for 3 hours, or until the meat is very tender. Do not stir until serving time.

This is very good served with sesame-seed noodles.
Mrs. David Belcher

Beef Kebabs

2 to 3 servings

1 pound New York strip steak, 2 inches thick
8 cherry tomatoes
8 small whole green peppers or 1 large green pepper sliced into 8 pieces

Cut the steak into 8 2-inch cubes and marinate in the following sauce for 2 hours.

Beef Kebab Sauce

**2 spring onions, sliced
1/2 teaspoon salt
1/4 teaspoon freshly ground pepper
2 ounces sherry
1/2 teaspoon dried basil
1 tablespoon olive oil**

Alternate steak cubes, tomatoes, and green pepper on 4 skewers. Broil over a charcoal hibachi for approximately 20 minutes. Turn often and glaze with the remaining sauce. Serve on a bed of rice.

Mrs. George M. Garman, III

Marinated Sirloin

4 servings

**1 3-pound sirloin steak
1/2 cup lemon juice
3 tablespoons olive oil
1 tablespoon anchovy paste
2 cloves garlic, sliced
1/2 cup green olives, sliced**

Marinate the steak 2 to 3 hours in lemon juice, olive oil, anchovy paste, and garlic, turning often. Drain the steak, pat dry with paper towels, and grill to desired degree of doneness. Decorate with sliced olives.

Mrs. Douglas Warner, Jr.

The handles of this German early 18th-century knife and fork are done in colored beadwork.

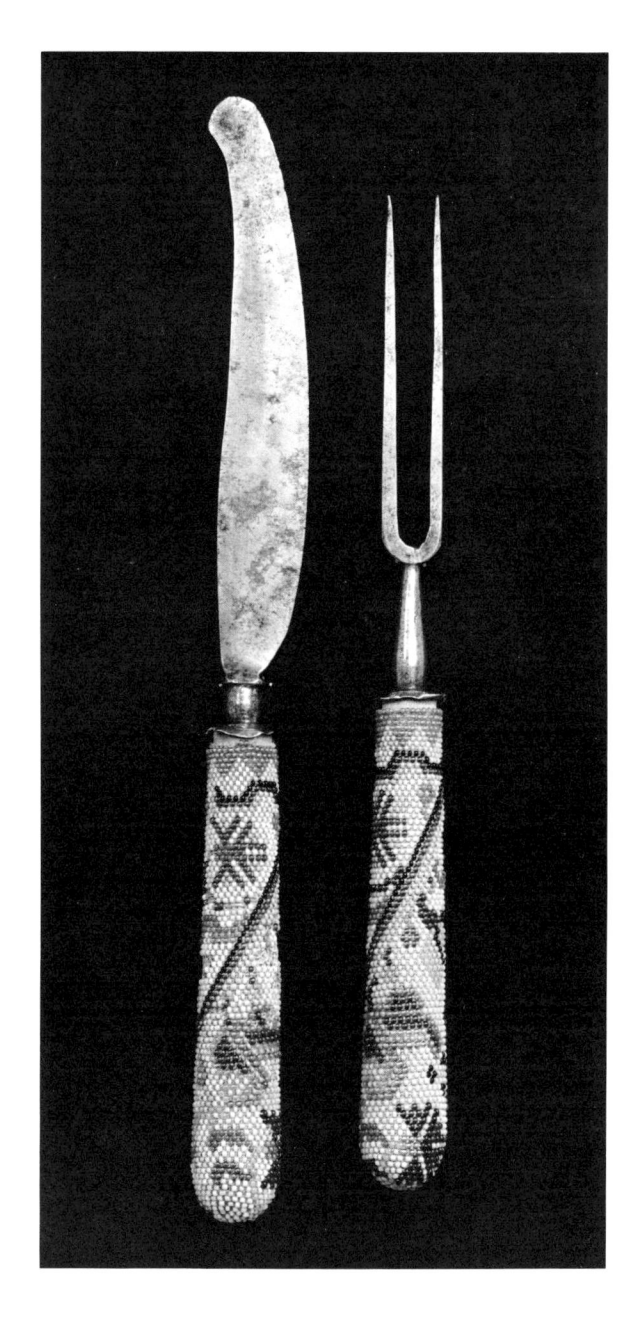

Marinated Flank Steak

4 to 6 servings

1 flank steak, 2 to 2-1/2 pounds
1/2 cup soy sauce
2-1/2 tablespoons brown sugar
2 tablespoons lemon juice
1 teaspoon ground ginger
1/2 teaspoon garlic salt

Trim fat from the steak. Score the meat on both sides and place in a shallow dish. Mix the remaining ingredients together and pour over the steak. Marinate overnight in the refrigerator or for 4 hours at room temperature, turning the steak occasionally. Drain the marinade, then broil 3 to 4 inches from the fire for 3 minutes on each side. Carve in thin diagonal slices immediately so that it will not cook a second more. *Mrs. James Grieves*

Baked Steak

350°

A sirloin or porterhouse steak, at least 2-1/2 inches thick
Salt and pepper
Mustard
Catsup
Worcestershire Sauce
Onion
Mushroom caps
Green pepper
Lemon

Salt and pepper the steak on both sides, lightly. Spread a thin layer of mustard on each side as well. The following adjuncts are excellent, but any one may be omitted; all together are excellent. On top of the steak, spread a thin layer of catsup and/or Worcestershire sauce. Sauté the onion after slicing it in thin rings and put them on top. Add some sautéed mushroom caps. How about some very thin slices of green pepper? And some thin circles of lemon? Measure the steak exactly in its thickest part and bake it 20 minutes for each inch of thickness. *Mrs. Arthur Stern*

Deviled Steaks

4 servings

4 tablespoons butter
1 cup Italian flavored bread crumbs
1 tablespoon vegetable oil
2 tablespoons lemon juice
1/4 cup minced shallots or scallions
2 tablespoons red wine, or red wine vinegar
2 tablespoons Dijon mustard
Dash of cayenne
2 teaspoons Worcestershire sauce
Salt
Pepper
MSG
4 cube or minute steaks or any small steak
Roquefort or Boursin cheese

Melt the butter in a saucepan and add 2 tablespoons to the bread crumbs. Mix well and set aside. To the remaining butter, add the oil, lemon juice, and the shallots or scallions and cook until just tender. Add wine or vinegar, mustard, cayenne, and Worcestershire sauce and simmer 2 minutes. Let this cool while you put salt, pepper, and MSG on steaks. Place the steaks in a shallow glass or stainless steel pan; spoon the marinade over, cover, and marinate, unrefrigerated, up to 6 hours. Refrigerate if marinated longer.

To cook, remove the steaks, dry on paper towels, and sauté them quickly in half oil, half butter. Put on a broiler-proof platter, spread with Boursin cheese or a Roquefort-and-butter mixture and press crumbs into the cheese. Broil 1 minute until crumbs are browned.

A small spoonful of Boursin is good on any big

steak or on lamb chops. A small spoonful of mustard butter is good on steak or chops.

Mrs. Benjamin Griswold, IV

Rare Roast Beef, Foolproof and Simple

A 2, 3, or 4-rib roast beef
Salt and pepper

Salt and pepper a roast of any size. Place it in a preheated oven set at 375°. Turn the heat off after 1 hour but leave the roast undisturbed, without opening the door. This must be done hours before dinner so that the heat will penetrate the meat sufficiently.

Before serving, reset the oven to 300° and reheat a 2-rib roast for 20 minutes, a 3-rib roast for 25 to 30 minutes, and a 4-rib roast for 35 minutes. The beef will be rare, warm, and juicy and the oven will not be spattered as it is in the revolutionary high-heat method.

Mrs. Benjamin Griswold, IV

Brisket with Chestnuts and Prunes

4 servings

1 pound brisket
2 cups prunes
2 onions
Brown sugar
2 cups canned or fresh chestnuts
1 tablespoon butter
1 tablespoon flour
1/2 cup vinegar or white wine

Cut up the brisket, add a little water, and simmer it until it is soft. Boil the prunes with the onions, thinly sliced, and the brown sugar to taste, in just enough water to cover them. Remove the prune pits if you like. Parboil the chestnuts, if fresh, and peel them, then add them to the meat and the prunes. Add the butter, sprinkle in the flour, then the vinegar or wine, and heat thoroughly. This may be made ahead of time and reheated.

Mrs. Walter Rosenbaum

Roast Tenderloin Charentais

350° / 6 servings

2-pound piece of beef tenderloin
1/2 cup olive oil
2-1/2 tablespoons wine vinegar
Bouquet garni
3 cloves
Dash nutmeg
3 thin slices salt pork
1/2 cup dry white wine
1 shallot, finely minced
Salt and freshly ground pepper
1 teaspoon tarragon leaves, finely chopped
1/4-1/3 cup heavy cream

The evening before serving, marinate the beef in olive oil, wine vinegar, bouquet garni, cloves, and nutmeg. Almost an hour before serving, remove the meat from the marinade, tie salt pork over the top and roast for 40 to 45 minutes or until your meat thermometer indicates that it is cooked but still rare. Baste it occasionally with the marinade. Remove to a hot platter and keep warm. Remove all but 1 tablespoon of fat from the roasting pan. Deglaze the pan with the wine and strain into a small saucepan. Add 1 teaspoon wine vinegar, the shallot, and salt and pepper, if needed. Simmer for 10 minutes. Then add the tarragon and 1/4 as much heavy cream as you have sauce. Reheat, then remove from heat and swirl in the butter. Slice the tenderloin and pour the sauce over it. French fried potatoes and sautéed mushrooms go well with this.

Mrs. Robert A. Russell

Spanish Roast Beef

350° / 18 servings

6 pounds rolled roast of beef
3 garlic cloves, minced
1 tablespoon salt
2 teaspoons paprika
1-1/2 teaspoons black pepper
1/2 cup red wine
1/2 cup red wine vinegar
1/4 cup olive oil
5 onions, chopped
4 tomatoes, peeled and chopped
2 green peppers, chopped
1/2 cup sliced mushrooms
1 bay leaf
1/2 cup stuffed olives, sliced

Mash together the garlic, salt, paprika, and the pepper, and rub the mixture into a 6-pound rolled roast of beef. Put it in an earthenware bowl, add the red wine and the wine vinegar, and marinate the beef in the refrigerator for 12 hours, turning the meat often and basting it frequently.

Remove the meat from the refrigerator 3 hours before roasting it, drain and dry it thoroughly, and reserve the marinade. Brown the meat in a roasting pan in the heated olive oil over high heat, turning it frequently to brown it evenly. Put around the meat the onions, tomatoes, green peppers, sliced mushrooms, and the bay leaf and add the reserved marinade. Roast the beef, basting frequently, allowing 16 minutes per pound for rare, 20 minutes per pound for medium, and 23 minutes for well-done. If necessary, add water to the pan.

Remove the meat to a heated platter and discard the bay leaf. Rub the vegetables and sauce through a sieve, add sliced stuffed olives, and season to taste. Reheat the sauce and serve it separately.

Mrs. Jon Alan Wurtzburger

Cold Fillet of Beef, Niçoise

425° / 6 servings

2 pounds fillet of beef
3 tablespoons olive oil
1 large eggplant
1 pound tomatoes
1 onion
2 green peppers
3 tablespoons olive oil
1 clove garlic
1/2 pint sour cream
1 teaspoon paprika
Lemon juice
2-1/4 cups aspic jelly
3 hard-cooked eggs
1/4 pound black olives

First, brush the fillet with the olive oil. For rare beef, roast for about 20 minutes or until the meat thermometer registers 120°. Set aside.

Slice the eggplant, score it with a knife, sprinkle it with salt and let it drain for 1/2 an hour, then wipe it dry. Skin and quarter the tomatoes and remove the seeds. Peel and slice the onion, halve the peppers, remove the fibres and seeds, and shred them. Heat 3 tablespoons of olive oil in a pan, and brown the eggplant on each side. Reduce the flame and cook the onions until translucent, then add the peppers and cook an additional 2 minutes. Then add the tomatoes; turn up the heat and cook one minute. Put in another dish to cool.

Make a dressing by crushing the garlic into the sour cream; season to taste with salt, pepper, paprika, and lemon juice.

Carve the beef and arrange around a platter, with slices overlapping; brush with cool aspic several times. Spoon the salad down the center of the platter, then decorate with quarters of egg and the olives. The dressing should be in a separate boat. Anchovy bread (recipe follows) is a good accompaniment.

Anchovy Bread

1 loaf crusty bread
6 anchovy fillets
A tube of anchovy paste
1/4 pound butter
Pepper

Cut the bread almost through to the crust. Mash the anchovy fillets, the anchovy paste, and the butter together, add some pepper if you like, and spread the slices with this flavorful mixture. Tie it with a string so that the slices don't fall apart; set it on a baking sheet and heat it at 400° for 10 minutes or until it appears crusty and brown.
Herbert Powell

Fillet Louis XV

450° / 8 servings

1 beef tenderloin
Duxelles
Sauce Béarnaise

Rub the beef tenderloin with salt and pepper. Place in a preheated oven for 40 minutes, then remove. While still warm, cut into 2-inch rounds. Spread a tablespoon of Duxelles (see below) on each steak, mask with sauce Béarnaise. Place under the broiler for about 3 to 4 minutes until brown and serve immediately.

Duxelles

1 pound mushrooms, chopped very fine
2-1/2 tablespoons butter
1/2 tablespoon oil
3 tablespoons shallots, minced
Salt and pepper
Dash of lemon juice

Heat the butter and oil in a large heavy pan and sauté the shallots until soft. Add the chopped mushrooms and cook until mushrooms are dry and hold together well enough to spread. Add salt, pepper, and lemon juice.
Mrs. John J. Smith

Tournedos Rossini

6 servings

6 tournedos (filets mignons)
6 tablespoons butter
6 rounds of bread, sautéed in butter
6 slices foie gras
18 slices of truffle
1/2 cup demi-glaze sauce or good brown sauce made with beef stock
1/2 cup Madeira

Sauté the tournedos in butter and place on sautéed bread rounds of the same size. On each tournedos place a round of foie gras and 3 slices of truffle which have been heated in pan drippings. Place the demi-glaze sauce and Madeira in the skillet, heat and pour around the tournedos. Garnish with watercress.
Mrs. Robert A. Russell

Tournedos Maria Pia

6 servings

4 ounces butter
1/3 teaspoon leaf marjoram
Salt and pepper
6 tournedos (1-inch thick slices of fillet of beef)
Kitchen Bouquet
1 cup dry white wine
2 teaspoons dry mustard
3 ounces Madeira
3 bay leaves
Brandy

Melt 2 ounces of the butter in a chafing dish; add the marjoram, salt, and pepper. Brush both sides of each tournedos with Kitchen bouquet. Sauté the tournedos just short of the desired degree of doneness, remove from the chafing dish, and keep warm. In the chafing dish add the remaining 2 ounces of butter, and the dry white wine in which the dry mustard has been dissolved. Add the Madeira and the bay leaves. Cook this over a hot flame until the sauce is reduced to about half its original volume. Remove the bay leaves. Return the tournedos to the chafing dish; heat and sprinkle lightly with brandy; ignite and serve.

If you wish to shorten the time of cooking at the table you can partially cook the meat under the broiler before putting it in the chafing dish.

Frank D'Amanda

Fillet of Beef with Mushroom and Truffle Sauce

450° / 8 servings

Beef tenderloin, about 4 pounds
Cracked Java pepper
1/4 cup Madeira
1/3 cup butter
1 cup brandy

Wipe the beef with a towel and place in a preheated oven. After 10 minutes, season the meat well with pepper and pour over it the Madeira and the melted butter. Bake 30 minutes for rare meat. Place the meat on a warm serving platter. Warm the brandy and pour it, lighted, over the meat. Serve with the following sauce.

Mushroom and Truffle Sauce

8 large mushrooms, chopped
1 or 2 large truffles, chopped
1/4 cup Madeira wine
1 cup beef bouillon
2 teaspoons arrowroot

Marinate the mushrooms and truffles in the Madeira. Heat the bouillon, saving some to dissolve the arrowroot. Combine the arrowroot with the bouillon and heat slowly for 5 minutes. Add the mushrooms, truffles, and Madeira and cook for 1 or 2 more minutes. The fillet may be served with a slice of chilled paté on each carved portion.

Miss Frances Faust

Glazed Lamb Mock Duck

325° / 8 servings

1 4-pound boned lamb shoulder, rolled and tied
1 6-ounce can frozen orange juice
4 tablespoons lemon juice
1/4 cup butter or margarine
1/2 teaspoon salt
1/2 cup finely chopped celery
1 tablespoon mint flakes

Place the lamb on a rack in a shallow roasting pan; roast it for 1 hour. Combine orange juice, lemon juice, butter, and salt and simmer for five minutes. Turn up the oven to 350°. Brush the lamb with the sauce; roast it uncovered for 1-1/2 to 2 hours or longer, brushing the meat with sauce every 15 to 20 minutes. Add the celery to the remaining sauce; cook for 5 minutes more. Stir in the mint; serve the hot sauce with the lamb.

Mrs. Percival C. Keith

Western Run House Leg of Lamb

500° / 6 servings

Garlic
Leg of lamb, about 5 pounds
Dry mustard
Water
Rosemary
Paprika

Cut the garlic into slivers and, making shallow incisions in the lamb with a knife, poke the pieces into it. Make a paste of dry mustard and water and coat the leg with this, then add a dusting of rosemary and paprika. Leave the lamb at room temperature for a while.

Roast the lamb uncovered and with no water in the pan for 15 to 20 minutes or until it is golden brown. Reduce the heat to 400° and leave it to roast 40 minutes more, basting it only if you have

the energy. Make an incision in the lamb, and if it looks too rare, leave it for an additional five minutes. This will be a unique experience for many lamb devotees.
Mrs. Jerome Kidder

Butterfly Leg of Lamb, Two Ways

6 servings

FOR ONE WAY:

A 5-pound butterflied leg of lamb, boned and flattened
Salt
Pepper
Lemon juice
Mustard butter

Season the lamb with salt, pepper, and lemon, then grill 10 minutes on the cut side and 15 minutes on the fell side. Spread with mustard butter and slice diagonally.

FOR ANOTHER WAY:

A butterflied leg of lamb, boned and flattened
1/2 cup olive oil
1 teaspoon ground pepper
1 clove garlic, crushed
1/2 teaspoon or more parsley
2 onions, minced
2 teaspoons salt
2 lemons, both juice and rind
1/2 teaspoon thyme
1/2 teaspoon oregano
1 bay leaf
1 pint red wine

With plenty of time and advance thought, a marinade may be made of the ingredients listed, and the lamb may be left in it, with occasional turning, for a day or a night. Then the lamb is drained and grilled in the same way, outdoors or under the broiler.
Mrs. Curran W. Harvey

Roast Lamb with Coffee

300° / 6 servings

5-pound leg of lamb
Salt and pepper
Dry mustard
Rosemary

Sauce:

1 cup strong coffee
2 tablespoons cream
2 tablespoons sugar
1 jigger brandy

Salt and pepper the lamb, and dust it all over with the mustard. Pat some ground rosemary into the top of the lamb. Roast in a slow oven 18 minutes to the pound if your intention is to have it well done, or 12 minutes if you like it pink. Baste it frequently with the sauce while it is in the oven. Then transfer it to a warm serving tray and let it stand 20 minutes before carving so that the juices will not run out and it can continue to cook internally the necessary amount of time.
Mrs. Morton Katzenberg

Pickled Sour Cherries

Red sour cherries
Cider vinegar
Sugar

Seed, then weigh the sour cherries, and cover them with the cider vinegar. Set them aside for 24 hours. Drain the vinegar from the cherries; it can be saved to use in salad dressings another time. Use an amount of sugar equal to the weight of the cherries and stir it into the fruit until it has more or less dissolved, then continue stirring it off and on for about 2 days. Pack it in jars or stone crocks. This is good as a relish with roast lamb.
Mrs. C. B. Bosley

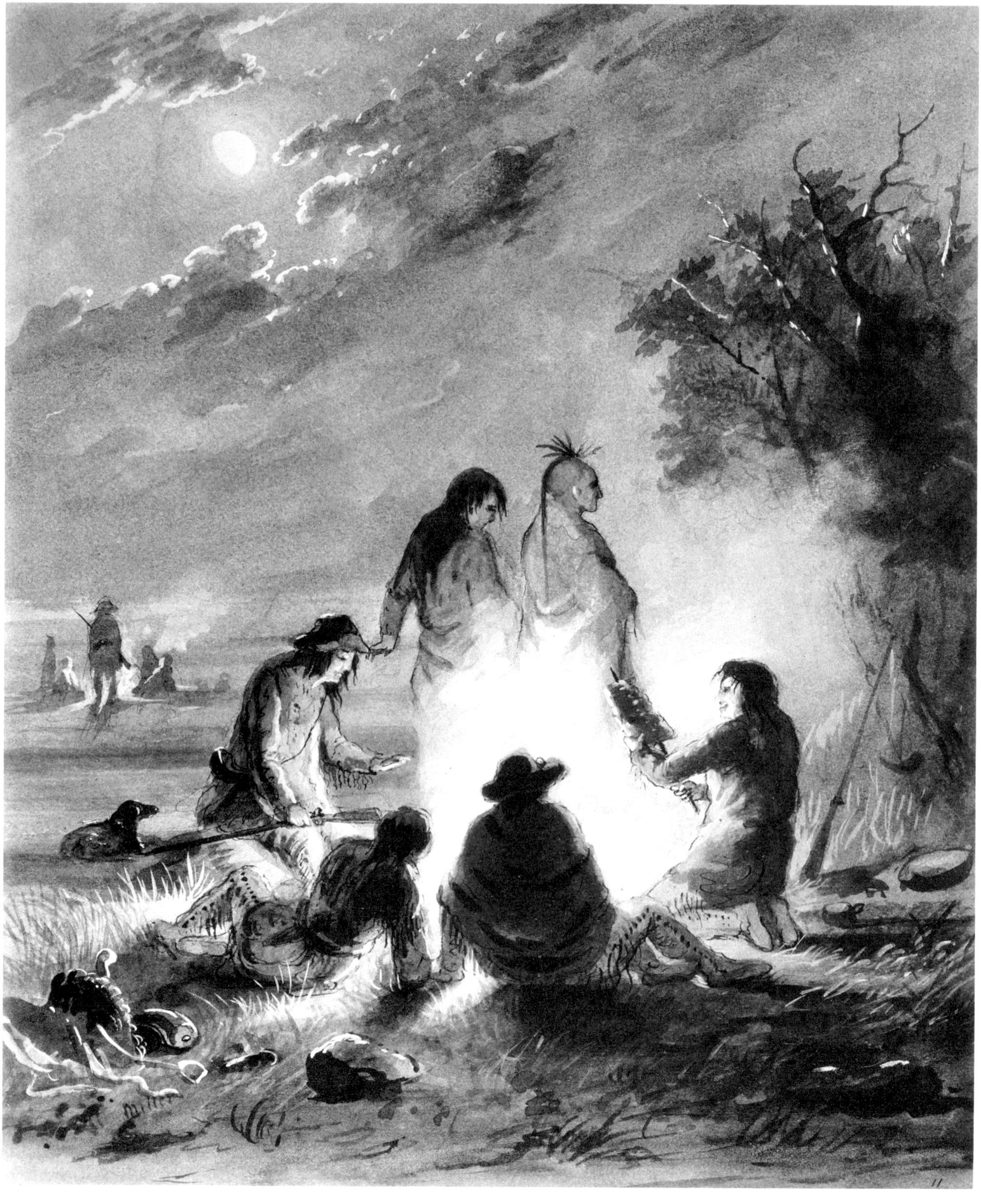

Shish Kabobs

6 servings

Leg of lamb, cubed, and/or pork tenderloin, cubed
Salt and pepper
Juice of 1 lemon
Juice of 1 orange
Oregano
1 cup olive oil
1 cup wine
1 clove garlic, minced
Small white onions, parboiled
Green pepper, seeded and cut in 1-1/2 inch squares

Use either leg of lamb or pork tenderloin or both. Combine the salt, pepper, lemon and orange juices, oregano, olive oil, wine, and garlic with the meat. Place in an earthenware bowl and cover. Allow the meat to marinate for 5 hours, turning it occasionally.

Drain the meat, thread on skewers, alternating the meat with peppers and onions. Broil on a grill or under the broiler, turning the skewers often.

Mrs. James N. Cianos

Individual Lamb Roasts

350° / 6 servings

6 loin lamb chops, 2-1/2 inches thick
Thin strips of salt pork
Butter
Salt
Pepper
Flour

Have the butcher remove the fat, bones, and tail from the lamb chops, then wrap around them a thin strip of salt pork, securing the pork strips with wooden picks. Brown them in butter after sprinkling them with salt, pepper, and a little flour. Place them in a roasting pan to roast for 25 to 35 minutes or until tender. If preferred rare, roast the chops for about 20-25 minutes.

Serve hot with mashed potatoes and garnish with bunches of watercress.

Mrs. Alan Wurtzburger

Buffet Curry of Lamb, Chicken or Shrimp

24 servings

3 cups stock (lamb, beef, or chicken)
2 cups shredded coconut, unsweetened
4 tablespoons bacon fat
2 medium-sized onions, sliced
2 apples, peeled and sliced
4 tablespoons flour
4 tablespoons curry powder, or to taste
7 pounds cooked lamb or chicken, cut into 1-inch cubes, or shrimp
1/4 cup seedless raisins
2 tablespoons sugar
Juice of fresh lemon

Bring the stock to a boil and keep it warm. Steep the coconut in 2 cups boiling water. Drain and save the liquid. Heat the fat in a large heavy kettle or Dutch oven over a low flame. Add the onion and apple and sauté until tender. Add the flour and curry powder and stir vigorously until a paste-like consistency is achieved. Immediately add the stock, stirring until it is as thick as gravy. Add the meat or shrimp; then add the coconut and as much coconut

Facing page: *Preparing the Evening Meal*, watercolor by Alfred Jacob Miller, 1849. The members of a fur trading expedition are seen roasting the hump rib of a buffalo, the favorite food of men of the prairies. The artist accompanied the expedition of the American Fur Company in 1836/37 and painted the watercolors on his return to Baltimore.

liquid as is needed to maintain the desired thickness. Add the raisins, sugar, and lemon juice. Heat over simmering water or over a very low flame for 2 hours or longer, stirring occasionally; additional liquid from the steeped coconut may be added if necessary.

Serve with rice and any or all of these accompaniments: quartered tomatoes, sliced banana, diced apple, diced melon, sliced hard-boiled eggs, roasted shelled peanuts, diced avocados, crushed pineapple, sliced peaches, sliced pear, and chutney. Beer, milk, or champagne should be served as the beverage.
Mrs. Irving Nudelman, Mr. Edward McCracken

Casserole Paysanne

450° / 24 servings

3 pounds smoked ham, in 1/2-inch cubes
4 cups thin cream sauce
1-1/2 pounds snappy cheese, cubed
5 tablespoons drained horseradish
3 tablespoons chili sauce
2 tablespoons Worcestershire sauce
2 bouillon cubes
3/4 teaspoon salt
1/4 teaspoon pepper
18 hard-cooked eggs, thickly sliced

Cut the ham into 1/2-inch cubes. Make the thin cream sauce in the proportion of 2 tablespoons each of flour and butter to 1 cup of milk, add to it the cheese, the horseradish, chili sauce, Worcestershire sauce, and bouillon cubes. Heat it in a double boiler until the cheese has melted; then add the salt and pepper. Fill a buttered casserole with alternate layers of the seasoned sauce, the ham cubes, and the thickly sliced eggs. Finish with a dozen or so ham cubes on top. Bake for about 40 minutes. Parsley on top adds to the decoration.
Mrs. Richard Lansburgh

Jambon à la Crème

4 servings

4 slices of ham, cut in 1/4-inch cubes
1 cup white wine
12 sliced mushrooms
Butter
1/2 teaspoon cornstarch
1 cup cream
1/4 cup Madeira or port
Salt and pepper

Heat the ham in the wine until the wine has evaporated. In another pan, sauté the mushrooms lightly in a little butter. Mix the cornstarch with a little cream; then add the rest of the cream, making sure it is not lumpy. Add Madeira or port to the cream; then pour it all into the pan with the mushrooms. Add the ham slices and heat it all thoroughly, but briefly.
Mrs. W. Boulton Kelly

Jambon Persillé

PARSLIED HAM IN ASPIC,
THE EASY WAY

10 servings

4 cups baked ham, coarsely chopped
4 cups well-flavored and clarified soup stock
1-1/2 cups dry white wine
6 shallots, chopped
1 bay leaf
A dozen or so peppercorns
3 envelopes gelatin
3/4 cup cold water
3 cups fresh parsley, finely chopped

Probably a 3-inch piece of baked ham will yield the required amount.

Make a delicious aspic with the stock, white

wine, and seasonings by boiling it until the right flavor is achieved. Strain it, add the gelatin which has been softened in water, and stir until the gelatin is dissolved. Mix a little aspic with the chopped ham and put the ham into a pretty serving bowl. Let the remaining aspic set until it begins to thicken, and then stir in the parsley. Spread it over the ham completely.

Miss Alice Newman

Ham in Fruit Sauce

350° / 4 servings

1/4 cup butter
1/4 cup flour
1 cup beef bouillon
1/2 cup white wine
3/4 cup raisins
3/4 cup currants
1 teaspoon lemon peel, very finely sliced
1 teaspoon wine vinegar
1 tablespoon sugar
Juice of half a lemon
Pre-cooked ham slices, about 3/8 inch thick

Melt the butter, add the flour, and cook two minutes to get rid of the starchy taste. Add all the other ingredients save the ham and simmer until the fruits are soft. You may need to add a little more bouillon and you may want some more sugar. Put the ham in a casserole, cover it with sauce, and heat for about 15 minutes. Serve with baked white or sweet potatoes.

Mrs. Walter G. Lohr

Pork Chops and Apple Casserole

375° / 6 servings

6 pork chops, 3/4-inch thick
1-1/2 teaspoons salt
1/4 teaspoon pepper
12 small white onions, peeled
4 apples, peeled and quartered
1/2 cup seedless raisins
1 tablespoon brown sugar
1 cup cider or consommé
1/8 teaspoon thyme
Bouquet garni of bay leaf and parsley
Dashes of thyme, mace, clove
2 tablespoons currant jelly

Season the chops with salt and pepper. In a skillet, brown the chops well on both sides, then drain. Arrange the chops in a greased earthenware casserole with the onions, apples, and raisins. Sprinkle with brown sugar, add the liquid and seasoning, and cover tightly. Bake for 1-1/4 hours, removing the cover for the last 20 minutes. If this is still too liquid, remove some of the juices with a baster. Add currant jelly to the remainder. Serve in the casserole.

Otto F. Kraushaar

Barbecued Pork Chops

350° / 4 servings

8 lean pork chops
4 tablespoons fat
1/2 cup catsup
1 teaspoon salt
1 teaspoon celery seed
1/2 teaspoon nutmeg
1/3 cup vinegar
1 bay leaf
1 cup water

Brown the chops on both sides in hot fat, then transfer the chops to a baking dish. Combine the remaining ingredients and pour over the chops. Cover and bake for 1-1/2 hours.

Mrs. Norman P. Ramsey

The Fruits of the Earth (detail), painted by Francesco Bassano in Venice, about 1580-1590.
This is one of a series of paintings which represented the four elements — earth, air, fire, and water.

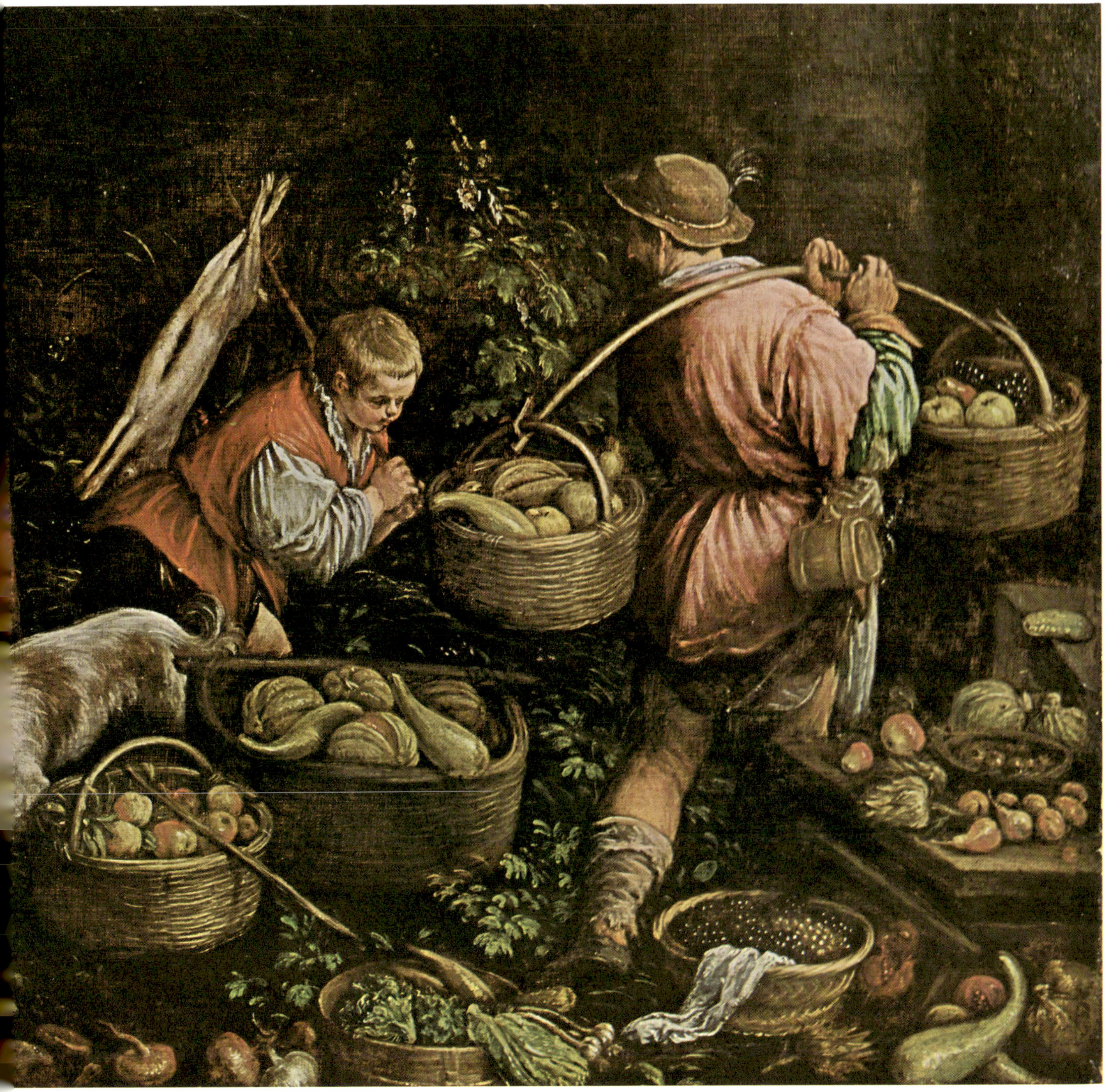

Hungarian Pork Chops

6 servings

**6 1-inch thick pork chops
3 tablespoons fat
1 or 2 onions, finely chopped
Salt
Paprika
3 or 4 green peppers, seeded
2 or 3 tomatoes, peeled
Caraway seeds
Sour cream**

One must have good flavorful paprika in all Hungarian recipes. This one is no exception. Trim the chops and brown them on both sides in a little fat in a heavy skillet. Remove the chops and in the same skillet sauté the onions only until transparent. Return the chops to the pan and sprinkle with both salt and the good paprika, at least a tablespoonful. Cut the peppers and the tomatoes into large pieces and cover the chops with these and then sprinkle them with as much caraway seed as you like. Cover and simmer until the meat is tender. If you find there is too much juice remove the lid until the liquid is reduced to the right amount. Right before serving swirl in generously some sour cream, not forgetting that the juices must not boil after this addition. *Mrs. S. Page Nelson, Jr.*

Creoled Pork Chops

350° / 6 servings

**6 thick pork chops
Salt and pepper
6 1/2-inch slices of Bermuda onion
6 1/2-inch rings of green pepper
6 teaspoons washed rice
1 can condensed tomato soup**

Salt and pepper the chops, then put them in a pan with a slice of onion and a slice of green pepper on each. In the center of the pepper, put a teaspoon of the rice. Pour the tomato soup into the pan and bake at 350° for 1-1/2 hours. Baste the chops frequently and, if necessary, add a small quantity of water from time to time to keep them from becoming dry. *Mrs. Jack Wasserman*

Butterfly Pork Chops

350° / 6 servings

**6 butterflied pork chops, 6-8 ounces each
Salt, pepper, and a pinch of thyme
3 tablespoons margarine or butter
1/2 small onion, chopped
1/4 cup beef consommé**

Wipe the pork chops dry with a paper towel and season with salt, pepper, and thyme. Sauté them in margarine or butter in a skillet until they are nicely browned on both sides, then add the onion and consommé. Cover the skillet tightly, place in the oven, and bake 45 minutes to 1 hour or until the chops are tender.

Mrs. Bertram Bernheim, Jr.

Suprêmes de Porc

300° / 6 servings

1 pork tenderloin, cut in 1-inch slices
Salt
Pepper
4 tablespoons clarified butter
2 shallots
1 tablespoon paprika
1 tablespoon flour
1 glass of sherry
1/2 cup cream
Sautéed mushrooms (optional)
Chopped parsley for garnish

Pound the fillets to a thinness of about 3/4 inch; dust them with salt and freshly ground pepper. Sauté them in the butter over low heat until they are just browned. Chop the shallots and add them with the paprika. Stir in the flour, then the sherry. Simmer a minute or two and then put the casserole in the oven, covered, to cook for about 40 or 50 minutes. Pour in the cream; sautéed mushrooms may be added at the same time. Let the dish stand for about 10 minutes before putting the chops on a warmed platter with the sauce over them.

This is an excellent buffet dish, for a little delay doesn't hurt it.
Miss Sara Anthony

Pork Piquant

300° / 8 servings

1 loin of pork, boned and cut into 8 or 9 chops
Fat for searing
1 No. 2 can pineapple chunks
2 tablespoons cornstarch
1/2 cup water
1/4 cup vinegar
1 teaspoon salt
1/8 teaspoon pepper
1/4 cup brown sugar
2 tablespoons lemon juice
2 tablespoons prepared mustard
2 tablespoons Worcestershire sauce
8-9 small cooked and peeled sweet potatoes
2 medium onions

Cut away the excess fat from the pork chops. Sear them in hot fat on both sides until they are a golden brown. Drain them well on paper towels before arranging them in a 3-quart casserole. Season with salt and pepper.

Drain the juice from the canned pineapple into a saucepan. Add to it the cornstarch, which has been mixed with water, the vinegar, salt, pepper, brown sugar, lemon juice, mustard, and Worcestershire sauce. Stir over moderate heat until the sauce has slightly thickened. Arrange the potatoes among the chops. (Drained canned ones do very well in this dish.) Peel and thinly slice the onions, separate into rings, and layer them over the chops and potatoes. Sprinkle with salt and pepper. Pour the sauce over all, cover and bake for 2 hours or less, just until the pork is tender. Uncover, add the pineapple pieces, and bake 15 minutes more. A molded spinach salad goes well with this.
Miss Hortense Reit

Sweet and Sour Pork

4 to 6 servings

2 pounds lean pork
1 tablespoon bacon drippings
2 tablespoons cornstarch
1/2 cup water
1/4 cup brown sugar
1/2 teaspoon salt
1/3 cup vinegar
1 tablespoon soy sauce
1 No. 2 can pineapple chunks
3/4 cup thinly sliced green pepper
1/2 cup thinly sliced onion

Cut the pork in 1-1/2-inch strips and brown the

pieces in bacon drippings. Drain the pineapple and reserve the juice. Stir the cornstarch into the water and combine it with the sugar, salt, vinegar, soy sauce, and pineapple juice. Cook this until it is clear and slightly thickened, about 2 minutes. Add the sauce to the pork and cook for about 1 hour, covered, over low heat or until the pork is tender. Chill it overnight. Before serving, heat it over a low flame until it is hot, then add the pepper, onion, and pineapple pieces. Cook for 2 minutes and serve with wild rice or a mixture of white and wild rice, which is an excellent and inexpensive substitute.

This is best cooked the day before and reheated with a few additions at dinner time.

Mrs. Keith McBee

Baked Canadian Bacon

450°-350° / 24 servings

2 whole sides of Canadian bacon
2 teaspoons dried thyme
1-1/2 teaspoons coarse-ground pepper
2 teaspoons orange rind
8 tablespoons Dijon mustard
1-1/2 teaspoons powdered mace
2 oranges, thinly sliced
2 lemons, thinly sliced
2 cups dry white wine
For garnish: stewed or pickled fruits, orange slices, mint leaves

Remove the casings from 2 whole sides of Canadian bacon and place them in a long, shallow baking pan. Make a paste of all the ingredients except the wine, sliced oranges, and lemons. Cover the bacons with the paste and put them in a 450° oven for 25 minutes. Do not disturb the pan. After 25 minutes, lower the temperature to 350°, when the paste should be set.

Place orange and lemon slices around and on the bacons. Slowly pour 2 cups of wine on the bacons and into the pan. Bake for another 40 minutes, basting frequently. Serve bacons thinly sliced on an oval tray, garnished with stewed or pickled fruits, orange slices, and mint leaves.

Miss Rita St. Clair

Piquant Beef Tongue

6 servings

1 beef tongue (about 2 pounds)
1/2 cup vinegar
2 small onions, sliced
3/4 cup raisins
1 lemon, sliced
3/4 cup brown sugar
3/4 cup almonds
Salt
Pinch of ginger
1 teaspoon allspice
3/4 cup cider (optional)
1 heaping cup of ground gingersnaps

Simmer the tongue for 4 hours in water almost to cover. Pour into a saucepan 4 cups of the water in which the tongue was cooked. Add all the rest of the ingredients with the exception of the ground gingersnaps. Simmer until reduced by half. Then add the gingersnaps to thicken the sauce. Skin and slice the tongue, add the slices to the sauce and let them simmer for a short time before serving.

Mrs. Sam Stabins

Braised Fresh Tongue

325° / 6 servings

1 3-1/2-to-4-pound fresh beef tongue
3 or 4 carrots, coarsely chopped
2 small or 1 large onion, coarsely chopped
3 ribs celery, coarsely chopped
1 large clove garlic, split
2 bay leaves
4 or 5 stalks parsley

2 or 3 whole cloves
1 bottle dry red wine
1/3 cup Cognac
1/2 tablespoon salt
6 to 8 whole peppercorns
2 cans (10-1/2 ounces) condensed beef broth
1 tablespoon of arrowroot (optional)

To Boil: Place the tongue in a heavy kettle, cover with cold water, and bring up to a boil. Boil for about 5 minutes, skimming off any scum that rises to the surface. Reduce heat, cover, and simmer for 2 hours. Drain and cover with cold water. When the tongue is cool enough to handle, pull off the skin. Where it is reluctant, run a small sharp knife between the meat and skin. Trim off the root and pull out any bones. Combine all the remaining ingredients except the beef broth and arrowroot in a large polyethylene bag. Add the tongue. Tie securely, squeezing out all air. Place in a bowl or pan to protect against leakage and marinate for a minimum of 6 hours. If overnight, refrigerate, turning occasionally so the meat is well soaked.

To braise: Preheat the oven to 325° for 15 minutes. Remove the tongue from the plastic bag and place the tongue, the marinade, and the beef broth in a large heavy enameled ovenproof casserole. Bring to a boil over a high heat. Cover tightly, then bake for 2 hours or until very tender when pierced with a fork. Turn the tongue after the first hour. Lift the meat from the liquid onto a warm platter and keep warm. Place the casserole over a high heat and reduce the liquid to about half. Taste here for seasonings. Strain. If the sauce seems too thin, mix 1 tablespoon of arrowroot with 2 tablespoons of wine until smooth. Add to the sauce and cook over a low heat, whipping constantly with a wire whip, until slightly thickened.

To serve: Slice the tongue and arrange the slices, overlapping, on a warm platter. Spoon some of the sauce over the meat, and serve the remainder in a warm sauce boat.
Helen McCully

Tongue and Asparagus in Aspic

24 servings

5 cups of aspic (see below)
72 asparagus tips, cooked
1/2 cup French dressing
Pimiento
Cucumber pickle
3 smoked tongues, cooked
2 truffles, or 12 large pitted black olives
Whites of 12 hard-cooked eggs

Coat 2 large platters with aspic and chill until the aspic has set. Marinate the cooked asparagus tips in French dressing for an hour, drain well, and arrange in bundles of 3 (tips to the center) on the aspic-coated platters. Cut the pimiento and pickle in narrow strips and drape one of each across each

Swan-shaped sauceboat made at Worcester in the earliest period, 1751-1783. The moulded surface of the porcelain is painted with leaves and butterflies.

asparagus bundle. Coat with aspic and chill until set. Cut the tongue into thin slices. Fold each slice in half and decorate with a slice of truffle or olive set in a circle of hard-boiled egg white. Overlap the tongue slices all around the edge of platter, coat with aspic and chill until set, too.

Aspic

5 cans double chicken consommé
2-1/2 packages gelatin

With wet towels, sop up the film of fat which accumulates on top of the cans of consommé, then boil up the soup with an egg white and strain it through a thick layer of cheesecloth. Soak gelatin in a little more than 1/2 cup of the clarified stock, then dissolve it in 5 cups of boiling hot consommé. It will be thick and clear when it is cold.

Mrs. Robert D. Meyers

Frankfurter Polonaise

12 servings

1 onion, chopped
Paprika
Butter
2 cans (6 ounces) tomato paste
2 cans (10-1/2 ounces) consommé
Salt and pepper
14 frankfurters
Mashed potatoes

Glaze a chopped onion and some paprika in a little butter and add the tomato paste, consommé, salt and pepper to taste, and let it simmer slowly until slightly reduced. Skin about 14 frankfurters, cut them into inch lengths, add to the tomato sauce, and let them poach in this for about 20 minutes. Serve in a tureen with mashed potatoes.

Miss Avonia Read

Molded Sweetbreads

375° / 10 servings

5 pairs of sweetbreads
1 cup white bread cubes
Milk
1/2 pint whipping cream
1-1/2 teaspoons Worcestershire sauce
Salt, pepper, and paprika
2 eggs

Soak the sweetbreads in cold water for 5 minutes. Drain; parboil at least 1 hour to release any blood in them. Firm them by putting them immediately into ice water. When they are cool, remove the tubes and any tough membrane. Soak the bread in a little milk and mix it with the sweetbreads, chopped up, the cream, seasoning, and slightly beaten eggs. Put this all in a well buttered 9-inch ring mold; set the mold, covered, in a hot water bath and bake for 45 minutes.

Serve with peas or glazed carrots in the center of the ring and chopped parsley over all.

Mrs. James Donovan

Creamed Sweetbreads and Mushrooms

4 servings

1 pair calf's sweetbreads, 1-1/4 to 1-1/2 pounds
1 cup rich chicken or veal stock
1/2 pound fresh mushrooms (smallish ones)
4 tablespoons butter
1 tablespoon finely minced onion
4 tablespoons flour
2/3 cup heavy cream
2 egg yolks, lightly beaten with 1/3 cup light cream
2 teaspoons very dry sherry or other dry white wine
Salt and pepper to taste
Pastry shells

Simmer the sweetbreads in stock, covered, about

20 minutes. Drain, reserving the broth. Cool the sweetbreads quickly by putting the pan containing them in ice water. When cold, remove the gristle, tough membrane, and fat, but not the thin membrane covering the sweetbread. Cut in uniform bite-sized pieces.

If the mushrooms are clean-looking, wipe them with a damp paper towel, otherwise rinse and drain. Trim, slice, and sauté in 2 tablespoons butter with the onion until the onion is soft and clear. Melt 2 tablespoons butter in another saucepan, add the flour and cook, stirring until bubbly. Add the reserved broth from cooking the sweetbreads and cook over medium heat, stirring constantly, until quite thick. Add heavy cream and egg yolks mixed with thin cream; continue to cook over *low* heat until the egg yolks have lost their raw taste and the sauce has thickened to a heavy cream consistency. Stir in the sherry.

Pour the sauce over the mushroom-onion mixture and mix gently; then add the sweetbreads and stir and taste, adding salt and pepper and perhaps a dash of lemon juice as required. This may be cooled and refrigerated overnight and reheated over hot water the next day. When ready to serve, ladle into pastry shells. *Miss Grace Farmer*

Sweetbreads Joseph

4 servings

2 pairs sweetbreads
Vinegar
1/4 cup sherry
1 cup cream
Salt
Almonds

Soak 2 pairs of sweetbreads in cold salted water for 1 hour, then drain. Place in a pan of water to which a little vinegar has been added, bring to a boil, and let cook for 20 minutes. Plunge them into ice-cold water to firm, then remove all the skin and membranes.

Place sweetbreads in a skillet and pour on 1/4 cup of sherry, cover tightly, and let them steam for a few minutes. Scald 1 cup of cream, add a pinch of salt, and pour it over the sweetbreads. Let them poach slowly for 15 minutes, basting frequently. Cover with the sauce from the pan and over all sprinkle slivered, browned, and salted almonds. Garnish with chopped parsley.

Mrs. Joseph T. Brennan

Terrine de Ris de Veau

Taillevant Restaurant, Paris

2 pounds sweetbreads
2 carrots, finely chopped
1 medium onion, finely chopped
3 shallots, finely chopped
8 tablespoons sweet butter
1 clove garlic
Salt and pepper
1 cup dry white wine
1/4 cup port
1/2 cup Madeira
1 bay leaf
1/4 teaspoon thyme
2 tablespoons chopped parsley
1/2 pound fat pork
1/2 pound veal
1/4 pound cooked ham
1 egg, beaten
1/2 cup cream
3 ounces truffles or some pistachio nuts
1-3/4 cups veal stock
4 tablespoons port for aspic
1 tablespoon gelatin
Thin crêpes to line the terrine

Parboil the sweetbreads; remove the tubes and membranes and weight them with a heavy plate while you continue the terrine. Chop the vegetables finely; sauté them in some of the butter and season them with salt and pepper. In the remaining butter, sauté the sweetbreads after slicing them lengthwise in half. Then combine the vegetables and sweetbreads, add the wine, port, Madeira, bay leaf, thyme, and parsley. Cover the pan and simmer for 40 minutes. Remove the sweetbreads; reduce the liquid somewhat and strain it, pushing all the juices through the strainer. Mix the pork, veal, ham, beaten egg, and cream together; add salt and pepper.

While most terrines are lined with fatback or bacon, this one, lined with thin crêpes, is more unusual and much less rich in fat. In lining the dish allow the crêpes to hang over the edges of the terrine or suitable ovenproof dish, saving a few crêpes for the top. Now, put a layer of the mixed meats in the crêpe-lined terrine, sprinkle with a little of the reduced stock from stewing the sweetbreads and vegetables, add a layer of sweetbreads, strew a few whole pistachio nuts or sliced truffles over them, and continue layering forcemeat, sweetbreads, and nuts, judiciously sprinkled with stock, until the terrine is well filled. Fold the edges of the crêpes over all, adding a few crêpes to cover the casserole completely. Put a piece of baking paper or foil over the top, add the lid, and bake for 1-1/2 hours. Remove the lid. Weight the terrine, when barely cold, with a plate made heavy by cans of soup or some other kitchen objects.

If you choose to unmold the paté, rather than to serve it from the terrine, make an aspic of veal stock, flavored with the port wine, using a tablespoon of gelatin dissolved in it if it does not jell naturally. Run a knife around the cold terrine so that the stock can run in, and pour in enough aspic to cover the top.

A simple way to cut it for serving is to cut through the slices before unmolding, then to turn it all out on a serving plate. Pass this with Melba toast.

Milton S. Eisenhower

Kidney Stew

2 servings

2 beef kidneys
1 or 2 tablespoons butter
1 medium onion, chopped
1-1/2-2 tablespoons flour
1/2 cup stock or water
1/2 cup sherry or white wine
Salt and pepper
Chopped parsley
Sliced hard-boiled eggs

Cut away the white tissue from the kidneys. Soak the kidneys for 4 hours in salted water, drain, and then slice them thinly. Melt the butter and sauté the kidneys lightly and set aside.

Brown the onion just until limp and translucent. Stir in the flour, add the stock, the wine, and the kidneys and simmer for 45 minutes. Correct the seasoning of this thick stew. Add chopped parsley and garnish with sliced eggs. This is good with English muffins or waffles.

Mrs. James D. Atkinson

Sautéed Veal Kidneys

2 to 4 servings

2 veal kidneys
Salad oil
Vinegar
2 tablespoons butter
2 chopped shallots
Hot water as needed
2 tablespoons flour
1/2 cup red wine
Salt and pepper
1/4 beef bouillon cube
Minced parsley

Slice the veal kidneys lengthwise. Remove the fat and strings and cut them into small cubes. Heat a small amount of oil in a skillet, add the kidneys, and stir until the color changes; then add a few drops of vinegar. Place the kidney pieces in a strainer and hold under running water for a few minutes. Heat the butter and add the shallots, cook briefly, then blend in the flour and let it brown. Stir in the red wine, seasoning, and the bouillon cube; then add enough hot water to make a sauce of the desired consistency. Cook for several minutes, then return the kidneys just long enough to heat them through. Garnish with minced parsley.

Serve with green salad and fried potatoes. Boil the potatoes first, then slice and fry them with onions until they are golden and crisp.

Mrs. Harry E. Foster

Veal with Artichoke Bottoms

6 servings

2 pounds leg of veal in 2-inch cubes
4 tablespoons butter
3 tablespoons apple brandy
3 tablespoons flour
1/2 pound mushrooms, small and left whole
3 tablespoons flour
1/2 cup chicken stock
1/2 cup white wine
1/4 cup rich cream
Salt and freshly ground pepper
3 firm cooked artichoke bottoms
Noodles, al dente
Chopped parsley for garnish

Heat 3 tablespoons of butter in a heavy skillet large enough to dispose the veal in a single layer (though it may be done in several takes). Brown the pieces over moderate heat and set them aside. Warm the apple brandy, ignite it and flame the veal. Then set the meat aside. In the same heavy skillet, sauté the mushrooms lightly, adding more butter, if necessary. Sprinkle the mushrooms with the flour, add the stock and wine and stir until the sauce comes to a boil. Add cream and seasoning and let it cook over high heat to reduce it a bit and then combine it with the veal.

All this can be done in advance. The dish may be finished by simmering very slowly on top of the stove or, perhaps with less trouble, in the oven at 325° for somewhat less than an hour, or until the veal is tender. Sauté the artichokes, cut into serving-size pieces in hot butter, and add to the veal at serving time. This can be served on noodles or accompanied by the noodles. In any case, chopped parsley should be ready to strew over the top of the veal.

Miss Alice Newman

Veal Provençal

8 servings

4 pounds leg of veal, cut into 1-inch cubes
4 tablespoons olive oil
8 tablespoons butter
2 cups stock (veal, beef, or chicken) or 2 cups water
4 tablespoons flour
Wine
4 medium-size yellow onions, peeled and sliced
8 tomatoes, peeled, quartered, seeds scooped out
2 cloves garlic, minced
1 pound mushrooms, sliced
6 tablespoons chopped parsley

Brown the veal in the olive oil and butter in a large heavy skillet. When the veal is browned, transfer it to a casserole. Add the stock to the skillet and deglaze the pan. Sprinkle the meat with flour and stir. Add the stock and wine and stir until the mixture comes to a boil. Season and simmer, covered, until the meat is tender (about an hour.) Cook the onions and tomatoes with garlic in 1 tablespoon butter over slow fire for 10 minutes. Add to the meat. Sauté sliced mushrooms in 1 tablespoon butter and add them. Serve in the casserole with parsley on top. *Miss Alice Roberts*

Veal in Sour Cream

6 servings

3 tablespoons butter
3 pounds boneless veal, cut up into cubes
1 pint sour cream
1 package onion soup mix
1 teaspoon salt
1/4 teaspoon pepper
2 teaspoons dill seed

Melt the butter in a Dutch oven and brown the veal well on all sides. Combine the sour cream, onion soup mix, salt, pepper, and dill seed. Mix thoroughly with the meat. Simmer, covered, for about an hour or until tender. This may also be done in a 300° oven for the same length of time.

Mrs. Arthur P. Korach

Veal Chops with Eggplant

6 servings

6 tablespoons olive oil
6 loin or rib veal chops, cut 1/2 inch thick
1/2 cup dry white wine
1 eggplant, peeled and sliced
1/4 cup flour
3 tomatoes, peeled and cut in eighths
1-1/2 teaspoons salt
1/2 teaspoon freshly ground black pepper
1 clove garlic, minced

Heat 3 tablespoons oil and sauté the chops over low heat for 35 minutes or until tender. Transfer to a serving platter. To the juices in the pan, add the wine and bring to a boil, deglazing the pan. Pour over the chops, and keep them warm until the vegetables are ready.

While the chops are cooking, prepare the vegetables. Dip the eggplant in the flour and in a separate pan heat the remaining 3 tablespoons of oil and brown the eggplant on both sides. Set aside. In the same skillet cook the tomatoes, salt, pepper, and garlic over low heat for 10 minutes. Return the eggplant, cook for 1 minute, then cover the chops with the mixture and serve.

Mrs. Milton Walker

Veal Oscar

6 servings

12-14 slices veal tenderloin, pounded thin
Seasoned flour
Sweet butter
2 1-pound packages frozen king crab meat
1 pound fresh asparagus
Sauce Béarnaise

Dredge the veal in seasoned flour. Sauté in sweet butter. Place on an ovenproof platter. Top each slice of veal with lightly sautéed king crab meat and cooked fresh asparagus. Place in a warm oven. Serve topped with Béarnaise and accompanied by tomatoes stuffed with wild rice.

Mrs. Irwin Nudelman

Escalopes de Veau à la Crème

6 servings

3 pounds veal scallops
2 tablespoons oil
6 tablespoons butter
3 tablespoons minced shallots or green onions
1/2 cup dry wine or 1/3 cup dry vermouth or Madeira
2/3 cup brown stock or canned beef bouillon
1-1/2 cups whipping cream
1/2 tablespoon arrowroot or cornstarch blended with 1 tablespoon water
1/2 pound sliced fresh mushrooms
Salt and pepper

Dry the veal slices thoroughly with a towel, then brown them quickly on each side in 1 tablespoon oil and 2 tablespoons butter. Remove the veal to a serving dish and keep warm. Leave 2 tablespoons of fat in the pan and add 2 more tablespoons of butter. Stir in the shallots or green onions and cook slowly for 1 minute. Pour the wine and stock or bouillon into the skillet and scrape up all the coagulated cooking juices with a wooden spoon. Boil rapidly until the liquid has been reduced to about 1/4 cup. Pour the cream and starch mixture into the skillet and boil for several minutes until the cream has reduced and thickened slightly. Remove from the heat and season.

In a separate skillet heat the remaining 1 tablespoon oil and 2 tablespoons butter until they foam. Cook the mushrooms until they brown slightly and add to the sauce. Return the veal scallops to the sauce and heat briefly before serving.

Mrs. Donald Brown

Veal Casserole

6 servings

1-1/2 pounds boneless veal shoulder
1 cup thick velouté sauce
2 cups mushroom caps
1 bay leaf
Black pepper, freshly ground
1 teaspoon salt
2 teaspoons chopped onion
2 slices of lemon
2 cups cooked peas or lima beans
1/4 cup cream

Cut the veal to small cubes about 1-1/2 inches in size and parboil for 5 minutes in salted water to remove the scum. Wash and drain the veal and place it in a covered buttered casserole. Season the velouté sauce, made with chicken or veal stock, with black pepper and salt, and pour it over the veal pieces. Put the mushroom caps on top of this with a bay leaf, the chopped onion, and the lemon slices. Simmer slowly for 1 hour in the covered casserole, although it may be tender in less time.

Before serving, remove the bay leaf and lemon slices, pile the cooked vegetable on top of the meat, pour in the cream, and heat through. Serve with thin noodles topped with buttered bread crumbs, or with wild rice.

Mrs. Charles Marburg, John Puckett

Paupiettes de Veau Richelieu

375° / 6 servings

6 thinly sliced veal scallops
1/2 pound sausage meat
A pinch of allspice
1 shallot, chopped fine
1 egg
1/2 wineglass dry white wine
Chopped parsley
A swallow of Cognac
Salt and pepper
Butter
Oil
1 large onion, chopped fine
2 cloves of garlic, minced
2 cups chicken stock
1 teaspoon tomato paste
Bouquet garni
3 tomatoes
Parsley

Pound the veal on a wet board with a wet meat hammer. Mix the sausage, allspice, minced shallot, egg, white wine, parsley, cognac, salt, and pepper together. Spread this evenly over the scallops and roll them up. Tie with string as you would a parcel. Roll in flour and before cooking roll again in flour. Melt some butter and oil in a sauté pan; when hot put in the veal birds to color them, which should take about 10 minutes. Keep turning them slowly to brown on all sides. When the veal has browned, remove it from the pan and pour out the fat.

Using the same pan, heat some butter, add the chopped onion, and cook until the onion has begun to color. Then add the garlic, stock, tomato paste, and a bouquet garni. Put the paupiettes back in the pan and cover. Put them in the oven for 15 minutes. Turn them and cook 15 minutes more. Cut off the strings as you remove them from the pan.

Reduce the sauce by half. Then add a liqueur glass of heated brandy and flame. Add a teaspoon of butter. Amalgamate by shaking the pan, not stirring the butter in, and then add another small piece of butter and shake again. Have ready some sautéed tomatoes, cut in half and fried in butter or cooking oil on top of the stove. Salt and pepper them and sprinkle with a modicum of sugar. These can be kept warm enough in a warm oven. Put them on a heated serving dish with the veal on top, then the sauce poured over them. Be sure to sprinkle parsley over them finally.

Mrs. Sol Kann

Veal Birds with Rice

12 servings

12 veal scallops
1 onion
1 tablespoon butter
4 hard-cooked eggs
4 tablespoons chopped chives
4 tablespoons butter
3 tablespoons brandy
2 tablespoons flour
2 cups veal stock
1/2 cup white wine
1 teaspoon tomato paste
1/2 teaspoon glace de viande
Boiled rice

Place veal scallops (cut to about 5 x 3 inches) between waxed paper and pound them very thin. Sauté a finely chopped onion in 1 tablespoon butter until it is golden brown, then combine with finely chopped eggs, chives, salt and pepper to taste. Spread the veal slices with the filling, roll up the slices, and tie them with a string. Brown them on all sides in the 4 tablespoons of butter. Flame with heated brandy and remove from the pan.

Stir in the flour, add veal stock, wine, tomato paste, and glace de viande. Cook, stirring, until it comes to the boil. Return the birds to the pan, reduce the heat and cook, covered, for 15 minutes or until the meat is tender. Carefully remove the strings, arrange the birds on a bed of rice, and spoon the sauce over them.

Mrs. Sol Kann

Scaloppine al' Marsala

4 servings

1-1/2 pounds veal cutlet, sliced thin
Salt, pepper, and flour, with a touch of garlic powder
Butter
Vegetable oil or Crisco
1/2 cup Marsala
1 tablespoon water

Pound the cutlets very thin between sheets of waxed paper; then cut the veal into pieces about 6 inches square, or smaller. Dredge in the seasoned flour. Melt butter in a large frying pan, adding a little Crisco or vegetable oil to keep the butter from burning. Brown the veal pieces over moderately high heat. As the veal is browned, remove it to another pan. When it is all done, put the other pan on a high burner and pour in Marsala and water and let it sizzle. The liquid will thicken slightly. Remove and serve with the sauce poured over the veal.

The veal may be cooked an hour or two before serving, kept in the second pan, and then returned to a burner. When it gets hot, add the Marsala and water and let it sizzle briefly.

Frank D'Amanda

The Prodigal Son Carrying Swill to the Swine is a detail of a twenty-seven foot tapestry of the story of the Prodigal Son. Silk and wool tapestry, Flemish (Brussels), about 1500.

Osso Bucco Milanese

6 servings

3 whole shanks of veal, cut in 3-inch pieces
1/4 cup olive oil
1/4 cup butter
Pinch of sage
1 bouillon cube
Stock
Pepper
Juice of 2 lemons
A little white wine or water
Grated lemon rind
Chopped parsley

Heat the butter and oil with a pinch of sage in a heavy casserole, then sauté the meat in it until it is golden brown. Add the bouillon cube dissolved in a little stock, pepper, juice of 2 lemons, and if it is too dry, add a little more stock or water. Cook slowly, covered, for 2-1/2 hours, turning the pieces every half hour. Less time may be needed, but it is the long very slow cooking which gives the flavor. Put the meat on a serving platter, swirl the essence in the pan with grated lemon rind and parsley, and pour over the meat. Serve with the following risotto:

Risotto Milanese

4 tablespoons butter
3 tablespoons chopped onion
1 cup raw rice
4 cups veal, beef, or chicken stock
Pinch of saffron

Heat the butter in a heavy pan, and sauté the chopped onion until limp and golden. Add the rice and stir over medium heat until it is opaque. Add 1 cup of boiling hot stock and cook, stirring constantly, until the stock has been absorbed. Add another cup of stock and continue cooking. Add the remaining stock, 1/4 cup at a time, until the rice is tender. Stir in the saffron, which has been moistened in a little stock. *Mrs. Pumphrey Nes*

Foxcroft Mulligan Stew

24 servings

4 pounds veal, cut up
1 duck, cut up
4 tablespoons salt
3 1-pound-12-ounce cans Italian tomatoes
1 can tomato paste, rinsed out with 1 can water
4 packages frozen lima beans
4 packages frozen cut corn
1 bunch celery, cut in 1/2-inch pieces
1 pound onions, chunked
1 pound rice
2 teaspoons black pepper
1/2 pound butter
2 pints cream

Simmer veal and duck in water to cover 2 hours, with 2 tablespoons salt. Divide in half and use 2 very large pots. Let them cool overnight, then remove and discard the cake of grease on top. Pull the meat off the skin and bones and put back in the stock in which it was cooked. Cut the duck pieces up so the meat isn't in long strings. Add tomatoes, lima beans, corn, celery, onions, and rice (half to each pot) and cook 4 hours or until all the meats have disappeared. Stir frequently, as the rice sticks easily. If it scorches on the bottom a little, it will taste more like the old school product than if it doesn't. Finally add the butter and cream and the rest of the seasonings. This freezes very well and is well worth making. It is easier than it sounds and everybody loves it. This has been a favorite at Foxcroft School, Middleburg, Virginia, for many years. This is really a very thick soup and is served in bowls.

To serve Mulligan Stew as a stew for a crowd, cook additional veal (1 pound for every 6 people) and add to the already made Mulligan Stew. Serve over barley (recipe follows) on plates instead of in bowls.

Barley
1 pound of barley for every 10 people
Stock
1 stalk of celery
Salt and pepper
Butter

Cook the barley in boiling stock with a stalk of celery for about 2 hours. Or you can add the barley directly to the stew with or instead of the rice. Season to taste with salt, pepper, and butter.

Mrs. Bradford Jacobs

Osso Bucco

BRAISED VEAL KNUCKLES

6 servings

3-1/2 to 4 pounds knuckle of veal
3 or 4 carrots
1 large onion
2 stalks celery
3 tablespoons olive oil
3 tablespoons butter
Salt and pepper
1 tablespoon flour
1 cup tomato pulp
1 cup white wine
Veal stock or water
Herb bouquet of parsley, rosemary, and thyme
Strip of lemon peel
Chopped parsley

The knuckles of veal (your butcher may call it shin or shank) must be sawed, not chopped, into 3-inch lengths, as the marrow must remain inside the bone. Chop the vegetables very fine and put them in a large heavy pan with the oil and half the butter. Add the meat and season highly with salt and pepper. When the meat and vegetables are well browned, add the remaining butter worked with 1 tablespoon of flour. Stir and cook until the flour begins to brown, then add the tomato pulp, wine, and sufficient stock or water to barely cover the meat. Add the herb bouquet. Simmer gently, covered, for 1-1/2 to 2 hours or until the meat is tender.

Ten minutes before serving, remove the meat from the pan, strain the sauce, removing the herb bouquet. Put both meat and sauce in a serving dish, adding the lemon peel and more finely chopped parsley.

Otto F. Kraushaar

Vitello Tonnato

COLD BRAISED VEAL with TUNA SAUCE

6 to 8 servings

3 pounds boneless veal, in one piece and tied
4 anchovy fillets
2 cloves garlic
2 quarts chicken stock, or 1/2 stock, 1/2 white wine
Several carrots, onions, and stalks of celery
2 bay leaves
Parsley
12 peppercorns

Place the veal in a heavy pot, pour water over it, and bring to the boil to blanch it. Put it in cold water to rinse off the scum. If you wish, make incisions in the meat and insert pieces of anchovy and garlic. Otherwise just put the anchovies and garlic in a pot along with the veal and the other ingredients. Simmer, partially covered and very slowly, for about 1-1/2 hours or until just tender. Let the veal cool in the stock, but take about 3/4 of a cup of the stock to strain and to use in the tuna sauce.

When the veal has cooled, drain it, remove both fat and gristle, and slice the veal. Put the tuna sauce (below) between the slices and over all and refrigerate, closely covered with plastic wrap or waxed paper for a whole day. Before serving, arrange the slices in a pleasing pattern, overlapping in a serving dish. Spoon some sauce over them and sprinkle with lots of chopped parsley. Authentic garnish: capers, lemon slices, and black olives.

Tuna Sauce

1 cup olive oil
1 large can (7 ounces) tuna fish in olive oil
2 egg yolks
3 tablespoons lemon juice
Flat anchovies, washed and drained
1/4 cup heavy cream
3/4 cup cooled, strained veal stock
2 tablespoons capers, washed and drained
Salt and pepper

In a blender, put the olive oil, tuna, egg yolks, lemon juice, and washed anchovies, and purée them. Add the cream and enough of the stock to make a smooth sauce as thick as a good mayonnaise. Stir in the capers; rectify the seasoning.

Miss Alice Newman

A Roman wine strainer with elaborate perforations. Silver, 1st century A.D.; said to have been found near Lake Trasimeno.

POULTRY

Barcelona Chicken Breasts

8 servings

4 large chicken breasts
1/4 pound butter
1/2 pound fine noodles or spaghettini
1 pound mushrooms, chopped
1 tablespoon chopped onion
1 tablespoon chopped parsley
1/2 cup fine bread crumbs
3 tablespoons butter
3 tablespoons flour
3 cups milk
1/2 teaspoon salt
Pepper
1/2 cup wine
2 egg yolks
1/2 cup whipped cream
1/2 cup grated Parmesan cheese

Sauté the chicken breasts in the butter over low heat until tender and golden. Meanwhile, cook the noodles according to the package directions and drain thoroughly. Mix them with a pat of butter and add some pepper. Keep them warm. Sauté the mushrooms and the onions (in the butter left from sautéing the chickens) until the vegetables are tender. Add chopped parsley and bread crumbs to them. Put the noodles in a warm flat casserole with the chicken breasts on top and put a mound of the mushroom mixture on each breast. Keep the casserole warm while you make the sauce.

Melt the butter, stir in the flour, then the milk. (If you have scalded the milk, the process of thickening goes more quickly.) Add salt, pepper, and wine and cook for 10 minutes, stirring it well. Beat the yolks well, add spoonfuls of the hot sauce to them, and then finish the liaison by pouring the yolks back into the sauce. Cook carefully over low heat (do not boil) until it is thick and smooth. Fold in the whipped cream, pour it all over the chicken, sprinkle with Parmesan cheese, and glaze under the broiler until brown and bubbly.

Mrs. Sven Peuleché

Chicken Breasts all'Alba

2 servings

2 whole chicken breasts, skinned and boned
Flour to dredge
4 tablespoons butter
Salt and white pepper
1 small can white Italian truffles
4 slices Fontina cheese

Halve the chicken breasts, pound carefully between sheets of waxed paper until 1/4 inch thin, dredge with flour, and sauté in butter until done, 5 to 6 minutes on each side. Remove the breasts to a shallow pan, season with salt and white pepper. Slice the truffles thinly and place them on the breasts. Cover each breast with a slice of Fontina cheese. Broil the breasts just long enough to melt the cheese. Serve at once. *Mrs. John J. Smith*

Chicken Breasts and Oysters

400° / 8 to 10 servings

6 large chicken breasts, boned
Chicken stock
1 pint oysters
1/2 cup dry white wine
Salt and pepper
Nutmeg
3 tablespoons flour
3 tablespoons butter
Grated Parmesan cheese
Fine bread crumbs

Poach the chicken breasts in chicken stock to cover them until just firm; do not overcook. Poach the oysters in their liquid and the white wine until the edges curl. Combine the oyster liquid and the stock in which the breasts were cooked and boil rapidly to reduce to 2 cups. Season with salt, pepper, and nutmeg. Make a roux with 3 tablespoons butter and 3 tablespoons flour. Strain the chicken-oyster liquid into the hot roux, stirring constantly. Cook until thickened; the velouté should have the consistency of heavy cream.

Butter a soufflé dish or any ovenproof casserole about 9 inches in diameter and 3 inches deep. Arrange layers of the well drained oysters, the chicken breasts cut into serving pieces, and the sauce and finish with a layer of the sauce. Sprinkle the top lightly with a mixture of grated Parmesan cheese and fine bread crumbs. Dot it with a few small pieces of butter and heat for 15 minutes, until the top is lightly browned and the casserole hot. Serve in the casserole. *Mrs. William Garvey*

Sweet and Sour Chicken Breasts

6 servings

1 tablespoon oil
2 tablespoons butter
4 chicken breasts, skinned, boned, and cut into 3/4-inch strips
1/4 cup brown sugar
1/4 cup vinegar
1-1/2 tablespoons cornstarch
1 green pepper, cut in strips
1 cup unsweetened pineapple chunks
Soy sauce to taste, perhaps 1 tablespoon

Melt the butter and oil in a heavy skillet. Sauté the chicken strips quickly, turning to brown on all sides. Do not overcook.

In a saucepan, combine the sugar and cornstarch with the vinegar and the liquid from the pineapple. Cook, stirring constantly, until the sauce is thick and shiny. Add soy sauce to taste. When ready to serve, add the chicken, green pepper, and pineapple to the sauce, and heat to the boiling point. Correct the seasoning and serve at once with rice.
Malvina C. Kinard

Chicken Breasts Amandine

12 servings

12 chicken breasts, split, boned and skinned
1/2 pound butter
3/4 cup sherry
1-1/2 cups blanched and slivered almonds
1 clove garlic, minced
3 tablespoons flour
3 cups chicken stock
1-1/2 cups dry white wine

9 leaves tarragon or 1 teaspoon dried tarragon
1-1/2 pints sour cream
Salt
Pepper

Brown the breasts lightly in 3 tablespoons of the butter and pour heated sherry over them. Cook about 3 minutes more. Remove the chicken from the pan and keep warm. Add the remaining butter, garlic, and 1 cup of the almonds to the pan. Stir over low heat for about 5 minutes. Add the flour and stir until smooth. Slowly add most of the chicken stock and then the wine. Add the tarragon and sour cream. Season well. Return the chicken to the sauce and cook slowly for about 10 minutes more or until tender. Place the chicken breasts on a hot platter; cover them with the sauce and sprinkle with the remaining 1/2 cup of blanched, slivered almonds, which have been gently browned for about 10 minutes in a 350° oven.

This dish may be made ahead and reheated in a slow oven. *Mrs. S. Page Nelson, Jr.*

Fool's Chicken

300° / 8 to 10 servings

8 or 10 chicken breasts
1 package chipped beef
4-5 slices bacon
Pepper
Chicken livers (optional)
1 can mushroom soup
1 cup sour cream
A dollop of sherry

Line a buttered baking dish with the chipped beef. Place half a slice of bacon on top of each chicken breast and place the breasts on top of the chipped beef. Sprinkle lightly with pepper. If you like, you may put chicken livers, lightly sautéed, between the breasts. Mix the mushroom soup with the sour cream and the sherry and pour over the chicken. This can stay in the refrigerator any number of hours, even overnight. Bake for 1-1/2 hours. Thighs and legs of chicken may be used in the same way.

Mrs. Carter Burns, Mrs. E. Walker Englar

Szechwan Spicy Chicken

6 servings

4 whole chicken breasts, skinned and boned
1 lemon
4 bunches scallions, trimmed and washed
4 tablespoons soy sauce
4 tablespoons sherry
4 tablespoons catsup (optional)
4 tablespoons chili sauce (optional)
4 teaspoons sugar
1-1/2 teaspoons salt and pepper
3/4 to 1-1/2 teaspoons red hot pepper flakes
6 tablespoons peanut or salad oil, divided
6 tablespoons minced fresh ginger root or 2 teaspoons ground ginger
8 minced garlic cloves
1/2 small can water chestnuts

Cut the chicken in half-inch cubes, squeeze the lemon over them, and set aside. Cut the white part of scallions in 1/4 inch diagonal slices; cut the green stalks in 1-inch diagonal slices and set them aside.

In a small bowl, combine soy sauce, sherry, catsup, chili sauce, sugar, salt and pepper, and the hot pepper flakes; set aside. All this may be done ahead. Heat a wok or a skillet till hot, add 4 tablespoons oil and heat. Fry ginger and garlic 1/2 minute, stirring. Add the scallions and water chestnuts and fry one minute, stirring. Push the vegetables up on the side of the wok; if using a skillet remove scallions and water chestnut mixture to a dish while cooking the chicken, then stir back into the pan. Add the remaining 2 tablespoons oil to the pan; stir-fry the chicken cubes, a few at a time, for one minute, pushing the cooked pieces to the side, or removing them before adding more. Stir the scallion mixture and chicken together. Add the reserved sauce; stir to coat the chicken. Let the mixture simmer for 1/2 minute or until hot through. Serve immediately. This can be cooked at the table in a chafing dish. Serve with lots of rice.

The spiciness of this traditionally very hot dish depends on the amount of red hot pepper flakes used. Try with the lesser amount the first time and increase to the full amount if you like.

Mrs. Thomas E. Allen, Jr.,
Mrs. Benjamin Griswold, IV

Sherried Chicken

350° / 4 servings

1/2 cup flour
2 tablespoons salt
4 large chicken breasts
1-1/4 sticks butter
1/2 cup dry sherry
2 tablespoons soy sauce
2 tablespoons lemon juice
1/4 cup finely chopped preserved ginger

Combine flour and salt and coat the chicken pieces with the mixture. Melt 1/2 cup (1 stick) butter, brown the chicken on all sides, and place it in a covered baking dish. In a saucepan combine the remaining butter, sherry, soy sauce, lemon juice, and ginger. Bring to a boil, stirring, and pour over the chicken. Bake, covered, in a preheated oven for about 1 hour or until tender. Turn chicken once during baking.

Mrs. Morton Baum

Chafing-Dish Chicken Curry

5 or 6 servings

3 tablespoons butter or margarine
1 large apple, peeled and chopped
1 large sweet onion, finely chopped
1 clove garlic, minced
1 scant tablespoon mild curry
1 tablespoon flour in 1 cup chicken stock
3 whole chicken breasts, cooked and cut up
Salt and pepper to taste

In a large chafing dish directly over a flame, melt the butter or margaine and sauté the apple, onion, garlic, and curry powder until the onion is transparent. Blend in the flour, add the chicken stock and, stirring constantly, simmer until it is thick and smooth. Add the chicken pieces and heat through, then season with salt and pepper before serving. Serve in a chafing dish with hot rice, favorite curry condiments, and a green salad.

Mrs. Sidney Silber

Chicken Kiev

4 servings

4 half chicken breasts (not frozen)
1/8 pound sweet butter
1 clove garlic, crushed
1/2 teaspoon rosemary
Salt and pepper
About 1/2 cup flour
2 beaten eggs
1 cup bread crumbs
Salad oil for deep frying
1 bunch watercress

Skin and bone the chicken breasts. Place each half between pieces of waxed paper and, starting in the center, beat them with a meat mallet until they are about 1/4 inch thick. Remove the paper. In the middle of each half breast put a small finger of firm cold butter, a bit of garlic, some rosemary, salt and pepper. Roll them up, tucking in the ends. Dust lightly with flour, brush with beaten egg, and roll in the bread crumbs. Then brush with more egg and roll in the crumbs again. The double dipping insures a leak-proof roll. Italian bread makes the best bread crumbs for this.

The next step is to fry them in deep fat at 350° from 3 to 5 minutes, until the rolls are golden brown. Drain them on brown paper and serve immediately, garnished with the watercress.

The chicken breasts may be prepared up to the final step as far ahead as the day before, leaving the chicken in the refrigerator. In that case, bring the rolls back to room temperature before frying.

Frank D'Amanda

Chicken Ceci

350° / 6 servings

3 chicken breasts, halved
2 cans (10-1/2 ounces) chick peas, drained
1 medium red onion, chopped
4 celery stalks with leaves, chopped
1/2 pound ham, diced
1 small pepperoni sausage, in 1/4-inch slices
1 cup olive oil
1/4 cup red wine
3/4 teaspoon Spice Islands Italian Herb Seasoning

Put chicken breasts in the bottom of a baking casserole and pour all the ingredients, mixed together, over them. Marinate them in a refrigerator all day or all night and then bake for 45 minutes.

Miss Jose Wilson

Melting Chicken

6 servings

3 whole chicken breasts, skinned and boned

Marinade:

1 cup coconut cream
1 clove garlic, minced
1 teaspoon salt
White pepper
1 cup unsalted peanuts, finely ground
2 hot peppers (red or green), chopped
Chicken stock

Mix the marinade ingredients and marinate the chicken for 5 hours. Remove the chicken and drain it. Broil it 20 minutes. Deglaze the pan with a little of the marinade, add a little chicken stock to it, and pour over the chicken at serving time.

Mrs. W. Boulton Kelly

An unusual medieval aquamanile (water urn) in the form of a centaur. In his hands the figure held a pair of candlesticks. German, early 15th century.

"Muddles Green" Green Chicken

8 servings

8 cups chicken stock
1/4 pound butter
1 whole head celery and some leaves
3-4 leeks, white and green parts
3 large handfuls parsley with stems
3-4 slices toasted white bread, cubed
Salt and pepper
Quartered chickens for 8 people
Bouquet garni
2 egg yolks, or flour and butter
1/2 pint heavy cream
1-1/2 pounds fresh shelled green peas or their frozen equivalent, cooked
Hot unsweetened scones or English muffins

Make a chicken stock of necks, backs, and feet of chicken; strain, chill, and degrease it, or failing that, use an excellent canned broth which has been simmered with vegetables until flavorful.

Heat 1/4 pound butter in a large shallow pan large enough to hold the chicken pieces later, spread out. In the butter, sauté the celery, leeks, parsley, all chopped, and the bread and seasoning until the vegetables are soft. Lay the chicken pieces on top, add stock to cover, the bouquet garni, salt, and pepper and simmer until the chicken is tender.

Remove the chicken to keep warm, strain the contents of the pan, and pass the solids through a sieve or mouli mill (but not a blender, as the texture should not become too refined). Add the strained vegetables to the hot stock and consider the thickness of the sauce-soup. It should be that of a thick bisque. If necessary, thicken the sauce with a beurre manié of equal parts of butter and flour rubbed together, or beat some of the sauce little by little into 2 egg yolks, then return the yolks to the rest of the sauce to reheat and thicken. Add the cream, adjust the seasoning, and reheat the chicken in the sauce.

Serve from a tureen into old-fashioned soup plates, with the hot peas ladled on top. Pass the scones or muffins for dunking or mopping. The chicken should be tender enough to eat with a spoon and fork.

Lady Penrose

Poulet Sauce Moutarde et Pernod

2 to 3 servings

1 chicken or an equivalent amount of breasts and thighs
Butter
Oil
1/2 pint good cream sauce
2 tablespoons Dijon mustard
A scant 1/4 cup Pernod
Salt and pepper

Joint the chicken, salt and pepper it, and sauté it in half butter, half oil. When cooked, put it into a hot covered dish to keep warm. Pour the cream sauce in the sauté pan, add the mustard and Pernod, and cook until the sauce is thoroughly blended. Season to taste and pour it over the chicken.

Mrs. Peter Dane

Poulet aux Choux

300° / 8 servings

1-1/2 pound ham slice, with a rim of fat
1 clove garlic, crushed
6 scallions
2 chickens, 2-1/2 pounds each
1 white cabbage
1 pint rich chicken stock
1 glass white wine
1 pony brandy

Cut the ham in cubes, chop the scallions fine, quarter the cabbage, and truss the chickens for baking. Brown the ham with the garlic and scallions, and when some of the fat is fried out, brown the chickens. Put the cabbage in a large deep casserole, add the stock, and then place the ham, chickens, and seasonings on top. Cover and braise in the oven for about 1-1/2 hours or until the chickens are tender. Add a glass of white wine and a pony of brandy before serving.

Mrs. William C. Trimble

Chicken Inigo Jones

8 servings

2 2-1/2 pound fryers, cut up
1/4 pound butter
1/2 cup onion, minced
2 cloves garlic, minced
1 cup Chablis or other dry white wine
1 tablespoon chicken stock base
1/2 teaspoon salt
1/4 teaspoon white pepper
A pinch of dried tarragon
1 package frozen artichoke hearts
1 can (12 ounces) sliced mushrooms with liquor
1-1/2 teaspoons cornstarch for thickening
1 cup seedless grapes

Wash and dry the chicken. Melt the butter in a frying pan with a tight fitting cover. Sauté the chicken pieces, uncovered, until golden on all sides. Remove them while you sauté the onions and garlic. Return the chicken pieces to the pan, pour the Chablis over them, and then add the chicken stock base, salt, pepper, and tarragon. Cover the pan tightly and simmer until the chicken is tender, about 30 minutes. Add the frozen artichokes and cook them until they are tender, about 10 minutes, then remove both chickens and vegetable to a serving platter to keep them in a warm oven while you quickly make the sauce.

Drain the mushrooms and with the remaining ingredients in the pan make a sauce by adding cornstarch to the mushroom liquor and reducing the sauce to the consistency of heavy cream. Add the mushrooms and grapes to heat through thoroughly. Spoon some of the sauce over the chicken, putting the rest in a sauceboat after you have corrected the seasoning. Garnish the platter with finely chopped parsley. Wild rice, a green salad, and hot bread complete the meal.

Mrs. Charles Amster

Baked Marinated Chicken

350° / 4 to 6 servings

2 chickens of 2-3 pounds, cut in serving pieces
1/4 pound butter
1/2 cup soy sauce
Juice of 1 lemon
Paprika
Parmesan cheese

Melt the butter, add the soy sauce and lemon juice, and marinate the chicken for several hours at room temperature. Before baking, put the chicken pieces on a foil-covered baking sheet, skin side up, add any extra sauce, and sprinkle with paprika and Parmesan cheese. Bake for 40 to 50 minutes, depending on the size of the chickens.

Mrs. Philip Gottling

Honey Baked Chicken

350° / 6 servings

1 3-1/2-pound fryer, cut up, or 3 large chicken breasts, halved
1/4 cup honey
1 tablespoon prepared mustard
1 teaspoon curry powder
1 teaspoon salt
1/4 cup butter

In a 13 x 9 x 2-inch baking pan, melt the butter; add honey, mustard, curry powder, and salt and mix well. Coat both sides of the chicken pieces with the honey mixture as you place them in the pan, skin side down. Bake 1/2 hour on each side, basting occasionally. Serve with rice.

In place of the mustard and curry, lemon juice and grated lemon peel may be substituted.

Mrs. Sidney Silber, Mrs. Charles Newhall, III

Chicken with Champagne Sauce

375° / 45 to 60 servings

9 3-1/2-pound chickens, cut in serving pieces
At least 1 pound of butter
2 cups minced onions
Salt
Pepper
1/2 teaspoon nutmeg
2 cups flour
1/2 cup Cognac
3 bay leaves
12 cups chicken broth
1 bottle dry champagne
6 sprigs fresh thyme or 1 teaspoon dried thyme
1 quart quartered mushrooms
1 quart and 1 cup heavy cream
Chopped or sliced truffles (quite optional)

If possible, place 3 chickens, cut up, in each of 3 casseroles. Melt a pound of butter and pour it over the chicken pieces to coat them lightly. In a skillet, sauté the onions in butter until they become limp and transparent and divide them among the casseroles. Sprinkle the chicken pieces with salt, pepper, and nutmeg, then sprinkle with flour (this amounts to 2/3 cup for each casserole), tossing the chicken so the flour is well distributed. Now combine the Cognac, bay leaves, chicken broth, champagne, and thyme and divide among the casseroles. Bring each pot to the boil on top of the stove.

Prepare the quartered mushrooms by pouring 1 cup of cream over them, bringing them to the boil, and simmering for 2 minutes. Add the mushrooms to the chicken, cover the pots, and bake for 45 minutes. Remove the chicken and put all the sauce into one pot for convenience as you strain it. Reduce the sauce by 1/3, then add 1 quart of cream and boil briskly until it has reduced still more and seems thick enough to coat the chicken. Arrange the warmed chickens on heated platters, cover with sauce, add the truffles, and offer the rest of the sauce separately. Sprinkle parsley over the platters of chicken and present with large bowls of rice.

Mrs. Robert Berney

Tarragon Chicken

375° / 6

Use an earthenware beanpot, just big enough to hold the chicken and vegetables.

1 3-pound chicken
2 cups chopped onions
2 cups chopped carrots
2 cups chopped celery
1-1/2 teaspoons tarragon
1-1/2 teaspoons oregano
Pepper to taste
1/2 teaspoon salt
1/2 teaspoon Accent
3/4 cup white vermouth
Chicken broth

Disjoint the chicken, skin it, snip off the wing tips, and remove the fat. Put the neck, giblets, and wing tips in the casserole; cover with half the chopped vegetables, then the chicken, the herbs and seasonings, and finish off with the other half of the vegetables. (More herbs may be added to taste.) Add the vermouth, then add enough chicken broth to just cover the vegetables and bring to a simmer on an asbestos mat on top of the stove. Cover and cook in the oven for 35 to 40 minutes. This is good hot with rice, or cold, as the jelly will set.

Percival C. Keith

Chicken in Cucumber Sauce

4 servings

1 cup sour cream
1 cucumber, peeled and diced
1 3-pound chicken, cut up
1/2 cup bacon drippings
1 medium onion, minced
Tarragon

Pour the sour cream over the cucumber and set it aside while you make the other preparations. Brown the chicken pieces in bacon fat, then add the minced onion, salt, pepper, and tarragon to the pan and cook until the onion is golden. Stir in the cucumber and sour cream, cover the pan, and simmer it all gently for about 40 minutes or until the chicken is tender. Serve with finely chopped parsley strewn on the top.   *Mrs. James Grieves*

Tajin of Chicken with Prunes and Almonds

8 servings

2 2-1/2 to 3-pound chickens
1 teaspoon cinnamon
1/2 teaspoon saffron, crushed or powdered
1/2 teaspoon ginger
Salt and pepper
2 medium onions, sliced
1 pound prunes, soaked in water for 1 hour
3 ounces slivered almonds, roasted in oven with
  1 tablespoon oil
3 tablespoons chopped parsley

Put the chickens in a large heavy pan with cinnamon, saffron, ginger, salt, pepper, and onions and cover them with water. Bring to a boil, then simmer until the chickens are tender (about 45 minutes). Remove them to a warm, deep serving dish and keep warm in a very low oven, covered. Boil the sauce to reduce it somewhat; then add the prunes and cook for 15 minutes. To serve, pour the prune sauce over the chickens and top with roasted slivered almonds. Serve with buttered rice, sprinkled with parsley.

This dish can be made with lamb. Also, the prunes can be replaced by pears or quinces. If the dish is made with lamb, a good accompaniment is buttered couscous. Couscous can be found in some Middle Eastern groceries or at large supermarkets.
  Mrs. Douglas N. Sharretts

Poached Chicken With Vegetables

8 to 10 servings

1 4 or 5-pound chicken
1/2 lemon
1 carrot, sliced
1 onion, sliced
1 stalk celery, sliced
2 teaspoons salt
Peppercorns
1 bay leaf
White wine
1 egg
1/2 cup heavy cream
Accompaniments: cooked carrots, peas, and
  new potatoes

Wipe the fowl with a damp cloth, insert the peel from half a lemon in the cavity, and truss the bird. Put the chicken in a kettle with sliced carrot, onion, and celery, salt, several peppercorns, and a bay leaf. Add a mixture of boiling water and white wine to cover and simmer the chicken gently, covered, for 1-1/2 to 2 hours, or until it is tender when tested with a fork.

Reduce the stock to 2 cups and strain into a saucepan, add the juice of 1/2 lemon, and bring it almost to a boil. In a bowl, mix together 1 egg and 1/2 cup heavy cream. Very gradually stir in the hot stock. Return the mixture to the saucepan and heat it gently, stirring constantly until it thickens slightly. Do not let it boil.

Lift the chicken from the kettle, discard as much skin as possible, and drain. Place the chicken on a hot platter, pour some sauce over it, and surround it with the carrots, peas, and potatoes. Serve the rest of the sauce in a bowl. *Mrs. Warde B. Allan*

Chicken and Eggplant Casserole

325° / 4 to 6 servings

1 cup flour
1 tablespoon salt
1/2 teaspoon freshly ground black pepper
1 4-5 pound roasting chicken, disjointed
2 tablespoons butter
2 tablespoons vegetable oil
1 medium-sized eggplant, unpeeled, cut into 3/4 inch half-circles
1 large can Italian tomatoes, drained (or 3 cups fresh tomatoes, cut in chunks)
2 cloves garlic, minced fine
1 green pepper, coarsely chopped
1 large onion, coarsely chopped
1/4 pound fresh mushrooms, sliced
1/2 teaspoon dried basil
4 tablespoons chopped fresh parsley
1/2 teaspoon dried oregano
2 or 3 tablespoons grated Parmesan or Romano cheese (optional)
4 tablespoons olive oil, vegetable oil, or melted butter (optional)
Additional salt and freshly ground pepper if desired

Put the flour, salt, and pepper in a heavy brown paper bag, drop in the chicken pieces, and shake vigorously until each piece is well coated with flour. Remove the chicken from the bag and shake off the excess flour.

In a large, heavy skillet melt the butter with the oil over moderate heat. When the butter foam subsides, brown the chicken pieces, skin side down first; don't overcrowd the skillet. Set the chicken aside. Transfer half the chicken to a heavy oven-proof casserole, about 4-quart capacity. Arrange half the eggplant, tomatoes, garlic, green pepper, onion, mushrooms, basil, oregano, and parsley over the chicken. Sprinkle with additional salt and pepper if desired. Repeat, reserving remaining tomatoes and chopped parsley. Arrange the tomatoes and parsley on top, sprinkle with additional salt and pepper and grated cheese if desired. Bake, covered for 1-1/4 hours.

If you elect to eliminate browning the chicken pieces, bake the casserole, covered, in a pre-heated 425° oven, pouring the optional 4 tablespoons oil or melted butter over all the ingredients. Cook for 1 hour, turn the oven heat off and leave the casserole in the oven until needed. The grated-cheese topping (optional) will produce a golden brown crust if the hot casserole is placed under a moderately hot broiler for a moment or two.

Mrs. W. Scott Ditch, III

Coq au Vin

325° / 4 servings

1 5-pound chicken, disjointed
1/4 pound butter
Flour, salt and pepper
1 slice raw ham, fat removed
8-10 small white onions
A handful of small mushrooms, whole
2 ounces Armagnac or brandy
1 clove garlic, minced
Bouquet garni of parsley, thyme, bay leaf
1 cup red wine
Beurre manié (about 1 tablespoon each butter and flour kneaded together)

Brown the chicken pieces in the butter after

dredging them in seasoned flour. Remove the chicken pieces and brown the ham and onions, then the mushrooms. Put them all back in the pan and flame with the warmed brandy. Add the garlic, bouquet garni, and wine and cook slowly, covered, either in the oven or on top of the stove. It should take about an hour. Remove the bouquet garni; thicken the sauce slightly with some beurre manié. Dust the whole with finely chopped parsley. If less meaty pieces of chicken (from a broiler or fryer) are used, simply cut down on the cooking time. *Mrs. Arthur Stern*

Chicken and Sweetbread Salad

8 servings

1 4-5 pound chicken
4 or 5 celery ribs
1/2 onion
A handful of parsley
Salt and peppercorns
1 pair sweetbreads
1 cup celery
Homemade mayonnaise
Salt and pepper
Capers
Hard-cooked eggs
Watercress

Poach the chicken in water seasoned with the chopped celery, onion, parsley, and the salt and peppercorns, until the white meat is just done. Blanch the sweetbreads for 5 minutes, plunge them into ice water, and when cool remove the membranes and poach gently in 1/2 water and 1/2 chicken stock for approximately 10 minutes or until firm and no longer showing pink inside.

Cut both chicken and sweetbreads into bite-size pieces and combine these with diced celery and homemade mayonnaise. Season with salt and pepper, garnish with capers, sieved hard-boiled eggs, and sprigs of watercress. *Mrs. Arthur Waxter*

Chicken Casserole

350° / 6 servings

6 pieces chicken
Flour
1-1/2 pounds fresh mushrooms
10 small white onions
1 bottle chili sauce
Worcestershire sauce
1 cup sherry (or to barely cover)
2 boxes frozen peas

Brown the chicken pieces, which you have shaken in a bag to coat with flour, then put them in a buttered casserole. At the same time, so you don't have to wash the pan a second time, sauté the mushrooms (left whole or in very large pieces) and set them aside. Do not cook them overlong as they will be cooked more later. Put the small whole onions in the casserole and then pour in an entire bottle of chili sauce, a few shakes of Worcestershire, and enough sherry to cover the chicken. Bake 3/4 of an hour, add the mushrooms and the frozen peas, and bake an additional 15 minutes or until tender. *Mrs. Robert A. Milch*

Chicken and Wild Rice Casserole

6 servings

2 whole broiler-fryers (3 pounds each)
1 cup water
1 cup dry sherry
1-1/2 teaspoons salt
1/2 teaspoon curry powder
1 medium onion, sliced
1/2 cup celery, sliced
1 pound fresh mushrooms
1 package (12 ounces) long grain and wild rice with seasoning
1 cup sour cream
1 can (10-1/2 ounces) mushroom soup

Put the chicken in a deep kettle; add the water, sherry, salt, curry powder, onion, and celery and bring it to the boil. Cover the kettle and reduce the heat; simmer slowly for 1 hour or less. Because this must be reheated, do not overcook the chicken. Remove it from the heat, strain the broth to be used later, and refrigerate both broth and chicken. When cool enough to handle, remove the skin and cut the chicken into large cubes. Wipe the mushrooms and sauté them in butter. Measure the chicken broth and use it as part of the liquid needed to cook the rice, following the package directions for very firm rice. Combine the chicken, cooked rice, and mushrooms in a 3-1/2-quart casserole, reserving some of the best mushrooms to circle the top. Pour over this the sour cream and mushroom soup, which have been mixed together, and bake in a preheated oven for 1/2 hour or at least until piping hot.   *Mrs. S. Page Nelson, Jr.*

Oven-Baked Chicken

350° / 2 to 3 servings

1 broiler, cut in serving pieces
1/2 cup flour
Salt
Pepper
1 tablespoon melted butter
1/2 cup tart French dressing
1 teaspoon Worcestershire sauce
1/2 teaspoon dry instant coffee

Shake the chicken pieces in a paper bag in which you have put the flour, salt, and pepper. Have ready the French dressing to which you have added the Worcestershire sauce and the coffee. Place the floured chicken in a buttered baking pan and bake 35 minutes. At that time, coat each piece with the French dressing using a pastry brush. Put the chicken back in the oven and bake about 40 minutes longer or until it is tender.
Mrs. John H. Rice, Jr.

Chicken With Fresh Tarragon

300° / 2 to 4 servings

1 broiler or fryer, cut up
6 tablespoons butter
Pepper
Salt
1 tablespoon flour
1/2 pint heavy cream
1/4 cup fresh tarragon leaves, chopped

This chicken dish tastes strongly of tarragon so the amount may be lessened. Do not, however, use dried tarragon for the same result. Brown the chicken carefully in the butter. Sprinkle with salt and pepper and place it in a shallow casserole. Pour off all the butter but 1 tablespoon, stir in the flour, cook a minute or two, then add the cream all at once, and stir over heat until it is thick. Add the tarragon and correct the seasoning. Pour the sauce over the chicken and bake for 1 hour. Baste the chicken occasionally. Naturally all the preparation may be done well in advance, but in that case bring the casserole to room temperature before baking. It will take 45 minutes more if the casserole goes from icebox to oven.
Mrs. Frank Hoen

Picnic Chicken

2-pound broilers, split
Salt
Melted butter
Mild mustard
Bread crumbs

No amounts are given, for the quantities may be large or small; it is the method which is important. Use any number of broilers; split, clean and dry. Season them with salt, brush them with melted butter, and broil them until they are just done, about 20 minutes. Then brush a thin layer

of mustard over them, pat on dry bread crumbs, sprinkle with melted butter, and brown the crumbs under the broiler. Serve at room temperature.
Mrs. Alan George

Chicken with Curry Dumplings

4 servings

1 frying chicken, cut up
Salt and pepper
1 sliced onion
3 tablespoons oil
1-1/2 cups water
1 carrot, sliced in rounds
2 stalks celery, coarsely diced
Pinch of basil

Dumplings

1/2 tablespoon shortening
1 cup sifted flour
1/2 teaspoon salt
1 teaspoon baking powder
1/2 cup cool milk
1 teaspoon curry powder
1/2 teaspoon grated onion
1/2 teaspoon chopped parsley

Season the chicken pieces with salt and pepper and brown with the onion in a large pot in the hot oil. When brown, discard the excess oil; add the water, carrot, celery, and basil, and simmer gently until almost tender.

Prepare dumplings by cutting the shortening into the dry ingredients until fine. Add the liquid and seasonings all at once. Mix well with a fork, turn out on a floured board, and knead gently about 1/2 minute. Form a smooth long roll and cut diagonally into 8 pieces. Place the pieces on top of the simmering chicken stew, cover the pan, turn the heat low, and, without lifting the lid, cook 15 to 20 minutes. Serve the chicken and dumplings at once.
Mrs. Arthur Wilkoff

Creamed Chicken with Oysters

6 servings

1/4 cup butter
1 tablespoon chopped green pepper
1/4 cup minced celery
3 tablespoons flour
2 cups of rich milk or light cream
1-1/2 teaspoons salt
1/8 teaspoon of white pepper
2 cups cooked diced chicken
1/2 pint oysters

Melt the butter, add the green pepper and celery, and cook until tender; then add the flour. Mix well and add the milk or cream and any liquor from the oysters. Cook until thick. Add the salt and pepper, the chicken, and the oysters last. Heat until the edges of the oysters curl slightly and the chicken is heated through. Serve hot on buttered toast.
Mrs. Morton S. Busick

Chicken and Crab Meat Rosemary

325°

2 tablespoons chopped onion
4 tablespoons butter
2 tablespoons flour
1 teaspoon salt
1 teaspoon pepper
Paprika
Crushed rosemary
2 cups chicken broth
2 cups sour cream
3 cups cooked chicken, cut in bite-size pieces
1 cup cooked flaked crab meat
1-1/2 cups avocado cubes, sprinkled with lemon juice
1 cup fresh bread crumbs
Watercress for garnish

Sauté the onion in 2 tablespoons of butter until golden; stir in the flour, salt, pepper, paprika, and crushed rosemary. Cook for a few minutes; add the chicken broth and cook over low heat, stirring constantly, until it boils and thickens. Remove from the heat and stir in the sour cream slowly. Add the chicken and crab meat. Add avocado cubes and gently blend into the chicken mixture. Turn into a 2-quart baking dish and cover with bread crumbs sauteed in 2 tablespoons butter. Bake for 30 minutes just to heat through. Garnish with watercress.

Miss Janet Gross

Tandoori Chicken American Embassy

1 chicken, quartered and skinned
2 teaspoons curry powder
1 clove garlic, minced
1 tablespoon lemon juice
1 teaspoon salt
1/2 cup plain yoghurt
2 tablespoons vegetable oil
Red food coloring
Indian seasoning: 1 teaspoon mangoe powder, 1 teaspoon black cumin seed powder, 1 tablespoon methi powder
2 tablespoons melted butter
1 tablespoon lemon juice

Mix the curry powder, garlic, lemon juice, salt, yoghurt, and oil together. Spill in a little red vegetable coloring and marinate the chicken in this overnight. Broil it for 20 minutes, turning the pieces so they won't burn. When done, sprinkle the Indian seasoning all over the pieces, and if you like, although this is not traditional, pour the butter and lemon juice over the dish at serving time. This dish can be made outdoors over charcoal.

Spices for Indian seasoning can be bought at Bloomingdale's in New York. Fenugreek, a Mediterranean herb, is worth experimenting with when making flavorful Indian seasonings.

Mrs. Chester Bowles

Chicken in Cream with Tomatoes

4 to 6 servings

2 2-1/2-pound chickens, cut into serving pieces
Salt and freshly ground pepper
6 tablespoons butter
1 cup fresh sliced mushrooms
1/4 cup finely chopped shallots
1/2 cup cubed, peeled tomatoes
1/2 cup dry white wine
1 teaspoon chopped fresh thyme or 1/2 teaspoon dried thyme
1 tablespoon chopped fresh tarragon
1-1/2 cup heavy cream

Sprinkle the chickens with salt and pepper. Heat 4 tablespoons of the butter and brown the chicken pieces on all sides. Cook slowly about 30 minutes. In a separate skillet, cook the mushrooms in the remaining butter until wilted. Set aside.

When the chicken is done, remove it and keep it warm. To the skillet add the shallots and cook briefly, stirring. Add the tomatoes, wine, mushrooms, thyme, and tarragon. Cook 10 to 15 minutes and add the cream. Season to taste with salt and pepper. Return the chicken to the skillet and cook until chicken and sauce are piping hot.

Mrs. Henry Hays

Chicken Livers and Mushrooms

8 servings

1/2 pound bacon
2 onions, diced
1 green pepper, diced

3 tablespoons butter
2 tablespoons sweet paprika
1 pound mushrooms, sliced
2 pounds chicken livers
Salt
Pepper
4 tablespoons sour cream

Render the bacon, then drain and crumble it. Sauté the onions and green pepper in butter until the former is transparent, then add paprika and mix well. At this point, add the mushrooms and chicken livers and sauté over high heat until just done (about 3 minutes). Season to taste with salt and pepper, add the crumbled bacon, and stir in the sour cream. Serve immediately with a green salad and rice.
Miss Sarah Anderson

Chicken Livers with Cognac

4 servings

1/4 pound bacon slices, diced
1 cup finely diced leek or onion
1 pound chicken livers, halved
2 tablespoons warm Cognac
1/4 pound sliced mushrooms
1-1/2 tablespoons flour
1/2 teaspoon thyme
1/2 teaspoon marjoram
1/4 teaspoon summer savory
1 cup chicken or beef broth
Salt and freshly ground black pepper to taste
1/3 cup dry sherry
2 cups (about 4 ounces) thin noodles, cooked al dente and drained

Fry the bacon in a skillet until crisp. Then remove the pieces and set aside. In the fat remaining in the skillet, sauté the leek or onion until tender but not browned. Add the livers and brown quickly on all sides, then add the Cognac and ignite it. When the flame dies down, add the mushrooms and cook 3 minutes longer. Sprinkle with the flour and cook 1 minute while stirring. Add the thyme, marjoram, savory, and broth and bring to a boil. Simmer 3 minutes or until the livers are cooked but still pink in the middle. Season with salt and pepper and add the sherry. The cooked noodles can be added to the skillet and mixed in, or the chicken mixture may be spooned over the noodles. Sprinkle the bacon bits over the top before serving.
Mrs. Henry Hays

Chicken Livers with Sherry and Cream

4 servings

1 pound chicken livers
Flour
1/2 teaspoon salt
1/4 teaspoon freshly ground black pepper
2 tablespoons butter
2 tablespoons vegetable oil
1/2 pound firm fresh mushrooms, sliced
1 tablespoon flour
1/4 cup dry sherry
1/4 cup chicken stock (canned chicken broth may be substituted)
1/2 cup cream
2 tablespoons finely chopped parsley

Wipe the chicken livers dry; cut large ones in two. Roll them in flour seasoned with the salt and pepper. In a heavy skillet over moderate heat melt the butter with the oil. When the butter foam subsides, add the livers and cook until brown on both sides. Do not overcook; 5 to 8 minutes in all is sufficient. Remove them from the skillet. Sauté the mushrooms in the same skillet about 5 minutes. Remove them from the skillet too. To the pan juices add the flour and mix carefully. Let simmer a few moments, then add the sherry, chicken stock and cream, and simmer until thickened. If the sauce seems a trifle thick, dilute with a little additional chicken stock or cream. This much may be prepared in advance.

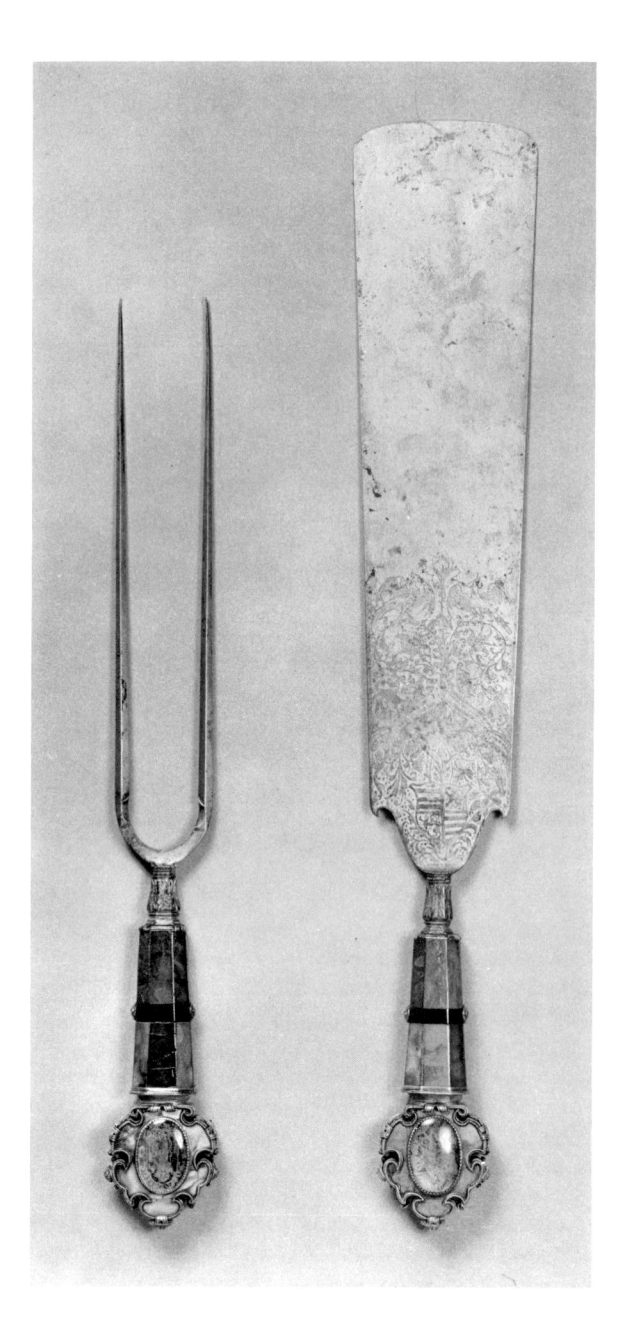

Just before serving, return the livers and mushrooms to the sherry sauce and reheat briefly without allowing the sauce to boil. Sprinkle with the chopped parsley and serve.

Mrs. Thomas Smith

Chicken Livers Charleston

4 servings

1/2 cup diced bacon
2 tablespoons chopped onion
2 tablespoons chopped green pepper
1 pound chicken livers
Flour
Thyme
1/2 cup red wine
1/2 cup pitted ripe olives
1/4 cup chopped parsley

In the top pan of a chafing dish over a flame, sauté the bacon, onion, and green pepper until the bacon is gently browned. Add the livers, lightly dredged with flour, and cook for 3 minutes, tossing them with a fork from side to side. Add a few leaves of thyme, then pour in the wine and cook for a few minutes. Add the olives and parsley and cook for another minute, stirring constantly. Serve on hot toasted English muffins. Add a green salad for lunch. *Mrs. Coleman Brownfield*

The official serving implements for the household of the Elector Palatinate of the Rhine. The handles are amber, inset with *verre eglomisé* panels, and the etched arms on the blade of the presentoir are gilt. German, 16th century.

2 Little Red Hens

425° / 2 servings

2 Rock Cornish hens
Stuffing of your choice
1-1/2 cups grapefruit juice
Juice of 1 lemon
2 cups whole cranberry sauce
1/3 cup raspberry preserves
Salt and pepper
1/2 teaspoon rosemary
1/2 teaspoon thyme
1/2 teaspoon poultry seasoning

Stuff the Cornish hens with your favorite rice or bread stuffing. Marinate the hens for 1 hour in a sauce made by combining grapefruit and lemon juice, cranberry sauce, and raspberry preserves. Sprinkle the hens liberally with salt, pepper, rosemary, thyme, and poultry seasoning. Fifteen minutes before roasting the hens, heat the oven to 425°. Reduce the heat to 350°, place the hens on a rack, cover with aluminum foil, and roast for 3/4 to 1 hour. Baste frequently with the sauce.

Mrs. Charles Eisman

Stuffed Cornish Game Hens

450°/6 servings

6 Cornish game hens
1-1/2 cups Uncle Ben's long grain and wild rice
1-1/2 teaspoons sugar
3/4 teaspoon salt
1/8 teaspoon pepper
1/8 teaspoon nutmeg
1/8 teaspoon allspice
1/3 cup slivered almonds, toasted

Wash and dry the Cornish hens. Cook the rice according to the package directions. Add wine, sugar, salt, pepper, and spices and mix well. Add the almonds, then stuff the mixture into the cavities of the hens. Place the hens in the oven in a roasting pan. Immediately turn the oven down to 350° and roast for 3/4 to 1 hour, basting occasionally with the following wine glaze.

1/4 cup red wine
3 tablespoons melted butter
1-1/2 teaspoons lemon juice

It is very convenient to prepare the birds a few hours in advance, leaving them in the refrigerator and then bringing them to room temperature before roasting time.

Mrs. Michael Ondo

Barlovento Duck

350°-400° / 4 servings

2 ducklings
1 package prepared poultry stuffing
1 egg, beaten
2 apples, peeled, cored, and chopped
2 oranges, peeled and chopped
1/2 cup raisins
2 cans frozen orange juice

Wash and salt the inside of the ducks. Mix the prepared stuffing, add the beaten egg, then add the apples, oranges, raisins and enough thawed orange juice to moisten them, reserving the remainder of the juice for basting. Season with nutmeg, salt, and pepper. Stuff the ducks with the mixture. Roast in a fairly hot oven for 2 to 2-1/2 hours, or until well browned, basting frequently. About 20 minutes before serving, drain off the excess fat and start basting with the remaining orange juice every 5 minutes.

Mrs. Walter Black

Pepper Duck

325° / 2 servings

1 duck for 2 people
Quantities of coarse freshly ground pepper

Cover an oven-ready duck with a heavy, heavy coat of coarse freshly ground pepper—tablespoons of it. (The pepper will become less pungent and take on a nutty flavor during the cooking.) Add salt. Roast on a rack a long time in a slow oven, about 3 hours. Prick it often to let the fat run out; it then becomes very crisp and fatless. To serve, quarter the duck with poultry shears. Dry white rice and red currant jelly are often served with it, but these accompaniments are unnecessary.

Mrs. Jon Alan Wurtzburger

Joe's Goose

350°

Canadian goose, ready to cook
Black pepper
Celery
Carrot
Turnip
Parsley
Apple
Onion
Butter

Sprinkle freshly ground black pepper generously in the vent and inside the carcass of the Canadian goose. Stuff it with celery, carrot, turnip, parsley, apple, and onion. Coat the breast with melted butter. Wrap the bird tightly in aluminum foil in such a manner that it can be easily opened for basting. Roast 1 hour and 20 minutes or until the goose is tender. Open the foil and baste under the broiler until browned to your taste.

Joseph B. Browne

Wild Goose Breasts

350° / 2 servings

2 wild goose breasts
Red wine
Vegetable oil
1 tablespoon crushed black peppercorns
Flour, seasoned with salt and pepper
3 tablespoons olive oil
2 tablespoons butter
2 cloves garlic, crushed
Rosemary
Paprika
1/2 cup white wine

With a sharp knife, skin and bone the breasts. Make a marinade of 1/2 part red wine to 1/2 part oil and the peppercorns. Marinate the goose breasts for 4 to 6 hours.

Remove the breasts from the marinade. Pat dry with paper towels, dip lightly in seasoned flour and sprinkle with paprika. Combine olive oil and butter in a skillet; add the crushed garlic and rosemary to the warming oils. Brown the breasts on both sides. Add the wine and cook over medium heat 20 to 30 minutes.

Mrs. John Eager

Cold Breast of Pheasant

6 servings

3 large pheasant breasts, cut in half
1 small onion, peeled and sliced
Salt and pepper
2 cups water or chicken stock
2 pounds fresh asparagus
1/3 cup freshly grated Parmesan cheese
1 cup Italian salad dressing
1/3 pound mushrooms
2 tablespoons butter
Lemon juice
Bibb lettuce
Mayonnaise

Skin the pheasant breasts and search them carefully for shot. Put them in a Dutch oven or heavy casserole with the onion, salt, pepper, and 2 cups of water or stock. Simmer for 30 minutes, remove the breasts from the broth and cool.

Cut the asparagus in 4-5 inch lengths and cook until just tender and not a second more. Put it under cold water immediately to freshen it and stop the cooking. Drain it well. Mix the cheese with the salad dressing and pour half of it over the asparagus, then set it aside until the dish is assembled. Sauté the mushrooms in the butter very lightly and sprinkle with lemon juice.

On a large serving platter arrange the Bibb lettuce leaves, lay the asparagus pieces over them, and top with the overlapping breasts. At both ends pile up the mushrooms attractively. Blend the mayonnaise with the remaining cheese dressing and spread over the breasts. Serve chilled for a cold buffet.
Mrs. W. Scott Ditch, III

Scallops of Turkey Breast

4 servings

4 turkey scallops (raw slices cut from the breast)
Flour
Salt and pepper
4-6 tablespoons butter
1 tablespoon oil
4 slices lean cooking ham
8-10 tablespoons mushrooms, thinly sliced
Pepper
Chopped parsley
4 slices Fontina or Gruyère cheese, thinly sliced
1/4 cup or more of chicken or turkey stock

Pound the turkey slices evenly and shake them in a bag containing the seasoned flour. Shake off any excess flour. Heat the butter and oil without browning. Cook the turkey slices over low heat about 5 minutes on each side. (This dish will taste like its veal counterpart, only more tender.)

On top of each turkey slice put a slice of ham, trimmed to the same size, and cover with a thin layer of mushrooms which have been sautéed in butter. Shake pepper over these, and a little chopped parsley. Cover this with the cheese slices. Put this all in a pan with a closely fitting lid, pour the stock in, cover the pan and cook over low heat on top of the stove for about 10 minutes. Serve with chopped parsley or sprigs of watercress. Some rice or noodles and a green salad, with a fruit dessert, go well with this filling entrée.

Miss Margaret Masters

A lady's ivory mirror case carved with a scene of lovers out hawking. The subject often was used for the symbol of the month May. French, 14th century.

Two Game Birds

350° / 2 servings

1 pheasant, about 2-1/2 to 3 pounds, ready to cook
1 tablespoon melted butter
Salt and freshly ground pepper to taste
1/2 cup celery leaves
1 small whole apple
1 small whole onion
1 slice lemon
1 whole clove of garlic
4 thin slices salt pork

Rub the cavity of the pheasant with the melted butter and some salt and pepper. Put the other ingredients, but not the salt pork, inside the bird and truss it. Because the pheasant meat is naturally quite dry, lay thin slices of the salt pork over the breast of the bird and roast uncovered from 15 to 30 minutes to the pound, depending on your taste. (Wild birds of dark meat are usually served rare while the white-meat varieties are best well done.) Baste the bird with the pan juices once or twice while it is cooking. Transfer the bird to a heated platter to keep warm and serve with the following sauce.

Apricot Sauce for Roast Pheasant

**1-1/2 cups chicken stock
1 cup canned pitted apricots
1 teaspoon grated orange rind
1/4 cup port or sherry
Pheasant liver, coarsely chopped
Salt and pepper
1 teaspoon cornstarch mixed with 2 teaspoons water**

Pour off the fat from the pan in which the pheasant was roasted. Add the chicken stock to the pan, stir it over moderate heat scraping up all the coagulated good juices, then reduce, over high heat, until only about 3/4 cup remains. Rub the apricots through a sieve and add to the pan with 1/2 cup of the apricot juice, the orange rind, port or sherry, the pheasant liver, salt, and pepper. Reduce the heat and simmer the sauce for 5 minutes. If it seems much too thin, add the cornstarch and heat, but do not boil, until it has thickened somewhat. Put some of the sauce over the bird but pass the rest separately.

Wild duck may be roasted in exactly the same way, and served with a Madeira sauce made by the same method as the apricot sauce, but eliminating the apricot and orange and substituting Madeira for the sherry.

Mrs. W. Scott Ditch, III

FISH

Bluefish in Gin

6 servings

6 bluefish fillets
1/4 pound butter
6 teaspoons onion flakes and Jane's Krazy Mixed-up salt
3 ounces gin

Place the fish in a flat ovenproof dish. Melt the butter and pour half of it over the fish. Sprinkle with the onion flakes and Jane's salt (about 1 teaspoon for each fillet). Broil until they start to brown, then add the gin to the rest of the butter, warm it, and pour it over the hot fish. Flame it and put the dish under the broiler again to brown, which should take about 10 minutes from start to finish.
Mrs. James Grieves

Bluefish with Sour Cream Topping

375° / 4 servings

1 good-sized bluefish, cut in fillets
Salt and pepper
Butter
1-1/2 cups sour cream
3 tablespoons chopped chives
3 tablespoons lemon juice
1/2 cup mayonnaise

Wash, dry, and salt and pepper the fillets. Put them in a buttered earthenware baking dish. Mix the sour cream, chives, and lemon juice into a good mayonnaise, preferably homemade, and mask the fish with it. Bake for fifteen minutes or more, until the fillets flake slightly, then put them under the broiler briefly to brown.
Mrs. Curran W. Harvey

Mussels, Three Versions

I

18 mussels
1 green pepper, seeded and chopped
1 red pepper, seeded and chopped
2 small onions, peeled and chopped
1 cup vinegar
1/4 cup olive oil
1 teaspoon salt

Clean and beard the mussels, scrubbing them well, and place them in a 450° oven for about 15 minutes until they open. Take off the top shell. Mix the chopped vegetables with the vinegar, oil, and salt and put a teaspoon or more of the mixture on each mussel.

II

18 mussels
1 onion
1/2 bottle white wine
1 quart salt water

Steam the mussels in a court bouillon made of the other ingredients for 10 minutes. Make the following sauce and use it as a dip for the mussels.

2 tablespoons vinegar
4 tablespoons olive oil
Salt and pepper
2 teaspoons capers
2 tablespoons chopped parsley
2 teaspoons chopped chives
1 teaspoon dried tarragon

III

18 steamed mussels

Garlic Sauce:

8 tablespoons butter
1 clove garlic, minced
2 teaspoons lemon juice
1 teaspoon chopped parsley

Melt the butter, season it with the garlic and lemon, and add the parsley. Use it as a dip for the mussels at cocktail time. *Mrs. W. Boulton Kelly*

Cold Rock Bass or Striped Bass with Lemon Sauce

2 servings
1 2-pound rock bass or striped bass
8-10 stalks of celery and their leaves
6 large sprigs of parsley
3 tablespoons beef base
2 teaspoons salt
1 onion, sliced
1 teaspoon white peppercorns
Juice of 1 lemon
1 whole lemon, sliced
2 quarts of water

Clean the fish, leaving on both head and tail, and put it in a flat wide dish or fish poacher. Make a court bouillon of all the ingredients but the fish, and after it has simmered until it is flavorful, about 15 or 20 minutes, pour enough of it over the fish to come halfway up the dish. Measure the fish through the thickest part. Bring the bouillon to the boil, turn the heat down, and simmer the fish 10 minutes for each inch of thickness. Remove the fish; strain the bouillon to be used later in the lemon sauce. Before the fish is cool, skin it, then cut it in portions and cool completely before covering it lightly with lemon sauce (below). Garnish the platter with watercress and lemon quarters. Serve the remainder of the sauce in a sauce boat.

Lemon Sauce

2 tablespoons flour
2 tablespoons butter
2 cups fish bouillon
2 egg yolks
1/4 cup lemon juice
Salt and pepper

Make a velouté sauce by melting the butter, adding the flour, cooking 2 minutes, and then pouring in the fish bouillon. Stir it thoroughly until smooth. Make a liaison by adding some of the hot sauce to the well beaten egg yolks and then pouring that mixture back into the sauce; beat carefully. Add the lemon juice to make the sauce creamy.

Mrs. Stanford Z. Rothschild

Salmon Mold with Dill Sauce

6 servings

1 tablespoon gelatin
1/4 cup water or white wine
3 tablespoons shallots, chopped fine
1 tablespoon butter
1-1/2 cups fish stock
1-1/4 pounds cooked (or drained canned) salmon
2 tablespoons brandy
Salt and pepper
Paprika
1/2 cup whipping cream
1 tablespoon capers, washed and drained
Lemon slices (for garnish)
Watercress (for garnish)

Soften the gelatin in the water or wine. Sauté the shallots in the butter, add the fish stock and the softened gelatin, and heat until the gelatin has dissolved. (You may substitute half bottled clam juice and half water for the stock.) In a blender, put some of the stock and some of the fish; purée this in small quantities to make it easy. When it is all puréed, add the brandy, salt and pepper, and paprika to taste and finally fold in the cream. Put this in a buttered mold, and chill it until it has set. Serve it with a dill sauce (recipe follows). Surround it, when unmolded, with lemon slices, watercress, and capers.

Dill Sauce

1 egg
1 teaspoon each salt and sugar
1/4 teaspoon pepper
4 teaspoons lemon juice
1 teaspoon grated onion
2 tablespoons finely snipped dill
1-1/2 cups sour cream

Beat this all together and chill.

Mrs. John H. Rice, Jr.

Baked Shad Roe

350° / 2 servings

1 pair shad roe
Salt and freshly ground pepper
3 tablespoons soft butter
1 teaspoon dried dill
2 tablespoons chopped parsley
2 tablespoons dry white wine or dry vermouth
Lemon wedges
Slices crisply cooked bacon

Sprinkle the shad roe on all sides with salt and pepper. Spread butter on a sheet of aluminum foil large enough to enclose the roe envelope-fashion. Sprinkle dill and parsley on the butter. Place the roe in the center of the foil and bring up the edges. Add wine and seal closely. Bake 25 minutes or longer, depending on the size of the roe. Serve with lemon wedges and bacon.

Mrs. W. Gibbs McKenney

Shad Roe in White Wine

350° / 4 servings

4 pairs of shad roe
Butter
3 onions, chopped
2 tablespoons parsley, chopped
2 tablespoons shallots, chopped
12 large mushrooms, peeled and sliced
2 cups white wine
1 tablespoon flour
Bread crumbs
Lemon juice
Parsley

Wash and dry the shad roe. Butter an oblong baking dish and sprinkle the bottom with the onions, parsley, and shallots. Lay the roe on this. Sauté the mushrooms lightly in 1 tablespoon butter. Add with their juice to the roe. Add salt and pepper, then pour 2 cups white wine over them. Bake 20 minutes, basting frequently. Remove from the oven and drain off the juice. Melt 1 tablespoon butter in a saucepan. Add 1 tablespoon flour and 1 cup of the fish juice. Cook a few minutes and pour it over the roe. Sprinkle with bread crumbs, lemon juice, and parsley. Garnish with lemon.

G.O.K.

Herbed Shad

300°

1 shad, 2 to 4 pounds dressed (leave on head and tail)
Lemon-and-pepper seasoning
1 cup white wine or dry vermouth (optional)
2 stalks celery, chopped
1 small onion, chopped
2 bay leaves

Wash the shad and dry it with a paper towel. Sprinkle the fish inside and out with lemon-and-pepper seasoning. Put the fish on a rack in a baking pan. Add water to a level just under the fish. If desired, substitute 1 cup of white wine for part of the water. Add the celery, onion, and bay leaves. Cover tightly and steam in the oven for 5 hours. Baste frequently.

NOTE: The secret of softening the bones is to make sure that the pan cover fits tightly and to cook the fish for the full amount of time. If these directions are followed exactly, even the large backbone will be soft enough to be eaten, and most of the small splinter bones will disappear.

Miss Eleanor Holliday Cross

Shad Roe Ring

6 servings

2 cans (7-1/4 ounces) shad roe
1/2 cup cold water
2 tablespoons gelatin
1 can (10-1/2 ounces) chicken consommé
3/4 cup celery stock
1 teaspoon salt
2 teaspoons lemon juice
1/2 cup homemade mayonnaise

Drain the shad roe. Discard the skin and separate the little beadlike eggs with a fork. Pour 1/2 cup of cold water into a bowl large enough to hold all the ingredients, sprinkle with gelatin, and set aside until needed.

Bring to the boiling point the consommé and the celery stock or, if celery stock is not available, any vegetable stock or plain water. Add the salt and pour the hot liquid into the gelatin, stirring until the gelatin is dissolved. Let the mixture stand until cold. Then add the lemon juice and pour the gelatin mixture in a thin stream into 1/2 cup mayonnaise, beating as you pour. Lightly mix in the roe. Leave it in the bowl until it has thickened enough to keep the roe from settling to the bottom, gently folding it over occasionally to insure an even mixture. Turn into a quart ring and chill until set. Serve with chopped cucumbers folded into sour cream and parsley.

Mrs. Frank Thom

Shad Roe Florentine

6 servings

3 pairs of roe
6 tablespoons butter
6 shallots, minced
3/4 pound spinach, cooked and chopped coarsely
1-1/2 cups dry vermouth
2 cups heavy cream
Salt and pepper

Wipe the roe dry and put them in a sauté pan with the butter and the shallots. Sauté very lightly, then add the spinach and the vermouth and simmer uncovered for about 10 minutes on each side.

Remove the roe and the spinach; keep warm on a hot platter. Add the cream, salt, and pepper to the juices in the pan and reduce over a high heat until thickened; pour over the roe and spinach and serve.

Mrs. Bertram Bernheim, Jr.

Shark Fritters

6 servings

2 pounds shark, cut in strips about 3 inches long by 3/4 of an inch wide and thick
1 cup flour
1/2 teaspoon baking powder
1 teaspoon salt
1/4 teaspoon black pepper
2 beaten eggs
1/2 cup water
Butter

Dip the shark strips in a batter made of the flour, baking powder, salt, pepper, 2 beaten eggs, and 1/2 cup water. Fry the strips quickly to a golden brown in hot butter. Drain on paper towels.

Euell Gibbons

Finnan Haddie with a Mashed Potato Cuff

375° / 6 servings

1-1/2 pounds finnan haddie
Milk to cover fish
1/4 pound butter
3 tablespoons flour
2 cups milk
Salt and freshly ground pepper
4 hard-cooked eggs
2 cups mashed potatoes
2/3 cup grated American cheese

Select a thick slice of finnan haddie, cover it with milk, and simmer for about 20 minutes or until it can be easily flaked. Discard the milk, and when the fish can be handled, flake it in large pieces, discarding the hard ends.

Make a béchamel sauce by melting the butter, stirring in the flour, and simmering for about 2 minutes to rid the sauce of the floury taste. Add the 2 cups of milk which have been heated to a boil. Beat with a wire whisk until smooth. Season to taste, making sure not to salt it much as the fish is salty. Cut the eggs into eighths and then carefully combine the fish, eggs, and sauce and turn into a buttered casserole. With a pastry tube pipe an attractive border of mashed potatoes around the casserole. Carefully strew the grated cheese over all and bake for about 30 minutes or until brown. Serve at once.

This can be made with salt codfish, which has been soaked in many changes of water and then boiled till flaky. You may serve the fish over mealy hot baked potato halves. Shake chopped parsley and pepper over it.

Mrs. Roger Clapp, Mrs. Walter G. Lohr

Soy Swordfish

4 servings

1 large swordfish steak or 2 smaller steaks
1/2 cup soy sauce
1/2 cup strong tea
1/4 teaspoon oregano
Cloves
1/2 cup sherry
1/2 teaspoon cinnamon
Pepper
1 clove garlic mashed in marinade

Mix all the ingredients except the swordfish and marinate the fish for 2 hours. Drain and wipe the fish dry with a paper towel. Broil or fry in butter for about 15 minutes.

Mrs. W. Boulton Kelly

Baked Fish with Salmon Stuffing

350° / 6 servings

5-pound baking fish or 2 large fillets of sole

Stuffing:

**1/2 cup soft butter
2 egg yolks
6 slices bread, trimmed and crumbed
1/2 cup salmon liquid or milk
1 pound can salmon, drained and flaked
1 teaspoon salt
1/2 teaspoon white pepper
2 tablespoons chopped chives or parsley
1 small carrot, chopped
1 small onion, chopped
Pinch of thyme
1 cup fish or chicken stock
1/2 cup dry white wine or dry vermouth**

Sauce:

**1 cup fish liquid
1 cup cream
3 tablespoons soft butter
3 tablespoons flour
Squeeze of lemon**

Garnish:

**12 mushroom caps sautéed in 1 tablespoon butter
Parsley
Lemon wedges**

If you are using a whole fish, have it boned, leaving a pocket down the back of the fish as well as down the belly. Wash the fish well inside and out. Combine the 1/2 cup soft butter with the egg yolks, bread crumbs, salmon liquid or milk, salmon, salt, pepper, and chives. Stuff the fish both down the back and front with the salmon stuffing.

Butter a large baking dish and sprinkle the bottom with the carrot, onion, and thyme. Place the fish on a bed of vegetables and add fish or chicken stock and wine. Bake 45 minutes or until the flesh along the back flakes easily.

Transfer the baked fish to a warm platter and keep it warm while you make the sauce. Strain the liquid in the baking dish into a saucepan. Reduce to 1 cup and add the cream. Correct the seasoning and bring the liquid to a boil. Combine the soft butter and flour to a smooth paste and add gradually to the hot liquid, stirring until the sauce is thickened, but not too thick. Add a squeeze of lemon and pour into a sauceboat. Garnish the fish with the sautéed mushroom caps, parsley, and lemon wedges and serve the sauce separately.

This salmon stuffing is very delicate and easy to make and can be used to stuff trout or as topping on oysters, clams, or frozen fish, before baking.

Mrs. Duncan MacKenzie

Fish Mousse with Cucumber Mustard Sauce

6 servings

**1-1/2 pounds fillet of flounder or sole
3 cups white-wine fish stock (see following recipe)
Bouquet garni of 2 parsley sprigs, 1/8 teaspoon thyme, and 1/2 bay leaf, tied in cheesecloth
2 tablespoons gelatin
4 tablespoons white wine
3/4 cup chilled whipping cream
1-1/2 teaspoons dried dill weed
Salt and pepper**

Put the fish with the fish stock and the bouquet garni in an enameled skillet. Bring to a simmer, cover, and poach the fish about 6 to 8 minutes, or until just tender. Remove the fish to a bowl and flake it. Strain the liquid and measure 2 cups. Place the liquid in a saucepan and add the gelatin, which has been softened in 4 tablespoons white wine. Heat until the gelatin is dissolved. Pour the fish and liquid into a blender jar, cover, and blend at top speed for 1 or 2 minutes or until puréed. Pour into a bowl and chill.

Whip 3/4 cup cream lightly and fold into the chilled fish mixture. Add 1-1/2 teaspoons dried dill. Taste for seasoning and add pepper and salt if necessary. Pour into an oiled 6-cup ring mold or soufflé dish. Cover with waxed paper and chill in the refrigerator until set (several hours). Unmold onto a chilled platter. Decorate with watercress and serve with the following sauce.

Cucumber Mustard Sauce
1 cucumber, grated, peeled, and seeded
1 cup mayonnaise
1 tablespoon prepared mustard
1 tablespoon lemon juice
1 tablespoon chopped chives
Mix all the ingredients together.

White Wine Fish Stock
2 cups clam juice
1/2 cup water
1/2 cup dry white wine
1 thinly sliced onion
6 parsley stems
Simmer in a saucepan 20 minutes. Strain and taste for seasoning.

Mrs. Bertram Bernheim, Jr.

Mousse of Sole

350° / 4 servings

Place in a blender in the following order:
5 fresh fillets of sole
1 cup light cream
5 eggs
4 egg whites
2 tablespoons melted butter
Salt and pepper

Blend the mixture until smooth and combine with 1 more cup light cream and transfer into a casserole. Place the casserole in a pan of hot water and bake 30 minutes (or until a knife, inserted in the center, comes out clean.) Serve with hot hollandaise sauce. If you double the recipe, bake it 1 hour. *Mrs. Irving Steinbach, Mrs. Ralph N. Willis*

Poached Flounder

2 servings
2 tablespoons butter
2 flounder fillets
1/2 cup white wine (Graves is about right)
1 teaspoon finely chopped scallions or shallot
White pepper, MSG, and no salt
1/2 small can of flat anchovy fillets
1/4 cup heavy cream

Melt the butter in a large sauté pan and add the fish, wine, and onions. Dust with pepper and MSG and garnish with the anchovies. Poach gently until done (about 15 minutes.) Remove the fish to a warm platter, add cream to the pan, and whisk until it is at a simmer. Strain the sauce over the fish and serve at once.

Edward L. Brewster

Fillet of Sole with Oysters

375° / 4 servings
4 fillets of sole
Lemon juice
1 pint oysters
4 tablespoons butter
1 tablespoon flour
1 cup oyster liquor and white wine, combined

Place the fillets in a buttered shallow baking dish and sprinkle them with lemon juice. Drain the oyster liquor into a measuring cup and add enough white wine to make 1 cup of liquid. Make a velouté sauce by melting 1 tablespoon of the butter, blending in the flour, and adding the cup of oyster liquor-white wine, stirring until the sauce is slightly thickened.

Cook the oysters slowly in the remaining 3 tablespoons of butter until the edges begin to curl. Bake the sole fillets for 5 minutes in a preheated oven. Remove from the oven, pour half the sauce over the fillets, cover the fillets with the oysters, then top with the remaining sauce and brown quickly under a hot broiler. Spinach is an excellent accompaniment.

Up to the last step, everything can be done ahead of time and the dish can be briefly heated and browned under the broiler just before serving.

Mrs. Beverly Compton

Shrimp and Egg European

400° / 4 servings

1 pound shrimp
6 hard-cooked eggs
1 cup light cream
1 tablespoon chopped parsley
2 teaspoons minced chervil (a must)
2 teaspoons dry mustard
Salt and pepper to taste
1/2 cup (and more) Parmesan cheese
Butter
Paprika

Plunge the shrimp into boiling water, then simmer 3 minutes. Shell and devein them. Peel the eggs and cut them into shreds. Cut the shrimp into bite-size pieces. Combine the eggs and shrimp with the cream, parsley, chervil, mustard, and Parmesan cheese. Season with salt and pepper. Spoon into a deep-dish Pyrex pie pan and sprinkle with more Parmesan cheese. Dot generously with butter and dust with paprika. Bake until the mixture is heated through and golden on top, about 10 minutes.

Mrs. Sven Peuleché

Shrimp Polynesian

4 servings

1 medium green pepper, cut into 1-inch pieces
2 tablespoons butter
3 tablespoons cornstarch
1/4 cup water
2 teaspoons lemon juice
1/2 cup pineapple tidbits
1 can beef broth
1/2 cup pineapple juice
1 tablespoon soy sauce
1-1/2 cups cooked shrimp

Sauté green pepper in butter until tender. Mix cornstarch with water, then put all the ingredients but the shrimp into a skillet in no particular order until the sauce is thickened. Add the shrimp just long enough in advance to heat through. Serve over rice.

Mrs. Thomas P. Pratt, Jr.

Shrimp Broiled with Garlic Butter

6 servings

2 pounds uncooked fresh or defrosted shrimp in shells
1/4 pound stick of butter
1/2 cup olive or salad oil
1 tablespoon lemon juice
1/4 cup chopped scallions
1 tablespoon chopped garlic
1 teaspoon salt
Freshly ground black pepper
4 tablespoons chopped parsley

Shell the shrimp but do not remove the tails. Split them down the back and remove the intestinal veins. Wash under cold water and dry. Preheat broiler to the highest temperature. In a pan melt the butter, then add the oil, lemon juice, scallions, garlic, salt, and pepper. Add shrimp and broil 3 to 4 inches from the heat for 5 minutes. Then turn, broil 5 minutes on the other side. Serve on a platter with parsley and strained juices from the pan. *Mrs. William Hazelhurst*

Marinated Shrimp

3 pounds cooked and peeled shrimp

Marinade:

1-1/2 cups olive oil
3/4 cup white wine
1 bottle capers, drained, rinsed, and dried on paper towel
2-1/2 teaspoons celery seed
Tabasco sauce (optional)
2 bay leaves
2 large onions, sliced

Mix the marinade ingredients together. Marinate the shrimp overnight and serve with the marinade, strained. *Mrs. Ronald Diana*

Crevette et Champignon

12 servings

2 pounds shrimp
1/2 teaspoon crushed red pepper
2 bay leaves
1 teaspoon peppercorns
1 teaspoon dill seed
1 pound mushrooms (small ones, 3/4 inch in diameter)
1/2 cup (1 stick) sweet butter
1 medium leek (white part), chopped fine
1-1/2 tablespoons flour
1 pint cream
Salt and white pepper
1/2 teaspoon marjoram
2 egg yolks
1/4 cup sauterne-type wine (or the real thing)
Paprika to garnish

Boil the shrimp in salted water, to which the red pepper, bay leaves, peppercorns, and dill seed have been added, until they are pink and firm (about 5 minutes). Allow them to cool in the cooking water and then shuck them.

Wipe the mushrooms (or wash, if necessary) and remove the stems. Set the caps aside and boil the cut-up stems in 3 cups water; allow to boil down to 1-1/2 cups of essence. Melt the butter over direct heat in the top of a double boiler; add the leek and cook until soft. Add the flour, stir, and cook a bit longer so the flour forms a buttery roux. Blend in the mushroom essence and simmer gently until the roux no longer tastes floury. Remove from direct heat and place over boiling water. Stir in the mushroom caps and 1-1/2 cups of the cream. Allow them to steam for about 15 minutes. Add the shrimp, salt, pepper, marjoram and paprika and then heat until the shrimp are well heated through. Beat the egg yolks into the remaining 1/2 cup of cream. Add and stir in gently until the sauce is somewhat thickened. Stir in the sauterne, transfer to a warmed serving dish, and dust with the paprika to look pretty. Serve dry toast points with it.

Edward L. Brewster

Shrimp, Happily Married

4 servings

1 pound raw shrimp
1/2 cup lemon juice
1/2 cup olive oil
3 tablespoons butter
1/2 clove garlic
1/2 cup finely chopped nuts
Tabasco sauce
2 tablespoons dry vermouth
Hot rice

Devein and peel the shrimp and marinate them in the lemon juice and olive oil for 3 hours. Drain and then sauté in butter with the garlic. Discard the garlic and remove the shrimp to a serving dish and keep the dish warm while you make the sauce.

Add the finely chopped nuts (pecans, almonds, macadamia, or filberts will do nicely) to the butter in the pan, add the marinade and a little more lemon for a tart taste, plus 2 dashes Tabasco and the dry vermouth.

Simmer 5 minutes and pour over the shrimp. Serve with hot rice. *Mrs. William T. Baker*

Shrimp and Wild Rice Casserole

300° / 6 servings

1/2 cup thinly sliced mushrooms
1/4 cup thinly sliced green peppers
1/2 cup thinly sliced onion
1/4 cup butter
1 tablespoon Worcestershire sauce
Tabasco
2 cups cooked wild rice
1 pound undercooked shrimp
2 cups velouté sauce

Sauté the vegetables in the butter until soft. Add seasoning, rice, shrimp, and the velouté sauce. Place in a buttered casserole and heat through. (The shrimp are underdone so that they will not become tough and overcook when reheated.)

Mrs. John J. Smith

Shrimp and Grapefruit Combination

8 servings

4 cups diced cooked shrimp
2 cups diced celery
1/4 cup cut-up pimiento
1/2 green pepper, cut up
Salt
3/4 cup mayonnaise
4 cups sectioned grapefruit
Salad greens

Mix together with a very light touch the shrimp, celery, pimiento, green pepper, salt, mayonnaise, and 2-1/2 cups grapefruit. Turn out on crisp salad greens and garnish with the remaining grapefruit.

Mrs. Henry Hays, II

Louisiana Shrimp Gumbo and Variations

8 servings

1/2 pound raw ham or bacon, cut in pieces
2 pounds fresh okra, cut in pieces
1-1/2 cups onion, chopped
2 ribs celery, chopped (leaves too)
1/2 green pepper, chopped
2 garlic cloves, minced
1 sprig fresh thyme or 1/2 teaspoon dried

1 bay leaf
1-1/2 cups skinned fresh tomatoes or 2 No. 1 cans
6 cups water
2 pounds fresh shrimp, shelled and deveined
2 tablespoons chopped parsley

Sauté ham or bacon lightly in a skillet. Remove and set aside. Add okra and sauté until it is brown and has lost all its ropiness (about 10 minutes). Add the onion for the last 2 minutes. Then add celery, green pepper, garlic, thyme, bay leaf, tomatoes, and water. Bring the gumbo to a boil, then reduce the heat and add the ham, shrimp, and parsley. Simmer 1/2 to 3/4 of an hour. Serve over dry rice.

The seafood can be varied, but the more the better! Some suggestions for a more varied gumbo are: 1 pound crab meat, 1/2 dozen fresh soft crabs (cut in half), 2 dozen raw oysters. It is better to make this a day before you serve it so the seasoning has time to go all through it.

Mrs. Edwin A. Daniels, Jr.

Eight Boy Curry

8 servings

Curry:

1/2 cup minced onion
5 tablespoons butter
6 tablespoons flour
1 cup chicken broth
2 cups milk
1-1/2 teaspoons sugar
3 teaspoons to 3 tablespoons curry powder
1-1/2 teaspoons salt
3 pounds shrimp, cooked and cleaned
1 teaspoon lemon juice

Accompaniments:

Major Grey's chutney
Chopped peanuts
Sieved hard-boiled eggs
Crumbled bacon
Toasted coconut
Raisins
Chopped raw onions
French-fried onions
Chopped avocado

Brown the onion in butter, blend in the flour, broth, and milk and cook until smooth and thick. Add sugar, curry powder, and salt to taste. Add the shrimp and lemon juice and heat through. Serve over hot rice; pass the accompaniments, Chicken or veal may be substituted for the shrimp.

Mrs. Charles Eisman

Cucumbers and Shrimp with Mushrooms

2 servings

2 small cucumbers
Salt
1/2 cup mushrooms, thickly sliced
3 tablespoons butter
1 teaspoon flour
1/4 cup cream
1/4 cup chicken stock
1/4 cup shelled, chopped, cooked shrimp
Snipped chives, dill or basil for garnish

Wash and cut the cucumbers, unpeeled if they are young, into large dice. Blanch them in salted water, rinse and drain them. Cook the mushrooms in the butter slightly; add the cucumbers and simmer over a low flame for a few minutes. Shake the flour over these, stir it in, then add the cream, and the chicken stock. Bring it to a boil, season, then let it simmer until it is well flavored, just a few minutes. Stir in the shrimp, sprinkle with one of the herbs. Serves 4 as a first course.

Miss Margaret Masters

Shrimp Salad with Macaroni

8 servings

1-1/2 pounds fresh shrimp or 2 cans large shrimp
Salt
Tarragon
Lemon pepper
Rosemary
1/4 cup sherry wine
8 ounces macaroni
1/2 cup sour cream
1/2 cup homemade mayonnaise
Dash of lemon juice
1 box frozen peas
1 green pepper
2 hard-cooked eggs
4 tablespoons parsley
Lemon pepper
1/2 cup any nut meats (pecans, almonds, or cashews)

Cook the shrimp with the salt, tarragon, lemon pepper, and rosemary until just done. Shell and devein the shrimp. If fresh shrimp are not available, use 2 cans of large shrimp and marinate them overnight in sherry after washing them well in cold water and draining them. Cook the macaroni according to the directions, drain, run cold water over it, and drain again. Mix the sour cream, mayonnaise, and lemon juice. In a large bowl put the shrimp, macaroni, and the peas, which have been cooked but kept firm and chilled, the green pepper sliced and diced, the eggs, sliced, chopped parsley, lemon pepper, and salt, plus nut meats. Toss these all together to mix them well, using wooden forks for the purpose, and then pour in the mayonnaise mixture and mix it through thoroughly. Put the salad in a serving bowl, cover with plastic wrap, and let it season for several hours in the refrigerator before serving.

Miss Gretchen Siegloff

Shrimp and Rice Salad

6 to 8 servings

1 cup olive oil
1-1/4 cup tarragon vinegar
1-1/2 teaspoon salt
1/2 teaspoon freshly ground black pepper
1/2 teaspoon minced garlic
2 tablespoons grated onion
2 teaspoons chopped capers
2 pounds shrimp, cooked, shelled, and cleaned
1 green pepper, seeded and diced fine
8 black olives, sliced thickly
1-1/2 cups cooked, but firm, rice

Beat together the olive oil, vinegar, salt, pepper, garlic, onion, and capers. Pour over the shrimp, green pepper, and olives and let it all marinate for at least 2 hours. Add the rice just before serving and toss lightly. Serve on lettuce, with diced tomatoes and cucumbers around the dish.

Herbert Powell

Quick Shrimp and Artichoke Bake

450° / 4 servings

1 can (10-3/4 ounces) Cheddar cheese soup
1/3 cup water, dry white wine, or sherry
1 teaspoon Dijon mustard
Generous dash of Tabasco sauce
1-1/2 cups cooked shrimp (cut up if desired)
1 can artichoke hearts or 1 9-ounce package frozen artichoke hearts, cooked and drained
1 8-ounce package refrigerated biscuits.

In a shallow baking dish (about 10 x 6 x 2 inches) stir the soup with water or wine until smooth. Blend in the mustard and Tabasco sauce, then add the shrimp and artichokes. Bake 10 minutes, stir. Place biscuits on top of the hot mixture. Bake 15 minutes more or until the biscuits are browned.

NOTE: 1-1/2 cups of other seafood may be substituted for shrimp.
Mrs. Robert Berney

Shrimp Mousse

6 servings

4 hard-boiled eggs
1 cup cooked chopped shrimp
Salt and pepper
1 teaspoon curry powder
1 heaping tablespoon mayonnaise
1 tablespoon gelatin
1 cup frozen cream of shrimp soup
1/2 pint heavy cream, whipped
A few whole shrimp

Sieve the eggs and add to them the salt, pepper, curry powder, mayonnaise, and the shrimp. Soften the gelatin in 1/2 cup of cold shrimp soup and dissolve it in the remainder of the boiling soup. Add to the egg-shrimp mixture. Fold in the whipped cream. Turn into a soufflé dish until set. Decorate with a few shrimp, then float a little consommé aspic on top. Serve as a first course.
Mrs. Benjamin Griswold, IV

Cold Shrimp and Rice Salad

5 servings

1 cup raw rice
1/2 cup chopped chives
1/2 onion, minced
1 small green pepper, chopped
1-1/2 cups small shrimp, cooked and cleaned
1 cup mayonnaise
Pinch of ginger
Salt
Lemon juice to taste
Lettuce
Toasted sesame seeds

Cook the rice according to package directions and cool. Snip the chives and add them, the minced onion, and chopped pepper to the rice. Add the shrimp and mayonnaise. Season to taste with ginger, salt, and lemon juice. Refrigerate until serving time. Heap on lettuce and top with sesame seeds.
Mrs. Thomas Wright

Artichoke and Shrimp Salad

6 servings

3 cooked fresh artichoke bottoms or 1 package frozen artichoke hearts
24 medium shrimp
1 egg yolk
1/2 cup olive oil
1/4 cup Wesson oil
2 tablespoons vinegar
2 teaspoons Dijon-type mustard
2 tablespoons minced parsley
2 tablespoons chopped chives
1 tablespoon minced shallot

Cook the artichoke bottoms or hearts, fresh preferably, of course. (The expensive shrimp deserve the best kind.) Cook the shrimp only until they turn pink, then shell and devein them. Make a mayonnaise of the yolk, oils, vinegar, and mustard. Add parsley, chives, and shallot, and marinate the shrimp and artichokes for several hours, in the refrigerator. Don't forget to stir them up once in a while.
Mrs. Francis Kennedy

Shrimp Tequilla

6 servings

2 pounds shrimp
2 cups chopped parsley
Lemon slices
Cherry tomatoes
Olive oil

Avocado Dressing:

2 teaspoons salt
2 teaspoons dry mustard
4 tablespoons wine vinegar
1 cup oil (olive or peanut)
1/4 green pepper
1 tablespoon parsley, chives, tarragon, or basil
1 ripe avocado

Cook the shrimp until just done in simmering water; peel and devein them. Make an attractive presentation of a thick bed of chopped parsley, the shrimp, lemon slices, and cherry tomatoes which have been coated with olive oil. Pour over this an avocado dressing made by putting the avocado, peeled and pitted, and all the other ingredients into a blender. (The pepper should be charred, peeled and seeded, then minced. This is done by putting the pepper on a piece of foil in a 500° oven until it is scorched. The skin will rub off easily then. Red peppers are prepared in the same way.) *Mrs. Arthur Stern*

Shrimp Elizabeth

4 servings

1 pound shrimp
2 tablespoons olive oil
1 small onion, chopped
1/4 teaspoon minced garlic
2 tablespoons chopped parsley
1/3 cup diced green peppers
2 cups canned tomatoes, undrained
Dash thyme
1 teaspoon grated lemon rind
Dash marjoram

Peel and devein the shrimp. In a heavy skillet heat the olive oil, then sauté the onion, garlic, parsley, and peppers until they are soft. Add tomatoes (cut up) and seasonings and cook uncovered over medium heat until the liquid has evaporated to half. Add the shrimp, cover, and cook until the shrimp are just done. *Mrs. John Eager*

Crab Casserole

350° / 4 servings

1 pound back fin crab meat
2 tablespoons butter
2 tablespoons flour
1 cup milk
Salt
Pepper
Cayenne
1/2 teaspoon dry mustard
1/2 teaspoon onion juice
1 wineglass sherry
Small jar of chopped pimientos
2 tablespoons finely chopped green pepper
1 hard-boiled egg
Bread crumbs or cracker crumbs

Pick over the crab meat carefully. Make a cream sauce of the butter, flour, and milk; cook a few minutes to rid it of the floury taste, then add the seasoning, the sherry and the chopped pimientos and green pepper. Dice the egg and add that as well. Fold the crab meat into the sauce lightly and pour it all into a buttered casserole, cover with buttered bread crumbs, and bake until piping hot (about 30 minutes). Lacking the time to make the cream sauce, use a cup of canned mushroom soup instead.
Mrs. Francis C. Lang, Mrs. Russell E. Smith

Imperial Crab

400° / 3 to 4 servings

1 pound back fin crab meat
3 tablespoons mayonnaise
1/2 teaspoon Worcestershire sauce

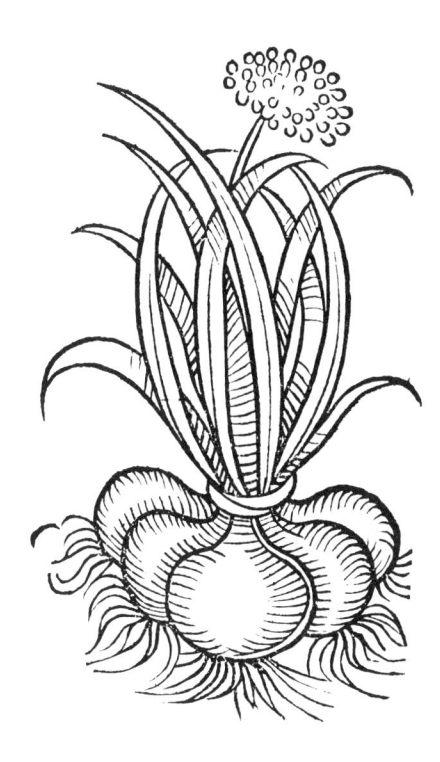

1/2 teaspoon Dijon mustard
1 tablespoon minced green pepper
1 tablespoon minced parsley
1 egg, well beaten
1 teaspoon salt (scant)
1/4 teaspoon white pepper
3 or 4 scallop shells

Pick over the crab meat and mix the other ingredients together. Pour them into the crab meat and toss gently with a fork to keep the crab meat from breaking. Have ready 3 or 4 scallop shells. Melt 1 heaping teaspoon of butter in each scallop shell and pile the crab mixture on top. Top each with 1 teaspoon additional mayonnaise and dust with paprika. Bake 20 minutes until browned.

Miss Eleanor Holliday Cross

Crab Bayou

3 to 4 servings

1 pound crab meat
6 slices lean bacon
2 small onions, finely chopped
1 clove of garlic, minced
1/4 cup tomato paste
1/2 pound lean ham, cut in thin strips
1/3 cup dark rum
1 pint white wine
1 tablespoon chopped parsley
A pinch of sugar
1/4 cup heavy cream
Hot boiled or steamed rice

Pick over the crab meat well. Fry the bacon until crisp, drain, crumble, and set aside. In the same pan, sauté the onion and garlic, then add the tomato paste and ham. Flame the rum and pour it into the pan, cook a few minutes, and stir in the crab meat. Add the white wine, parsley, and sugar and let it all simmer for 15 minutes. Stir in the heavy cream. Serve with or over rice. Garnish with the crumbled bacon.

Mrs. Francis Kennedy

New Orleans Crab Salad

8 servings

1 pound crab meat
2 cups cooked macaroni shells
1 cup chopped celery
1/2 cup chopped green pepper
1 cup mayonnaise
1/4 teaspoon curry powder
1 teaspoon salt
1 teaspoon lemon juice
1/4 cup flat beer
1/4 teaspoon dry mustard
Dash of pepper
1 teaspoon minced onion

Combine the crab meat, macaroni, celery, and green pepper. Make a dressing of the other ingredients, mix together with the crab meat, and chill in the refrigerator for a few hours before serving with lettuce.

For a summer luncheon one might serve this with thin rolled slices of bologna and boiled ham decorated with slices of pineapple and parsley, and a bowl of hot rolls. *Mrs. Gerald S. Wise*

Crab Cakes

4 servings

1 pound fresh crab meat
5 saltines, crushed
1 egg, beaten
1/2 cup finely chopped parsley
2 teaspoons dry mustard
2 teaspoons prepared mustard
Salt and pepper
2 tablespoons mayonnaise, preferably homemade

Search the crab meat for bits of shell, handling the crab lumps gently. Mix the other ingredients well and pour over the crab meat, tossing it all together with a fork. Press lightly into cakes and sauté quickly in half butter, half oil until golden brown. *Miss Martha Ann Peters*

Another Way with Crab Cakes

4 servings

2-1/2 tablespoons butter
2 tablespoons flour
1 cup milk
2 tablespoons dry white wine
1/2 teaspoon dry mustard
1/4 scant teaspoon white pepper
1/2 teaspoon MSG
1 pound crab meat
1 scallion, finely chopped
Parsley, finely chopped
Strip of green pepper, finely chopped
1 egg, beaten lightly

Make a white sauce in the usual way with the butter, flour, milk, dry white wine, dry mustard, white pepper, MSG, and salt to taste. Mix with 1 pound of the best crab meat you can afford, 1 medium scallion, finely chopped, some parsley, finely chopped, and a strip of green pepper, finely chopped. Lightly beat the egg and then combine everything, form into large cakes and fry in *hot* cooking fat. *Edward L. Brewster*

Baked Avocados with Crab Meat

350° / 4 servings

1 cup crab meat
1 cup thick cream sauce
1 teaspoon grated green pepper
1/4 cup sherry
2 avocados
Lemon juice
Grated cheese

Mix crabmeat lightly with cream sauce, green pepper, and sherry. Cut the avocados in half, remove pits, and rub the insides with lemon juice. Pile high with the crab mixture; cover with grated cheese. Place in a pan over hot water and bake until thoroughly hot and the cheese has melted. *Miss Alice Newman*

Soft-Shelled Crabs Parmesan

2 to 3 servings

6 soft-shelled crabs
Salt and pepper
Dry mustard
Parmesan cheese
1/4 pound butter

Clean the soft shelled crabs; season them with

salt, pepper, and dry mustard. Dust with Parmesan cheese. Melt the butter until foaming, add the crabs, and sauté, uncovered, over a medium flame until crisp and tender.   *Mrs. Jerrie Cherry*

Crab Soufflé

325° / 4 servings

1 pound crab meat
3 tablespoons butter
3 tablespoons flour
1-1/2 cups rich milk
1-1/3 cups grated cheese
Paprika
4 eggs, separated
Salt and pepper

Pick over the crab meat carefully. Make a cream sauce with the butter, flour, and milk; cook it several minutes, then add the grated cheese. Add the seasoning and cook it slowly until it is thick, smooth, and flavorful. Add the beaten yolks of the eggs, then lightly stir in the crab meat. This may be done at any time.

An hour before serving, fold in the stiffly beaten egg whites, pour the mixture into a buttered soufflé dish, set it in a pan of boiling water, and bake 1 hour. Serve on slices of broiled pineapple or with a thin cream sauce (made with cream) and garnish with watercress.

Mrs. Coleman Brownfield

Crab Meat in Ramekins

350° / 12 servings

4 tablespoons butter
4 tablespoons flour
1 cup chicken broth
1 cup light cream
4 egg yolks
1 cup mushrooms, sliced
3 pounds crab meat, picked over
4 tablespoons lemon juice or sherry
Buttered bread crumbs
Salt and pepper
Paprika
Dash of cayenne

Make a velouté sauce of butter, flour, chicken broth, and cream. Then make a liaison by adding some of this to the beaten egg yolks, then returning the yolks to the rest of the sauce. Add the mushrooms, which have been lightly sautéed in butter, and the crab meat. Add the lemon juice or sherry but not both. Season well and put in buttered ramekins. Top with buttered bread crumbs and bake for 30 minutes.

To freeze, cover tightly with foil, either before or after baking. In either case, bring to room temperature before reheating or baking.

Mrs. Richard H. Randall, Mrs. LeBaron S. Willard

Creamed Artichoke and Crab Meat

350° / 8 servings

12 canned artichoke bottoms
1 pound fresh crab meat or 2 packages frozen crab or lobster
4 tablespoons butter
4 tablespoons flour
2 cups whole milk
Sherry to flavor the sauce
1/2 cup grated sharp cheese

Wash the brine off the artichoke bottoms and put them in a buttered baking dish. On each put a portion of the crab or lobster meat. Make a sauce by melting the butter, adding the flour, and cooking for 2 minutes, then adding the milk all at once and then the cheese. Cook it for several minutes; then, off the stove, add the sherry. Pour it over the crab meat and bake 20 minutes in the oven.

Mrs. Arthur Waxter

Beurre Blanc Cottage

Annecy, France

2 tablespoons chopped shallots
1/4 cup dry Chablis
1/4 cup sweet butter
Pinch salt
1/4 teaspoons white pepper
1 teaspoon cornstarch
1/4 cup heavy cream or crème fraiche
Few drops dry vermouth

Cook the shallots in wine until the wine is reduced by half. Add the butter by bits, stirring constantly with a whisk. Make a paste of cornstarch and cream; add to the mixture and cook a few minutes more. Add a few drops of vermouth and serve at once with fish. *Malvina C. Kinard*

Crêpes with Lobster Newburg

375° / 7 to 8 servings

2 cups lobster meat
2 tablespoons butter
1 pound mushrooms, thinly sliced
2 cups medium cream sauce
1/4 cup dry sherry
3 egg yolks
1 cup cream
1 teaspoon paprika
Salt and pepper to taste
14-16 5-inch crêpes, using basic crêpe recipe

Cut the lobster into small pieces. Melt the butter in a large skillet and sauté the mushrooms very lightly, then add the lobster just to heat it through. Heat the cream sauce and add the sherry to it. Combine the egg yolks and the cream; add a little hot cream sauce, then return the mixture to the cream sauce but do not let it boil. Add the paprika and seasoning. Mix a third of the sauce with the lobster and mushrooms, reserving the rest for the topping. Put a spoonful or two of the mixture down the center of each crêpe roll and place seamside down in a buttered baking dish. Cover with the rest of the sauce and bake 20 minutes.
Mrs. Sol Kann

Sauce for Cold Fish

1 hard-boiled egg
2 dill pickles
1/2 bunch parsley
1-1/2 canned pimientos
1 green pepper
1/2 cup catsup
1/2 cup French's mustard
1/2 cup chili sauce
1/2 cup mayonnaise
1/4 teaspoon dry mustard
1 teaspoon sugar
Pepper and salt

Put the first five ingredients through a meat grinder. Add all the rest of the ingredients and mix them thoroughly. This fish sauce will keep almost indefinitely in the refrigerator.
Mrs. Allan Wetzler

Maine Deviled Lobsters

4 servings

4 1-1/2-pound live lobsters
1-1/4 cups sweet butter, well softened
2 tablespoons Dijon mustard
1 teaspoon Worcestershire sauce
Kosher salt
Cayenne
Fresh lemon juice

Place each lobster on its back and with a sharp knife split it open lengthwise. Remove the eye sac, the sandbag, and the intestinal vein and crack the claws. Place the lobsters on a broiling pan.

A small dish *(omphalos phiale)* decorated with fish, made in south Italy by Greek potters in the 4th century B.C.

Combine the butter, mustard, and Worcestershire sauce with salt, cayenne, and lemon juice to taste. Spread half of the mustard butter on the lobsters and broil them about 4 inches from the broiling unit for 7 to 10 minutes. Spread the remaining butter on the lobsters and continue broiling for 5 minutes longer. Do not overcook.

Arrange the lobsters on a platter. Sprinkle the tops with freshly chopped parsley and surround with decoratively cut lemon cups. Garnish with bunches of fresh parsley and serve with hot lemon butter (melted butter with lemon juice added to taste), served in individual small bowls.

Mrs. Irwin Nudelman

Lobster Mousse

24 servings

1 whole onion, cut in half
3 stalks celery
1 teaspoon thyme
3 bay leaves
8 lobster tails (or 8 cups cooked lobster)
6 envelopes unflavored gelatin
8 envelopes chicken bouillon powder
7 cups water
2 cups mayonnaise
1/4 teaspoon hot pepper sauce
1/4 cup lemon juice
4 tablespoons grated onion
2 teaspoons paprika
1-1/2 cups cream, whipped
1 cup finely chopped celery
1/2 cup drained capers
Salt, to taste

Use equivalent of two 6-cup molds, preferably in two different fish designs.

Boil 3 quarts of water with the onion, celery stalks, thyme, and bay leaves for approximately 10 minutes. Add the lobster tails and boil for 8 minutes more, depending on the size of the tails—meat should be firm but not tough; remove the lobster from the water, drain, and cool. Remove the shells and dice the meat in 1/2-inch cubes.

Soften the gelatin in 1/2 to 1 cup cold water. Add bouillon powder to 6 cups boiling water and dissolve the gelatin; then cool mixture. Add mayonnaise, hot pepper sauce, lemon juice, grated onion, and paprika. Chill until it begins to thicken, then fold in evenly the whipped cream, lobster, celery, and capers. Pour into molds and place in the refrigerator to set. Unmold by inverting each mold on a serving dish and placing a hot cloth on the mold to melt it slightly.

Decoration: **Stuffed green olives, black olives, flat anchovy fillets, pimiento strips, cucumber slices, and radish flowerets.**

Decorate by using all or any ingredients mentioned, plus a garnish of watercress or parsley around the mousse on the serving plates.

Miss Rita St. Clair, Mrs. William Speed, III

Lobster Bordelaise

12 servings

5 2-pound lobsters, cut in chunks, claws cracked
1-1/2 sticks butter
2 tablespoons olive oil
1 medium onion, chopped
2 medium carrots, chopped
2 shallots, chopped
1 bay leaf
1/8 teaspoon thyme
1/4 teaspoon tarragon
1/3 cup brandy
1/2 bottle dry white wine
1 small can tomato paste
1-1/2 cups fish stock
1/2 cup parsley, chopped
Salt and pepper
Cayenne

In a big spider, melt half a stick of butter with the olive oil. When it is quite hot, add the vegetables and the bay leaf, thyme, and tarragon and simmer without browning until very flavorful. Add another half stick of butter, then add the lobster pieces and sauté till the shells turn bright red. Heat the brandy, pour it over the pan, and ignite it. Add wine and simmer, then add tomato paste and fish stock. Stir it, then cover and simmer 10 minutes or so. Remove the lobster to a warm serving platter. Correct the seasoning of the sauce remaining in the pan, adding the cayenne and the remaining butter if you think it necessary. Bring it to a boil and pour over the lobster. Present this dish with parsley sprinkled over it.

This could be made with lobster tails if your purse were not up to the fresh lobster.

Mrs. Henry Hays

Memphis Jambalaya

6 servings

2 tablespoons olive oil
1 clove garlic, minced
1/3 cup chopped onion
2 tablespoons chopped green pepper
3 ripe tomatoes, peeled, seeded, and chopped
2 cups chicken stock
3/4 cup raw rice, washed
1/2 bay leaf
1/2 teaspoon chili powder
1/8 teaspoon each of cloves and thyme
1 teaspoon salt
Cayenne
1 cup raw shrimp, shelled and deveined
1/2 cup diced cooked ham
1 cup coarsely chopped ripe olives

Heat the oil in a saucepan and in it sauté the garlic, onion, and green pepper until the onion is transparent. Add the tomatoes, the chicken stock, washed rice, and the seasoning. Cover well and simmer 20 minutes. Add the shrimp, ham, and olives and cook for 10 minutes longer, until the rice is tender, the shrimp are pink, and the liquid has been absorbed.

Mrs. Eli Frank, Jr.

Chinese Paella

12 servings

2-1/2 pounds lobster tails
4 tablespoons salad oil
2 minced garlic cloves
8 cooked chicken breasts, sliced
2 cups water chestnuts, sliced
1 pound mushrooms, sliced
1-1/2 pounds snow peas, sliced
1 can bamboo shoots, sliced
4 cups chicken broth
Salt
1 teaspoon sugar
8 teaspoons cornstarch
1 cup walnut meats, chopped
3 hard-cooked eggs, chopped

Boil lobster tails 8 minutes and slice. Heat the salad oil with the finely minced garlic in a heavy pan. When sizzling hot, add the lobster pieces, chicken, water chestnuts, mushrooms, snow peas, and bamboo shoots. Cook 2 minutes and transfer to a large pot or casserole to be used over direct heat. Add boiling hot chicken broth, salt, sugar, and cover. Cook 4 minutes more. Stir 8 teaspoons cornstarch into a smooth paste with a little water. Add and cook 2 more minutes. The nuts and chopped egg are served beside this and it should be accompanied by rice, fluffy and hot.

Howard Benedict

Paella

12 servings

2 3-pound chickens, disjointed
Salt and pepper
2 garlic cloves, minced
4 tablespoons oil
1-1/2 pounds sweet Italian sausages, parboiled and sliced
2 lobsters, cut up, or 6 lobster tails, halved
2 pounds raw shrimp, peeled and deveined
2 cups Uncle Ben's or any long grain rice
4 cups liquid (white wine and chicken broth, mixed)
1/4 teaspoon saffron
4 mussels or cherrystone clams per person

Salt and pepper the chicken. In a large pan with a lid, sauté the garlic in the oil. Add the chicken and brown it. When it is almost done, in about 20 minutes, add the sausage and cook for 5 minutes. Then add the lobsters, cook for 10 minutes; add the shrimp then and cook 5 minutes more. Put the rice in the pan, stir the saffron into the liquid, and pour it over the rice. Give everything a big stir and put the lid on the pan. Cook it all slowly until the rice is tender. If by chance there is liquid still in the pot when the rice is just tender, draw it all off with a bulb baster. Finally add the mussels or clams and cover the pan again to steam them open.

This paella can be made outdoors on the grill, a change from steak. *Mrs. Ronald Diana*

A Party Fish Dish

400° / 8 to 10 servings

1 pound scallops
2 pounds fillet of haddock
4 tablespoons butter
5 tablespoons flour
1 cup heavy cream
1 cup chicken broth
1 tablespoon lemon juice
1 tablespoon Worcestershire sauce
1 tablespoon horseradish
4 tablespoons catsup
4 tablespoons parsley, chopped
1 large clove garlic, minced
1 teaspoon mustard
1 teaspoon soy sauce
2 teaspoons Accent
Salt
Cayenne
1/2 cup dry sherry
Bread crumbs
Chopped parsley for garnish

Cover the fish with salted cold water and let it stand 15 minutes. Drain well. Grease the top of a double boiler and place it over boiling water. Put the scallops in first, then the haddock. Cover and steam them 15 minutes.

Melt the butter in a saucepan and stir the flour gradually into the foaming butter, taking care that the flour takes on no color. Cook gently for 2 minutes. Gradually beat in, with a whisk, a mixture of cream and chicken broth, beating vigorously to produce an absolutely smooth sauce béchamel. Return the sauce to the heat and while stirring vigorously bring to a boil for 1 minute. Remove from the heat and add the lemon juice, Worcestershire sauce, horseradish, catsup, parsley, garlic, mustard, soy sauce, Accent, salt, and cayenne. Stir well, then add the fish and sherry. Place in a greased casserole, sprinkle the top with bread crumbs, and dot with butter. Bake for 1/2 hour. Garnish the top with chopped parsley.

This dish can be prepared a day or more in advance and refrigerated prior to being baked. Indeed, it can even be frozen. In either case, however, it should be allowed to come to room temperature before placing it in the oven.

Miss Grace Hatchett

Seafood Combination

6 servings

4 large lobster tails
1 pound scallops
1 pound shrimp
2 cups cream sauce
1/2 pound Cheddar cheese, grated
Salt
Pepper
2 slices bacon
1 can whole mushrooms
3/4 cup sherry

Remove the shells from the lobster tails and cut the lobster meat into bite-size pieces. Simmer the lobster tails and scallops in salted water un-

Giorgio Schiavone signed this unusual *Madonna and Child with Musical Angels.* He painted in Padua and as part of the signature noted that he was a student of Squarcione, a fact of which Mantegna was equally proud.

til tender. Steam the shrimp; shell and devein them. Make a medium cream sauce, add Cheddar cheese, salt and pepper to taste. Fry the bacon until crisp, drain it, then crumble it and add it to the sauce along with the mushrooms, sherry, cooked lobster meat, scallops, and shrimp. Heat in the top of a double boiler until ready to serve. Serve from a chafing dish with white rice.

Mrs. Sven Peuleché

Escabêche

18 servings

6 pounds of seafood (shrimp, scallops, sliced squid, bite-size fillets of rock bass, and flounder)
Flour for dredging
3 cups olive or corn oil
8 large cloves garlic, minced
3 medium onions, thinly sliced
1 teaspoon freshly ground pepper
3 tablespoons chopped parsley
1/2 teaspoon saffron
1-1/2 teaspoons crushed cumin seed
1 cup vinegar
6 tablespoons lemon juice
2-1/4 cups water
Salt
1-1/2 cups chopped scallions
12 lemon slices
6 bay leaves

Lightly dredge the fish with flour. Heat 1 cup of the oil and sauté the garlic and onion until soft. Remove from the pan with a slotted spoon and reserve. Sauté the fish in the same oil quickly until golden brown. Drain on paper towels and arrange in one or two shallow pans.

Mix the remaining oil, vinegar, lemon juice, water, pepper, parsley, saffron, cumin, and salt to taste. Pour over the seafood. Sprinkle with reserved onion, garlic, and chopped scallion. Add lemon slices and bay leaves. Marinate for 24 hours in the refrigerator. To serve, arrange the seafood on a shallow serving tray. Garnish with lemon slices and whole green onions. This can be used as an hors d'oeuvre or as a first course.

Miss Rita St. Clair

Coquilles Saint-Jacques

4 servings

1/2 pound scallops
2 cups light white wine
2 shallots, finely chopped
3/4 cup finely chopped mushrooms
6 tablespoons butter
1 tablespoon flour
Salt and pepper
3 egg yolks
1/2 cup whipping cream
1 tablespoon sherry or Madeira
4 scallop shells or small ramekins
2 tablespoons grated Gruyère cheese
12 small pretty mushrooms (for garnish)

Dice the scallops and cook them very gently in the wine until just tender, a matter of a very few minutes. Cook the shallots and the 3/4 cup of mushrooms in 3 tablespoons of butter. Make a velouté sauce of the remaining butter, flour, and the wine used for the scallops. Simmer for a bit to get rid of the floury taste, and season with salt and pepper. Beat the egg yolks, add the cream, then pour some of the sauce into them and beat together. Put the egg mixture in with the rest of the sauce. Heat this gently; add the scallops, and then the Madeira or sherry. Taste again for flavor. Divide this among the four scallop shells and sprinkle with the grated cheese. Slice the small mushrooms vertically down through the center of each cap and stem and arrange the sliced mushrooms around each dish, with the stalk ends fanning out to the edges. Put under a hot grill before serving. Don't let the sauce come to a boil or the dish will become liquid.

Miss Margaret Master

Scallop and Mushroom Casserole

375° / 4 servings

1 pound scallops
1/2 can bouillon
1 pound mushrooms
1 lemon or more
3 tablespoons butter
1 cup thin velouté sauce
Chopped parsley
White wine
Bread crumbs

Simmer scallops in 1/2 can bouillon. Simmer mushrooms in lemon juice and some butter in a covered pot until they wilt a bit. Then make a thin velouté sauce using the liquids from both saucepans. Cook until it thickens, and pour this over the drained scallops and mushrooms, which have been mixed together in a baking dish. Add salt, pepper, and parsley to taste (and white wine if you have some but it is not necessary). Cover with breadcrumbs and bake until bubbly (about 15 minutes). Two tablespoons of cheese may be added to the casserole, too.

Mrs. John Eager, Mrs. Jerome Kidder,
Mrs. Jesse Slingluff

Vol-au-Vent of Seafood

12 to 14 servings

1 cup chopped celery
1 cup chopped onion
1 cup chopped green pepper
4 tablespoons butter
4 tablespoons flour
2 cups light cream
1 cup milk
1 egg yolk
6 pounds cooked shrimp
4-6 oysters per person
1 pound crab meat
Salt and pepper
Juice of 2 lemons
1 cup sherry

Simmer the celery, onion, and green pepper in a little water until soft. Make a cream sauce of butter, flour, cream, and milk with an egg yolk added to thicken it. Heat the oysters until the edges curl, and heat the shrimp and crab meat. Add the drained cooked vegetables to the sauce and when it is well flavored, add salt, pepper, and lemon juice. Last, add the seafood and season all with sherry. Serve in a vol-au-vent pastry shell, which may be bought, or in a casserole. If the seafood is not to be served immediately, keep it hot in a double boiler before putting it in the vol-au-vent.

Mrs. Richard Lansburgh

Mock Terrapin Using Oysters

8 servings

2 quarts oysters
1/2 pound mushrooms, sliced
10 tablespoons butter
8 tablespoons flour
1 pint cream
1 pint milk
Yolks of 4 hard-cooked eggs
3 stalks of celery, minced
1/2 teaspoon grated onion
Red pepper
Pinch of mustard
Dash of Worcestershire sauce
Black pepper
Salt
Paprika
1/2 cup sherry

Put the oysters in a saucepan with their liquor and simmer just until they are plump. Drain them well, then cut them up in not too small pieces. Sauté the sliced mushrooms in 2 tablespoons of butter and set those aside. Make a béchamel sauce with the remainder of the butter, the flour, and the cream and milk. When it is thick and smooth, add the egg yolks, celery, onion, and all the seasoning. Keep stirring until it reaches the consistency of a soft mayonnaise, then add the mushrooms. When almost ready to serve, add the oysters and sherry.   *Mrs. Albert C. Bruce*

Oysters in Champagne Sauce

6 first-course servings

1-1/2 pints select oysters
1 cup plus 2 tablespoons champagne
2 tablespoons butter
1 tablespoon minced shallots
2 tablespoons flour
1/2 cup heavy cream
1/2 teaspoon salt
Pinch of white pepper
Dash of Tabasco
2 egg yolks

Put the oysters with their liquor and 1/4 cup champagne in a small non-aluminum pot. Cover and heat just long enough to bring the liquid to a rolling boil. Remove from the heat at once and drain well, reserving all the liquid.

In a heavy non-aluminum saucepan, heat the butter until foamy, add the shallots, cover and simmer a minute or two until they are soft but not brown. Stir in the flour. Cook and stir without browning at least a minute, then add 1/2 cup of reserved oyster liquid, strained carefully. Whisk until smooth and add 1/2 cup champagne, cream, salt, pepper, and Tabasco. Mix well, reduce heat, and simmer, uncovered, until reduced almost to half, about fifteen minutes. Strain the sauce, rinse the pot, and return the sauce to the pot. Add 1/4 cup champagne and bring back to simmer; cook slowly another ten minutes. Beat the egg yolks with 2 tablespoons warmed champagne until they are light and frothy. Pour about 1/4 of the sauce into the yolks and mix vigorously. Return this mixture to the pot with the rest of the sauce and heat just long enough to bring to a rolling boil.

Dry the oysters on a towel, then place 3 or 4 oysters in a scallop shell. Just before serving, reheat the sauce until hot, spoon over the oysters and broil for about three minutes, just until the sauce begins to have a few pinpoints of browning. Do not overcook. Serve at once with a teaspoon.

All the preparation can be done a few hours in advance. Once the oysters are in the scallop shell, cover with clear plastic and refrigerate them. Remove from the refrigerator to allow to come back almost to room temperature. Carefully drain off any liquid that may have collected before spooning on the hot sauce. This champagne sauce is also excellent cold.

Any bit of leftover sauce makes a splendid difference in a fish or lobster-tail salad.   *Carol Cutler*

Deviled Oysters

6 servings

36 medium oysters
1/4 cup Dijon mustard
1 egg beaten with 1 tablespoon salad oil
Fresh bread crumbs
Melted butter

Poach the oysters in their liquor until they come to a boil. Drain them well, then heat them for 2 minutes with the mustard and cool. Roll them in the beaten egg and then bread crumbs, and chill in the refrigerator for about 1 hour. Dribble butter over the top of the oysters and broil them for about 5 minutes on each side. Serve as a first course or on toothpicks as an appetizer.

Mrs. Bertram Bernheim, Jr.

Baked Creole Oysters

325° / 4 servings

1/3 cup olive oil
1 small onion
1 medium pepper
4 ribs celery
4 slices bread, made into crumbs
Grated rind of 1 lemon
1 pint oysters
1/2 cup water
1 tablespoon Worcestershire sauce
3 eggs
1/2 cup melted butter, or less

Put the olive oil in a skillet and add the 3 vegetables, all chopped, half the bread crumbs, and the lemon rind. Cook these, uncovered, until barely tender. Add the oysters with their liquor, the water and the Worcestershire sauce. Heat this slowly, stirring constantly, until the edges of the oysters curl. Let the mixture cool somewhat and stir in the beaten eggs. Pour into a greased baking-and-serving dish, sprinkle with the rest of the bread crumbs, and pour some melted butter over it all. Set the casserole in a pan of hot water and bake about 20 minutes. Serve with rice.

Mrs. Frank T. Gray

Oysters Cotton Patch

4 servings

1 pint select oysters
Pancake flour
2 eggs, well beaten
Cornflake crumbs
Safflower oil

Drain the oysters and pat them dry. Then dip them, one at a time, first in pancake flour, then into the beaten egg, and finally into the cornflake crumbs. Pat them again gently and set aside. When ready to serve, heat the oil, measuring about 3/4 inch in the skillet, and fry the oysters at medium heat, no more than 8 at a time, until brown on each side. Drain them on paper towels and keep warm until all the oysters have been fried.

Serve these an old Maryland way, as a side dish for chicken salad!

Mrs. Walter G. Lohr

Pickled Oysters

5 pints oysters
1 pint oyster liquor
1-1/2 tablespoon salt
1 dessertspoon of cloves
1 tablespoon mace
1 tablespoon allspice
1 tablespoon white peppercorns
1-1/2 pints white wine vinegar

Heat oyster liquor with salt to a boil and add the spices, bound in cheesecloth to be discarded later. Then add the oysters. Leave over high heat until they begin to curl around the edges and appear done and plump. Remove them immediately and place in cold water to stop further cooking. Add vinegar to the oyster juices and spices and boil once again. Strain and cool. Replace the oysters and serve with sliced lemon, as an appetizer.

Miss Louisa M. Gary

Poached Oysters and Cucumber Cocktail

24 large oysters
2 cups cucumber balls
1 cup chili sauce

Poach 24 large oysters in their liquid until the edges curl. Reduce the oyster liquid to 1 cup. Cool. With a small melon-ball cutter, cut about 2 cups of balls from the fleshy parts of peeled cucumbers, after discarding the seeds. Arrange the balls and oysters on a bed of lettuce or on sprigs of chicory. Mix the reduced oyster liquid with the chili sauce and spoon over the oysters and cucumbers. This cocktail is most attractive served in a stemmed coupe dish or wide champagne glass.

Mrs. William Garvey

Oyster Casserole

400° / 6 servings

1-1/2 pints fresh oysters or 2 12-ounce cans oysters
1 package Uncle Ben's long grain and wild rice
Salt and pepper
1/4 teaspoon paprika
1/4 pound sharp cheese, grated
1/2 cup soft bread crumbs
4 tablespoons melted butter
1/4 cup oyster liquor

Drain the oysters, reserving 1/4 cup of the oyster liquor. Cook the rice according to the package directions, to the moist stage. In a buttered casserole arrange 1/3 of the rice. Lay half the oysters on top, sprinkle with some salt, pepper, paprika, and 1/3 of the cheese. Add half the butter. Then repeat this process ending with a layer of the rice and cheese. Spoon the oyster juice over it. Top with bread crumbs, butter, and remaining cheese. Refrigerate for half a day, then bake for 30 minutes.

Mrs. Joseph D. Brown

Scalloped Oysters

375° / 3 servings

1 pint oysters
a stick butter
3 tablespoons chopped shallots
1-1/2 cup cracker crumbs
1/8 teaspoon pepper
1/2 teaspoon salt
1 cup medium cream

Butter a shallow 1-quart baking dish. Drain the oysters. Sauté the shallots in a little butter, then add them with the rest of the melted butter to the crumbs and mix well. Spread half the crumbs in the baking dish and arrange the oysters and seasoning over the crumbs. Pour the cream over them and top with the remaining crumbs. Bake until the crumbs are nicely browned, 20 to 25 minutes.

Miss Ann Gabhart, Mrs. Douglas Warner, Jr.

A Toast: "To the pleasures of life." Wood engraving by Grandville (French, 1803-1847) from *Scènes de la vie privée et publique des animaux*, 1842

Au sexe qui embellit la vie !!!...
Un murmure flatteur accueillit ce toast, qui fut porté par un aimable Hippopotame.

EGGS & CHEESE

Oeufs Froids Frou-Frou

6 servings

**6 eggs
6 small rounds whole grain bread
Set Mayonnaise (see below)
Sliced truffle
2 cups cooked peas
2 cups diced cooked turnips
2 cups diced cooked carrots
2 cups diced cooked green beans
Bunch of watercress**

Poach 6 eggs in a strong solution of vinegar and water. Drain them; place in a bowl of cold water. Remove the eggs and dry carefully on a cloth. Arrange on a cake rack on buttered whole grain bread, coat them with Set Mayonnaise, and decorate with a sliced truffle.

Carefully mix all the cooked vegetables together and add some of the mayonnaise. Spoon into an oiled mold and put to set in the refrigerator. Remove when set and turn out onto a round, flat serving dish. Garnish with the poached eggs and watercress.

Set Mayonnaise

**3 egg yolks
1 teaspoon salt, or more to taste
Dash of red pepper
1 teaspoon dry mustard, or more to taste
4 tablespoons tarragon vinegar
3 cups vegetable oil
1/2 cup light cream
2 tablespoons plain gelatin
4 tablespoons milk**

Put the egg yolks in a bowl. Add the salt, red pepper, mustard, and vinegar. Beat well and add the oil slowly, beating constantly. When the mixture has thickened, add the light cream and carefully mix in the gelatin, which has been softened in a little milk and dissolved over the fire.

Mrs. Robert A. Russell

Oeufs en Gelée

4 servings

**2 cans consommé madrilène (gelatin added)
1/2 large package cream cheese
1 teaspoon curry powder
4 poached eggs**

In a blender, mix 1 chilled can of madrilène, the cream cheese, and curry powder. Whirl it well and then pour it into either 4 traditional molds or a shallow casserole. Put the mixture in the freezer

briefly or the refrigerator while you poach the eggs; cool them in cold water, drain, and cut the ragged white edges from them. When the cheese mixture is firm, put the eggs on top. If 4 small molds are used, turn the eggs upside down so they will be right side up when unmolded. If the casserole is used, leave the eggs up as you will not unmold them. In either case, pour the other can of madrilène over them and chill it all well. Serve garnished with caviar, tiny shrimp, parsley, and watercress.
Miss Susan Pizzy

Hard-Boiled Eggs with Green Sauce

Hard-boil as many eggs as desired—8 is a good number for this amount of sauce.

Green Sauce

Handful of fresh chervil
Handful of fresh parsley
Handful of fresh tarragon
2-3 shallots
1 lemon
4 tablespoons unsalted butter
1 teaspoon flour
2 egg yolks
1 teaspoon Dijon mustard
1 cup heavy cream
Salt and freshly ground pepper

Shell and cool the eggs. Make the sauce: chop herbs, shallots, and some of the lemon zest. Work the butter with the flour. Combine the herb and butter mixtures, egg yolks, mustard, and cream. Heat in the top of a double boiler, stirring constantly until thick. Do not allow it to boil. Season with salt and pepper; cool. Add the juice of a lemon just before serving. Mask the eggs with the sauce.

This sauce can also be used hot with poached fish or chicken.
Mrs. T. Garland Tinsley

Eggs with a Tapenade Sauce

4 servings

15 or so pitted black olives
6 anchovy fillets
2 tablespoons capers, washed and drained
1/4 cup tuna fish, drained
1/3 cup olive oil
Juice of 1 lemon
Few drops of brandy
1/4 teaspoon Dijon-style mustard
4 hard-cooked eggs

Using a mortar and pestle or a blender, make a thick purée of the olives, anchovies, capers, and the tuna. Then slowly add the olive oil, the lemon juice, and finally a few drops of brandy and about 1/4 teaspoon mustard. Spoon this over halved hard-cooked eggs which you present cut side down. Add a judicious sprinkle of parsley and serve, perhaps surrounded by garden lettuce, as a first course. The tapenade is an excellent cocktail spread when offered with Melba toast or crisp crackers.
Mrs. Arthur B. Waxter

Egg and Caviar Mousse

24 or more servings

5 tablespoons unflavored gelatin
1 cup cold water
24 hard-boiled large eggs
10 ounces black caviar
3 tablespoons Worcestershire sauce
Freshly ground black pepper
2 medium onions, grated
5 cups mayonnaise
2 cups heavy cream, whipped

Soften the gelatin in cold water and dissolve it over hot water in the top of a double boiler; then cool it. Put the eggs through a sieve or ricer and combine with all the remaining ingredients, except the whipped cream, adding Worcestershire sauce to taste. Add the cooled gelatin and fold in the well-whipped cream. Rinse two 8-cup molds in cold water and divide the mixture between them. Unmold at serving time and surround the mousse with cherry tomatoes.   *Mrs. Robert D. Meyers*

Open Sandwich

2 servings

2 slices bread
2 pimientos
3 eggs
Butter
1-1/2 tablespoons Boursin cheese

Prepare 2 slices of bread by removing the crusts and carpeting each one with a drained canned red pepper cup (pimiento) cut open to fit the bread. Salt them. Scramble 3 eggs in butter into large soft curds and when they are not quite finished, add the crumbled cheese, salt, and pepper. Let cool somewhat and pile this onto the pepper base. Garnish with strips of the pimiento and serve cold.
Lady Penrose

Brioche aux Oeufs Brouillés
BRIOCHE FILLED WITH
SCRAMBLED EGGS

6 servings

6 individual brioches
12 eggs
6 teaspoons water
Butter
6 fresh truffles, sliced, or 1 jar (1/2 pint) sliced truffles
Salt and white pepper

Cut the round heads off the tops of the brioches and hollow out the insides, leaving 1/4 inch thickness around the sides and bottom. Brush the shells with melted butter and toast them about 8 inches from the broiler element. Keep warm until the eggs are ready.

Whisk the eggs with the water until well blended and pour them into a buttered skillet. Add the sliced truffles, salt, and pepper, and scramble very slowly, stirring occasionally, just until the eggs are creamy and undercooked. Fill the brioche shells to the rounded top and replace the tops. If they are not to be served immediately, cover them loosely with tent-like individual pieces of foil, leaving air space and put them in a 200° oven until ready for use. Or, by setting a pan filled with the brioches in a water bath, they can be reheated later at 250°.

Please note that this French recipe takes no account of the price of truffles. Mushrooms or chopped black olives, sautéed, would be effective, too.
Mrs. Lawrence Bachman

Scrambled Egg Casserole

25-30 servings

1-1/2 sticks of butter
4 dozen eggs
1/4 cup Carnation milk

Scramble eggs lightly in butter in large skillet. Don't make them too hard. When finished, set them aside.

3 cans mushroom soup
3/4 to 1 cup sherry
1 large can mushrooms
1/4 cup chopped onion
3/4 cup grated Cheddar cheese

Heat the soup until smooth. Add the sherry, mushrooms, and onions. Then in greased oblong Pyrex dishes (you need at least two) layer eggs, then soup mixture, and then cheese. Repeat, ending with cheese. Refrigerate. The next day, put the dishes in a cold oven, turn to 300°, and bake them

for 1 hour or until bubbly. Garnish with paprika and parsley.
Mrs. Robert J. Koch

Bubbly Eggs

350° / 4 servings

8 hard-cooked eggs
1 package frozen chopped spinach, cooked and drained
1 teaspoon grated onion
1 teaspoon Worcestershire sauce
Tabasco
Salt and pepper
2 tablespoons melted butter
2 teaspoons lemon juice
1 can (10-1/2 ounce) condensed mushroom soup
1 small jar (8 ounces) Cheez Whiz
Buttered fresh bread crumbs
Parmesan cheese

Slice the eggs in half lengthwise and remove the yolks. Mash the yolks and combine with the well-drained spinach, seasonings, melted butter, and lemon juice. Mix all this well and fill egg-white cavities. Heat the soup and Cheez Whiz in a double boiler. Pour it over the stuffed eggs. Cover with buttered bread crumbs, sprinkle with the Parmesan cheese and bake until bubbly.
Mrs. Frederick J. Singley, Jr.

Baked Eggs Supreme

325° / 4 servings

4 tablespoons dry bread crumbs
8 eggs
6 tablespoons milk
Salt
Butter
3/4 cup grated American processed cheese or sharp Cheddar
Chives
Paprika

Grease 4 individual shallow ramekins. Into each sprinkle the bread crumbs, then break and slip in 2 eggs. Add 1-1/2 tablespoons milk, top with a shake of salt, a dot of butter, and 3 tablespoons of grated cheese. Bake 15 to 18 minutes or until the tops are golden brown and eggs are set. Sprinkle with chives and paprika. If desired, all may be baked in one 8-inch or 9-inch shallow baking dish.
Mrs. T. Garland Tinsley

Cheese Casserole

350° / 4 servings

8 slices bread, white or rye
Butter for spreading

1/2 pound or more of sharp cheese
1 tablespoon minced onion
4 eggs
2-1/2 cups milk
Salt, pepper, and Tabasco

Butter the bread, spread with cheese, and sprinkle with the minced onion. Cut the slices in half diagonally and arrange with points overlapping in a flat baking dish. Beat the eggs until well mixed; add milk and seasonings and pour over the bread. Let this stand a few hours or even overnight in the refrigerator.

Put the casserole in a larger pan containing an inch of hot water and bake for about an hour or until it is both puffed and brown.

Mrs. Douglas Warner, Jr.

Cheese Soufflé Using Bread

350° / 4 to 5 servings

1-1/2 cups scalded milk
1 cup small pieces of bread
1 cup small pieces of sharp Cheddar cheese
1 tablespoon butter
1 teaspoon salt
Paprika
Pepper
1 teaspoon baking powder
4 eggs, separated

Grease a 10-inch soufflé dish and tape a 3-inch collar to the top edge.

Combine the milk, bread, and cheese and cook over low heat until both melted and smooth. Add the butter and seasoning, the well beaten egg yolks, the baking powder, and finally fold in the stiffly beaten whites. Spoon the soufflé into the dish and bake for 40 to 50 minutes.

This may be prepared ahead up to the addition of the whites, which must be beaten at the last moment.

Mrs. T. Garland Tinsley

An Impressive Cheese Soufflé

(as served at The Plaza Athenée in Paris)
4 servings

4 poached eggs
Basic cheese soufflé recipe for a 7-1/2 or 8-inch mold
Finely chopped mushrooms or puréed spinach

The eggs must be just firm but soft. Spoon half of the soufflé mixture into the mold. Make 4 depressions in it with the back of a big spoon. Line the hollows lightly with a little sautéed mushrooms or puréed spinach. Put an egg in each, add salt and pepper, then spoon the rest of the soufflé over the top. Bake as usual.

Mrs. Jack Riboud

Tomato and Bacon Frittata

475° / 2 servings

6 strips of bacon
4 eggs
3 tablespoons hot water
Salt
2 firm tomatoes, peeled and coarsely chopped
1 green pepper, cored and chopped
Butter

Fry the bacon until crisp, then drain it and set it aside. Separate the eggs. Add the water to the egg yolks and beat them until light. Beat the whites with a pinch of salt until fluffy. In an iron skillet at low heat, melt some butter (it is hard to say how much without seeing the size of the skillet), and place the bacon, tomatoes, and peppers in it. Now fold the whites into the yolks and spoon over the other ingredients. Leave them at low heat for about 7 minutes, at which time the edges will look done.

Preheat either the oven or broiler and put the skillet in to brown. About 7 minutes should do the trick. With a knife, loosen around the edges.

Fold the omelet in two and roll onto a hot serving platter.   *Miss Elisabeth Packard*

Quiche Maison

350° / 6 servings

1 rich piecrust for a 9-inch pie plate
1/2 pound bacon, diced
1 small onion, chopped
1/2 pound ham, diced
1/2 pound pork sausages, sliced
1/2 cup grated Parmesan cheese
1/2 cup grated Cheddar cheese
1-1/2 cans evaporated milk
4 whole eggs
2 teaspoons chopped parsley

Line the pie plate with the crust, partially bake it, let it cool, and paint it with the yolk of a beaten egg to keep it from becoming soggy when you add the ingredients for the custard.

Sauté the bacon until crisp and drain it. In butter, sauté the onion until limp, set it aside, and sauté the ham and finally the sausage. Be sure to drain the sausage well, too. Mix the meats and onions together and spread on the pastry. Combine the cheeses and spread half over the meats. Beat the eggs with the milk and pour those in, too. Top with the remaining cheese, strew in the parsley, and bake for 30 minutes or just until the center is firm.   *Mrs. LeBaron S. Willard, Jr.*

Quiche aux Endives

375° / 6 servings

6 heads Belgian endive
2-1/2 tablespoons lemon juice
1/4 teaspoon salt
1 cup boiling water
Rich pastry (see following recipe)
10 slices bacon, fried crisp and crumbled
1 pound mushrooms, finely chopped and sautéed in lightly salted butter until liquid has evaporated
3 well-beaten eggs
1 cup light cream
1 cup grated Gruyère cheese, fresh

Leave endives whole, cutting off the discolored part of roots or any brown spots on the outer leaves. Put in a saucepan, add lemon juice, salt, and boiling water. Simmer for 20 minutes, then drain thoroughly and cut into 1/2-inch slices. Meanwhile, roll out the pastry to fit an 8-inch pie pan and flute the edges. Put 3/4 of the crumbled bacon on the bottom of the pie crust along with the sautéed mushrooms. Arrange the endive in a layer over them. Blend eggs, cream, and grated cheese with a wire whisk. Pour over the endive. Bake for 35 to 40 minutes or until the quiche filling is just set. Top with crumbled bacon. Serve warm as a first course or as a luncheon entrée.

Rich Pastry

3/4 cup lightly salted butter, softened
6 tablespoons vegetable shortening
1-1/2 cups sifted all-purpose flour
1/2 teaspoon salt
1/2 cup ice water

Blend butter and shortening until smooth. Then add the flour, salt, and ice water; mix well and roll into a ball. Cover with waxed paper and chill for 2 hours or more. Roll out the dough on a floured pastry cloth to fit the pie pan.

Mrs. Irwin J. Nudelman

Tarte aux Oignons à l'Alsacienne

350° / 4 to 6 servings

2 cups Spanish onions, minced
6 tablespoons sour cream
1 egg
Salt and pepper to taste

Bits of raw bacon
A paté brisée pie crust or any other short pastry to line a 9-inch pie tin

In a heavy skillet, cook the onions, using a very little water, until they are translucent and there is no water left. Don't let them brown. Remove the pan from the heat and add about 6 tablespoons of sour cream, just enough to give the mixture a nice creamy consistency. Stir in the egg, slightly beaten, and add the seasoning. Pour the mixture into the prepared crust and garnish it with bits of bacon. Bake on the lower rack 45 minutes. To make a larger tarte use a pizza tin.

Mrs. Harry E. Foster

Spinach Pie

425°-350° / 6 to 8 servings

3 cups chopped frozen spinach
2 9-inch pie shells
6 tablespoons minced shallots
4 tablespoons butter
1 teaspoon salt
1/2 teaspoon pepper
1/8 teaspoon nutmeg
6 eggs
3 cups cream
1/4 teaspoon pepper
1/4 teaspoon nutmeg
1 cup Gruyère cheese, slivered
2 tablespoons butter, cut into tiny pieces

Barely cook the spinach and squeeze it completely dry. Bake the pie shells in a 425° oven for about 10 minutes or until lightly browned. Cook the shallots for a minute in butter. Add the spinach and stir to evaporate all its water. Stir in the salt, pepper, and nutmeg. Adjust the seasoning. In a bowl, beat the eggs, cream, 1/4 teaspoon pepper and 1/4 teaspoon nutmeg. Gradually stir in the spinach mixture. Pour into the partially cooked pastry shells. Distribute cheese and the butter kernels evenly on top. Bake in a 350° oven for 25 to 30 minutes, until the custard has set. This will wait; it doesn't have to be served hot, and it is quite good cold as well. The cream may be replaced by either milk or cottage cheese.

Mrs. Henry Hays, Miss Rita St. Clair

Egg and Spinach Galette

4 servings

4 eggs
4 tablespoons spinach purée
2 tablespoons milk or cream
Salt and pepper
Pinch of nutmeg
Butter (about 2 tablespoons)
Thick tomato sauce
1 cup good cheese sauce

Beat the eggs with a fork, add the spinach purée, milk or cream, and seasonings. Heat a small omelet pan (6-7 inches diameter on the bottom), drop in a nut of the butter and a quarter of the eggs, and cook on both sides like a pancake. Make 4 rounds and pile in layers with a spoonful or 2 of tomato sauce between each layer. Reheat in the oven, pour cheese sauce over and serve, cutting like a cake. *Mrs. A. Holland Mills*

Ham and Mushroom Crêpes

8 servings

4 ounces butter
1/2 pound mushrooms, coarsely chopped
Juice of 1 lemon
2 shallots, finely chopped
4 tablespoons flour
2 cups milk
1/2 pound boiled ham, diced
4 tablespoons parsley, chopped
Salt, and freshly ground pepper
8 5- or 6-inch crêpes
Grated sharp cheese
Paprika

Heat half the butter, add the mushrooms and lemon juice and sauté them for a short while. Set them aside. In another pan, melt the rest of the butter and sauté the shallots in it. Stir in the flour and simmer a bit until smooth. Add the milk and cook slowly until the sauce is smooth and thick. Then add to this the mushrooms, parsley, and ham, and taste for seasoning. Have ready 8 thin pancakes, divide the mixture among them, and roll up. Put the stuffed crêpes in a baking dish, strew with grated sharp cheese and a little paprika, and put under a hot broiler until the cheese has melted.

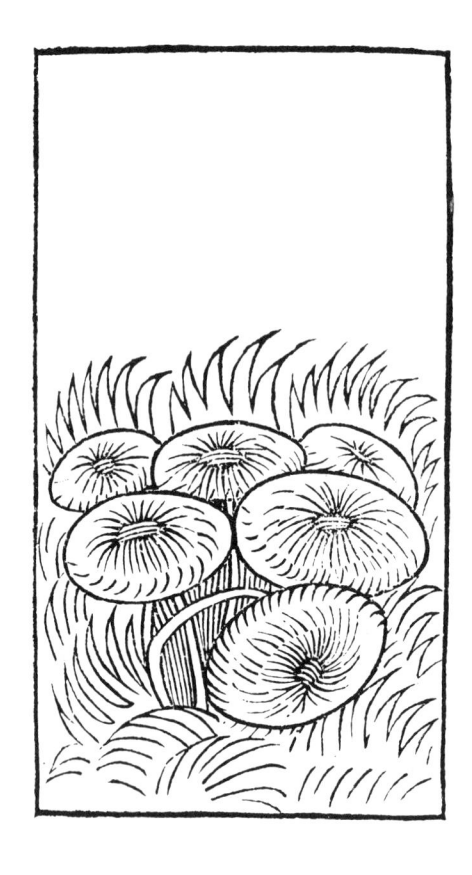

Mrs. John J. Smith

VEGETABLES

Sautéed Artichoke Hearts

3 or 4 servings

1 package frozen artichoke hearts
Lemon juice
Flour
2 tablespoons butter
2 or 3 tablespoons olive oil

Separate the artichoke hearts. With a sharp knife, slice each half artichoke vertically into 2 or 3 thin slices. Let them thaw and dry on paper towels. Sprinkle with lemon juice, salt, and pepper; let them stand 1/2 hour, and then dust with flour. Heat in a skillet the butter and oil. When the fat is quite hot, put in the artichoke slices and cook over moderate heat for 4 or 5 minutes on each side until well browned and a little crisp. Serve with steak or roasts.

Mrs. Donald Brown

Artichoke Bottoms with Asparagus Tips

350° / 6 servings

6 cooked artichoke bottoms
12 tablespoons Mornay sauce
18-24 asparagus tips
Grated Gruyère cheese

Mornay sauce is a thick béchamel with grated Gruyère cheese added: about 2 ounces to 1 cup of sauce.

Place a tablespoon of sauce in the center of each artichoke bottom. Cover with asparagus tips which are cooked just until tender. Add more sauce and put additional grated cheese on top. Heat for 15 minutes or until lightly browned. Serve with game or roast chicken.

Miss Leslie Hays

Hearts of Artichokes

350°

1 can hearts of artichokes packed in brine
Melba toast rounds
Melted butter
Salt and pepper
Garlic, crushed
Sliced almonds or sesame seeds

Drain and rinse the artichokes thoroughly and cut in half, best done with kitchen shears. Place each artichoke half, cut side up, on 1 Melba round. Pour the melted butter generously into the artichoke crevices, allowing some of it to run over on the rounds. Add the seasonings to taste (or these can be stirred into the melted butter). Sprinkle sliced almonds or sesame seeds over the artichokes.

Bake for 10 minutes and then brown lightly under the broiler.   *Frank D'Amanda*

Artichokes à la Constantinople

AGINARES A LA POLITA

4 servings

12 peeled baby white onions
12 small pieces of carrot
12 small peeled new potatoes
1 teaspoon salt
4 tablespoons finely chopped fresh dill
1/2 cup olive oil
Juice of 1 lemon
1 teaspoon flour
1 large can artichoke bottoms

Put onions, carrots, and potatoes in saucepan with salt and dill. Add water almost to cover. Beat together olive oil, lemon juice, and flour. Blend into the water in the saucepan, bring to a boil, and simmer the vegetables, covered, for 30 minutes or until tender. Add drained artichoke bottoms to the saucepan during the last few minutes, just to warm through.

Arrange the vegetables on individual hot plates or one hot serving dish, placing the artichokes in the center and the vegetables around them. Reduce the sauce a little and pour over the vegetables.
Miss Alice Roberts

Syrian Asparagus

4 servings

1 onion, thinly sliced
1/4 cup olive oil
1/3 cup hot water
1-1/2 pounds asparagus, washed and trimmed
Salt and pepper
Chopped parsley
Lemon wedges

Sauté the onion in the oil in a large skillet until tender. Add 1/3 cup hot water, the asparagus, salt and pepper to taste. Cook, covered, until the asparagus is just tender. Sprinkle with parsley and garnish with lemon wedges.   *Mrs. Peter Dane*

Whipped Broccoli

6 servings

2 or 3 large heads broccoli
3 tablespoons flour
2 tablespoons butter
1-1/2 cups milk
Onion juice
Salt
Pepper
Oregano

Cook the broccoli in rapidly boiling salted water until tender. Drain well and run it through the finest blades of a meat grinder. Make a heavy cream sauce of the flour, butter, and milk. Stir in the ground broccoli, season with the onion juice, salt, and pepper, and place in a double boiler. Whisk briskly to the consistency of mashed potatoes. Sprinkle lightly with oregano. Serve hot.
Mrs. Joseph T. Brennan

Spirited Broccoli

8 servings

1 bunch fresh broccoli
1-2 cloves garlic, mashed
3 tablespoons cooking oil
1/2 cup water
1/2 teaspoon salt

Sauce:

1/4 cup water

1 tablespoon cornstarch
1/4 cup blended whiskey
2 tablespoons soy sauce
1 tablespoon sugar
1/2 teaspoon MSG

Soak broccoli in water with 1 teaspoon of salt added, for 15 minutes. Cut off the tough ends of the stalks, cutting on the diagonal, and discard them. Peel the remaining stalks and cut into uniform pieces. Separate the heads into serving portions. In a large skillet, over medium heat, heat oil, garlic, and salt. When fairly hot but not smoking, add the broccoli, turning to coat all the pieces. Add 1/2 cup water and cover. Cook 6 to 8 minutes, turning occasionally, until crisp-tender.

In a measuring cup combine the cornstarch and 1/4 cup water. Stir until dissolved. Add the whiskey, soy sauce, sugar, and MSG. Add enough water to make 1 cup. When broccoli is finished cooking, remove the cover, turn up the heat to high, and add the sauce ingredients, stirring constantly. As soon as the sauce boils, remove it from the heat and serve.

Howard Fong

Beets in Orange Sauce

6 servings

2-1/2 cups diced cooked beets
1 tablespoon butter
4 tablespoons brown sugar
1-1/2 tablespoons flour
3/4 cup orange juice
2 tablespoons grated orange peel
Salt
Paprika

Melt the butter, add the brown sugar and flour, stir, and add the orange juice with the grated peel. Cook until thick, stirring constantly, then season with salt and paprika. Prepare this ahead and at serving time add the beets to heat through.

Miss Alice Newman

Beets with Cheese

6 servings

3 cups sliced or diced beets, cooked
1/2 cup sour cream
6 tablespoons grated cheese

Put the beets in a greased baking dish, mix well with the sour cream, sprinkle the cheese over the the top, and put under a moderate broiler until the dish is piping hot and the cheese has melted.

Mrs. Sven Peulechè

Brussels Sprouts in Onion Cream

8 servings

1-1/2 pounds Brussels sprouts
1/2 cup chopped onion
2 tablespoons butter
1 pint sour cream

Steam sprouts less than 10 minutes, or until tender. Sauté the onion in butter until a rich brown. Then stir in the sour cream and heat, stirring constantly. Add Brussels sprouts and mix well.

Mrs. Mary F. Barada

Danish Red Cabbage

4 servings

1 pound red cabbage
3 tablespoons butter or bacon fat
1 tablespoon sugar
1 tablespoon vinegar
1/4 cup water
1/2 cup red currant jelly
2 good hard apples, peeled and chopped
Salt and pepper
1/4 cup sherry (optional)

Remove the tough outer leaves and shred the cabbage. Rinse and drain well. In a heavy casserole heat the butter and melt the sugar in it. Add the cabbage and cook 3 minutes. Add the vinegar and water. Simmer covered for 2 or 3 hours, or until very tender. Stir occasionally and add more hot water if necessary to prevent it from scorching. Half an hour before it is done, add currant jelly, cubed apples, salt, pepper, and sherry. This should be sweet and sour, so more sugar and vinegar may be added to taste.

This is a delicious German dish, which keeps well and freezes beautifully.

Mrs. Charles Newhall, III, Mrs. Sven Peuleché

Holishes

6 servings

1 medium-size head of cabbage
1 package square noodles (Pennsylvania Dutch style)
1 cup cooking oil
Salt and pepper
1/2 teaspoon minced garlic

Shred the cabbage on a grater. Let it stand 15 minutes. Boil the noodles until just done (do not overcook), drain, and set aside. Heat the oil in a deep fryer. Put in a layer of cabbage; season with salt, pepper, and minced garlic. Next place a layer of noodles; repeat until all of the cabbage and noodles are in the pan. Fry, stirring occasionally until the cabbage and the noodles are brown, which will take 15 minutes. Correct the seasoning if necessary and drain on absorbent paper.

Mrs. Jules Horelick

Brandied Carrots

8 servings

3 or 4 bunches carrots, peeled and cut into julienne strips
1/2 pound butter
2 tablespoons sugar
1/2 teaspoon salt
1/3 cup brandy
Chopped parsley

Place the carrot strips in a baking dish just large enough to hold them comfortably. Melt the butter and pour over the vegetable. Sprinkle with sugar and salt and add the brandy. Cover and bake in a moderate oven for 1 hour. Add chopped parsley at serving time.

Mrs. Henry Hays, Mrs. Edward Stimpson

Glazed Carrots

Small carrots (several per person)
1/4 cup honey
1/4 cup butter
Dash of salt

Cut the carrots, after scraping them, into pieces resembling large-sized French fried potatoes. Cook them in the smallest amount of water possible in a covered heavy skillet or an electric frying pan. When the carrots are tender add the honey, butter, and salt. Remove the cover and continue to cook the carrots, turning them so they become glazed and evenly browned.

Mrs. Sven Peuleché

Potato Carrot Casserole

350° / 8 servings

4 large potatoes, peeled
1 pound young carrots, scraped
1 cup light cream
1 egg yolk
1/4 pound softened butter
Dijon mustard
Salt and pepper

Cook separately in boiling water both the carrots and the potatoes until tender. Drain them well

and then put them through a potato ricer. Put them in a bowl, adding the cream, egg yolk, and butter. Season well with the mustard, salt, and freshly ground pepper. Beat it all together until light and very fluffy, and then bake in a buttered casserole until piping hot.
Edward L. Brewster

Carrot Soufflé

350° / 3 servings

1 cup cooked carrots, mashed
1 cup fresh bread crumbs
1 cup milk
3 eggs, separated
1 tablespoon grated onion
1 cup shredded cheese
Salt, pepper and cayenne

Soak the crumbs in the milk for about 10 minutes. Then combine the crumbs with the beaten egg yolk, carrots, onion, cheese, and seasoning. Beat the whites stiffly and carefully fold into the carrot mixture. Pour into a 1-quart buttered casserole and bake for about 40 minutes or until set.
Mrs. F. Barton Harvey, Jr.

Carrot Tart

450° / 6 servings

6 tart shells
6 cups peeled sliced carrots, or 3 10-ounce packages frozen sliced carrots
3 tablespoons butter
1/2 cup heavy cream
Salt and pepper
Sugar
Nutmeg

Cook 1 cup sliced peeled carrots in water. Drain well and set aside. Cook the remainder in 1/2 cup of water, a pinch of sugar, and 3 tablespoons of butter. Purée them and beat in the heavy cream. Season to taste with salt, pepper, a little sugar, and a pinch of nutmeg. Fill the shells with the purée and arrange the sliced carrots in concentric circles on top. Brush with melted butter, dust with sugar, and bake for 10 to 15 minutes.
Mrs. Arthur Stern

Mashed Celery Root

4 to 6 servings

2 celery roots
1 cup peeled potato
2 tablespoons butter
2 cups stock or bouillon
Salt
Chives
1/4 cup cream (optional)

Blanch the celery roots in water for 5 minutes, then peel and chop coarsely with the potatoes. Melt the butter in a saucepan; add the vegetables and enough liquid and stock to cover. Simmer for 20 minutes, covered, and purée them in a blender or through a sieve. Add the cream and top with chives before serving.

This can be put into a buttered ring mold, held in the oven for a short time, and then turned out, putting peas or sautéed mushrooms in the center.
Mrs. W. Boulton Kelly, Mrs. Arthur Stern

Corn Pudding

325° / 6 servings

2 cups of fresh corn, cut from the cob
2 cups milk, scalded
2 tablespoons melted butter
1/4 teaspoon pepper
2 eggs, beaten
1-3/4 teaspoon salt
2 teaspoons sugar

Mix together and pour into 1-1/2-quart greased

A woman kneeling before a table of offerings, from an Egyptian wall painting of the Middle Kingdom.

casserole. Sprinkle paprika on top. Place the casserole in a pan of hot water and bake for about 1 hour and 15 minutes or until set.

Mrs. Douglas Warner, Jr.

Cucumbers in Cream

6 servings

2 pounds cucumbers, peeled, seeded, and cut into baguettes or balls
2 tablespoons butter
1-1/2 tablespoons flour
3/4 cup milk
Salt and white pepper
1/2 cup heavy cream
1 tablespoon chopped fresh tarragon or dill

Cook cucumbers in boiling, salted water for about 15 minutes or until just tender. Drain and keep warm. Make a béchamel sauce of the butter, flour, milk, and seasoning. Simmer the sauce a few minutes, then take from the fire and stir in the cream. Pour over the cucumbers and garnish with the tarragon or dill.

Edward L. Brewster

A More Successful Way with Eggplant

450° / 4 servings

1 eggplant
Sauce vinaigrette
Sour cream
Chives

Marinate (for about 2 hours) large cubes of eggplant in a well-seasoned sauce vinaigrette. Then bake them for about 30 to 40 minutes, until tender. Pour thick sour cream over them and return to the oven to get everything hot—only 1 or 2 minutes are needed. Garnish with snipped chives and serve.

Edward L. Brewster

Eggplant Soufflé

350° / 6 to 8 servings

2 eggplants
1/2 small onion, diced
2 garlic buds, minced
4 tablespoons butter
2 tablespoons flour
1 cup milk
4 eggs, separated
3 tablespoons tomato paste
1 cup grated Parmesan cheese

Peel the eggplants and cut into small pieces. Cook until tender in boiling salted water. Drain well and mash with a fork. Sauté the onion and garlic in half of the butter. Make a béchamel sauce of the remaining butter, the flour, and the milk, then make a liaison with the egg yolk by pouring some of the sauce carefully into the yolks, then returning the mixture to the sauce. Add the eggplant, the onion, garlic, tomato paste, and cheese. Let this cool.

An hour before dinner, beat the egg whites, fold into the eggplant mixture, and pile it into a buttered 2-quart soufflé dish. Place in a pan of hot water. Bake for 50 minutes. Serve immediately.

Miss Grace Hatchett

Eggplant Casserole

375° / 4 servings

1 medium eggplant
2 onions
1 pound ground beef
Salt and pepper
1 can (10-1/2 ounces) condensed soup (cream of mushroom, celery, or whatever you prefer)
Catsup to taste
Grated Parmesan cheese

Slice the eggplant without peeling it, mince the

onions, then layer these with the ground beef alternately in a casserole. Salt and pepper each layer well, pour soup, flavoured with the catsup, through all of it. Sprinkle with Parmesan cheese and bake uncovered for 1-1/2 hours or longer. Note that this may be arranged much in advance of baking.   *Mrs. Harrison L. Winter*

Ratatouille

6 servings

1 small eggplant, peeled and cut into 1-inch slices
2 tablespoons cooking oil
1 clove garlic, minced
1/2 cup chopped onion
1 green pepper, seeded and chopped
1-1/2 pounds zucchini, unpeeled and cut into 1/2-inch slices
2 pounds tomatoes, peeled, seeded, and chopped, or 1 large (28 ounces) can, well drained
1-1/2 teaspoons salt
1/4 teaspoon pepper
1 teaspoon fresh basil or 1/3 teaspoon dried basil
1 tablespoon olive oil

Place the eggplant slices on a paper towel; sprinkle with salt. Cover with another paper towel and place a plate on top. Let them stand for about 30 minutes to drain, then cut the eggplant slices into cubes. Put the cooking oil into a casserole or skillet; sauté garlic and onion. Combine the garlic and onion with layers of other vegetables; add salt, pepper, and basil. Drizzle olive oil over the vegetables. Bring the mixture to a boil; cover, reduce the heat, and simmer until the vegetables are just tender (about 25 to 30 minutes). During the cooking, stir occasionally and carefully so that each vegetable keeps its form. At the same time, baste off excess liquid and reduce it in a small saucepan. After the vegetables are tender pour some reduced liquid over the vegetables. Serve hot or cold.   *Mrs. Charles T. Hanson*

Green Bean Casserole

350° / 6 servings

2 packages frozen French-cut string beans
2 tablespoons butter
2 tablespoons flour
1 cup sour cream
1 teaspoon salt
1 teaspoon pepper
1 teaspoon sugar
1/2 teaspoon grated onion
1/4 pound Swiss cheese
1/2 cup crumbs of Ritz crackers
2 tablespoons melted butter

Cook the beans until tender. Make a béchamel sauce by melting the butter, blending in the flour, and adding the sour cream, salt, pepper, sugar, and onion. Remove from the heat and add the cheese in small pieces. Mix the beans with the sauce and pour into a casserole. Before baking, cover with cracker crumbs mixed with butter. Bake 20 to 30 minutes. This may be prepared ahead of time and brought to room temperature before baking.
   Mrs. Philip Gottling, Mrs. J. Richard Thomas

Piquant Green Beans

6 servings

1-1/2 pounds green beans
4 slices lean bacon, cut in 1/2-inch strips
2 tablespoons diced pimiento
1/4 teaspoon sugar
1/4 teaspoon dry mustard
2 tablespoons red wine vinegar
1 tablespoon Worcestershire sauce
2 drops Tabasco

Steam the beans until tender. Sauté the bacon, remove it from the fat, and add it to the beans. To the fat in the skillet, add the remaining ingredients and stir over high heat. Add the beans and mix thoroughly.   *Mrs. Mary F. Barada*

Green Beans in Cream

4 servings

1 quart green beans
1 teaspoon salt
1 cup medium or heavy cream

Prepare beans for cooking—either leave whole or cut them up. Place them in a saucepan and add cream and salt. Over moderate heat bring to a simmer, then lower the heat at once and simmer for about 3/4 of an hour, until most of the cream has boiled away. The beans will be "cooked to death" but delicious.
Mrs. Alan Victor

Lima Lima Beans

4 servings

4 cups shelled lima beans or 2 packages frozen ones
1-2 shallots, minced
2/3 cup chicken stock
1/4 cup butter
1 teaspoon celery seed
1/2 teaspoon sugar
2/3 cup heavy cream
Salt and pepper
2 teaspoons chopped parsley

Thaw the frozen beans slightly; place the beans and shallots in a heavy skillet. Add the stock, butter, celery seed, and sugar and cook, covered, over medium heat until the beans are just tender. If there is much liquid left, remove the lid, stirring the while to reduce it without scorching the beans. Drain the beans and keep them warm. Put any liquid along with the cream into a blender. Add half the beans and purée. Add the purée to the other beans, heat through, and sprinkle with parsley after adjusting the seasoning.
Mrs. Henry Hays

Lima Bean Casserole

350° / 4 to 6 servings

1 package frozen lima beans
1/4 pound mushrooms, sliced
3-4 tablespoons butter
1/4 cup chopped onions
1 cup shredded cabbage
1 teaspoon salt and some pepper
1 teaspoon soy sauce (or a little more)
2 tablespoons grated Parmesan cheese

Cook beans according to package directions, drain and turn into a shallow casserole. Cook sliced mushrooms, onions, and cabbage in butter until soft. Add to the beans along with salt, pepper, and soy sauce. Sprinkle cheese over the top and bake 15 to 20 minutes.

This may be served as a vegetable for 4 to 6 or as a one-dish meal for 2.
Edward L. Brewster

Romaine Soufflé

400° / 6 servings

1 large head romaine lettuce
4 tablespoons butter
3 green onions, chopped
3 tablespoons flour
1 cup extra-rich milk, heated
1 teaspoon Worcestershire sauce
1 teaspoon salt
Freshly ground pepper or 3 dashes Tabasco
4 eggs, separated
1 cup shredded Cheddar cheese
Grated Parmesan cheese

Cut off the end of the romaine, rinse thoroughly, and chop coarsely. Cook until wilted in a little water. Cool, drain, and chop fine. Melt 1 tablespoon butter and sauté the onions until soft but not brown. Add the lettuce and cook slowly until the liquid has evaporated. In a separate pan, melt

3 tablespoons butter and blend in the flour. Cook, stirring, for a couple of minutes. Add hot milk, salt, pepper, and Worcestershire sauce and cook, stirring, until thick and smooth. Remove from the fire and beat in the yolks one at a time. Add Cheddar cheese and put over low heat until melted and smooth. Stir in the romaine.

Whip the egg whites until they hold soft peaks, but are not dry. Stir half into the lettuce mixture, blending thoroughly, then gently fold in the remainder of the whites. Heavily butter a 1-1/2-quart soufflé dish, sprinkle with Parmesan cheese, turn to coat evenly, and then shake out the excess. Pour in the soufflé mixture; tap the mold on the table to settle and even it out. Sprinkle the top with more Parmesan cheese and bake for 25 to 30 minutes. *Philip S. Brown*

Spinach Stuffed Mushrooms

375° / 3 to 4 servings

12-16 large mushrooms
8 tablespoons butter
1-1/2 tablespoons minced onion
1 clove garlic, minced
1 package frozen chopped spinach
1/4 teaspoon nutmeg
1/2 teaspoon salt
1/8 teaspoon pepper
2 tablespoons Parmesan cheese

Dip mushroom caps in 6 tablespoons melted butter. Place them underside up in a buttered baking dish. Chop the stems and sauté with onion and garlic in 2 tablespoons butter until soft, not brown. Cook and drain the spinach and add it to the chopped mushroom stems along with the nutmeg, salt, pepper, and Parmesan cheese. Mix thoroughly and fill the mushroom caps. Bake for 15 minutes. *Mrs. Edward Fishman*

Mushroom Croquettes

4 to 6 servings

1 pound mushrooms, wiped clean
12 spring onions, chopped
2 tablespoons butter
Salt and pepper
1/4 cup sherry
2 heaping tablespoons butter
3 rounded tablespoons flour
3/4 cup soup stock
3/4 cup milk
3 egg yolks
1/4 cup minced parsley
Fine cracker crumbs
1 egg
Fat for deep frying

Grind the mushrooms, using the very finest blade. Fry the chopped spring onions with 2 tablespoons of butter until they are soft and yellow; then add the ground mushrooms and cook them together for a few minutes. Season with salt and pepper and moisten with the sherry. Simmer the mixture until most of the sherry has been absorbed. Make a sauce by melting 2 heaping tablespoons of butter with 3 rounded tablespoons of flour. Let it cook until the flour is blended, stirring constantly. Gradually pour in the soup stock and the milk and cook it until it is quite thick. Remove it from the fire and beat in the egg yolks and the minced parsley. Combine the sauce with the mushroom mixture and return it to the fire. Stir it constantly until it is thoroughly heated but do not allow it to boil. Spread the mixture out on a shallow buttered dish and when it is cool place it in the refrigerator until it is firm.

Form into croquettes, roll them in fine cracker crumbs, and then dip each one in egg which has been beaten with 1 tablespoon of water to each egg. Roll them in the crumbs again and let them stand about 10 minutes until the crumbs adhere to the croquettes. Drop a few at a time in hot but not smoking fat and fry them to a golden brown. This is also very good as a filling.

Mrs. Joseph T. Brennan

Mushroom Roll

350° / 8 servings

3 pounds mushrooms
6 eggs, separated
1/4 pound butter, melted
2 tablespoons lemon juice
A little grated onion
Salt and pepper
Nutmeg
1 pound sautéed mushrooms for filling

Grease a jelly roll pan (10-1/2 x 15 inches), line with waxed paper, then grease the paper. Chop 3 pounds of mushrooms fine and squeeze dry in a towel. Beat the eggs yolks until fluffy; add the mushrooms, butter, salt and pepper, nutmeg, lemon juice, and grated onion. Beat the egg whites to soft peaks and fold into the mushroom mix. Spread in the pan and bake 15 minutes. Turn out on waxed paper and when somewhat cooled peel off the top paper. (Don't let it get too cool or the paper will stick.) Roll it up. This may be kept overnight. At serving time, heat and cover with sautéed mushrooms and chopped parsley. *Miss Anne Barlow*

Mushroom Casserole

350° / 6 servings

1-1/2 pounds mushrooms
2 beef bouillon cubes
1/4 cup hot water
1/4 cup butter
2 tablespoons flour
1/2 cup half-and-half
1/2 teaspoon salt
1/4 teaspoon coarse black pepper
1/2 cup fine bread crumbs
1/2 cup grated Parmesan cheese
1/2 teaspoon onion salt

Wipe the mushrooms well, slice them, and put them in a 2-quart casserole. Melt the butter; add flour; dissolve cubes in water, and add; add the cream, salt, and pepper, and cook the sauce until it has thickened. Pour it over the mushrooms. Mix the crumbs, cheese, and onion salt and sprinkle it over the top. You will think the casserole mixture is too dry, but the mushrooms exude enough liquid to make the recipe exact as it is. Bake for 30 minutes.

Mrs. Gordon Leatherman

Stuffed Onions

350° / 4 servings

2 cups chicken stock
Juice of 2 lemons
Cayenne
1/2 teaspoon tarragon
4 large onions, peeled
2 hard-cooked eggs, riced
1 tablespoon cream
1/4 pound chopped mushrooms
1 tablespoon Italian bread crumbs
1/2 teaspoon oregano
Salt and pepper
Parmesan cheese, to taste
Butter

Simmer the chicken stock, lemon juice, cayenne, and tarragon until well seasoned, then parboil the onions in it for about 10 minutes. Scoop out the insides, leaving a shell and the root end (otherwise they would fall apart.) Make a stuffing of the riced eggs, cream, chopped mushrooms, bread crumbs, oregano, salt, pepper, and Parmesan cheese. Stuff the onions with this, dusting more cheese on top.

Put these in a close-fitting buttered baking dish, dust with more cheese, put a tablespoon of butter over each onion and bake, covered with foil, 1/2 to 3/4 of an hour.
Mrs. Charles Eisman

Onion Puffs

Cut Bermuda onions into 1/4-inch slices. Separate into rings and soak overnight in milk to cover. Drain and dredge in salted flour. Dip in milk and dredge in flour again. Fry in deep fat at 380° until pale brown. Drain well and set aside. These can be done at any time. Before serving fry them again. They will puff up like small doughnuts and will not smell oniony the second time. Allow 1 large onion per serving.
Mrs. James Donovan

Painter's Salad

Mushrooms diced
Ox-tongue, cooked and cubed
Carrots, diced
Onions, sliced thinly
Bacon, diced and fried crisp.

Sauté separately in butter until tender equal quantities of all the above. Season delicately with only salt and pepper, then combine them, reheating, just before serving. Serve as an accompaniment to a meat course.
Mrs. Frank Griffith Dawson

Onion Custard

350° / 6 servings

1 pound white onions
4 tablespoons butter
3 eggs
1 cup cream
1 teaspoon salt
1/4 teaspoon nutmeg
2 slices Canadian bacon, cut into small bits

Peel and thinly slice the onions. Sauté them in butter until cooked but not brown, about 15 minutes. Cool. Lightly beat the eggs. Beat in the cream, salt, and nutmeg. Mix with the onions. Place in a greased shallow baking dish that can be used for serving (about a 4-cup size.) Place the bacon on top and bake uncovered until set and lightly browned, 20 to 25 minutes.
Miss Alice Roberts

Sweet and Sour Onions

4 servings

2 pounds tiny pickling onions
2 teaspoons of sugar
White wine or consommé to cover
1 bay leaf
1/2 teaspoon of dried thyme
1 tablespoon of vinegar
Salt and pepper
Chopped parsley

Simmer the peeled onions slowly in the remaining ingredients, adding the salt and pepper toward the end of cooking. When they are tender, but not overcooked, remove the onions and reduce the sauce. Pour the sauce back over the onions, sprinkle them with parsley and serve either hot or cold.
Miss Sara Andrews

Peas with Celery and Mushrooms

4 servings

1 cup finely chopped celery
1 cup chicken stock
2 cups fresh garden peas
1/8 pound fresh mushrooms, sliced

1/4 teaspoon salt, or to taste
1 whole canned pimiento, chopped or diced

Cook the celery in chicken stock over moderate heat for 10 minutes. Add the peas and mushrooms, reduce the heat, and simmer uncovered for 5 to 10 minutes, cooking only until the peas are tender. Salt to taste. Garnish with the diced pimiento.
Herbert Powell

Hot or Cold Italian Stuffed Peppers

375° / 6 servings as an appetizer

6 medium-sized green peppers
1 cup tomatoes, peeled, seeded, and cut up
3 cloves of garlic
1 can anchovies with their oil
2 tablespoons olive oil
Dry bread crumbs
Butter

Cut the peppers in 4 pieces lengthwise. Scoop out the seeds and fibres. Chop the other ingredients, mixing them thoroughly with enough bread crumbs to make a firm consistency. Stuff the peppers, arrange them in an oiled baking pan, dot with butter, and bake for 1/2 hour or until tender. Serve hot or cold.
Mrs. Henry T. Rowell

Shannon Champ

6 servings

6 leeks, chopped
4 tablespoons butter
8 potatoes, peeled
1-1/2 cups hot milk
2 tablespoons butter
Salt
White pepper
Paprika

Sauté the leeks in 4 tablespoons of butter until soft. Boil the potatoes until tender; drain and mash with the hot milk and 2 tablespoons of butter. Combine with the leeks, add salt and pepper to taste, top with paprika, and place under a hot broiler for a minute or two.
Mrs. W. Boulton Kelly

Sauerkraut with a Dash of Gin

6 to 8 servings

1 can (1 pound 10 ounces) sauerkraut
1 cup water or chicken broth
1 apple, finely chopped
1/2 cup onion, finely chopped
2 ounces gin
3 tablespoons sugar
Coarse black pepper
1 small section of spareribs or a turkey neck

Rinse the sauerkraut in cold water and drain. Add 1 cup water or chicken broth, apple, onion, gin, sugar, pepper, and spareribs or a turkey neck and cook for 2 hours on top of the stove over low heat. Cool overnight. Remove the meat and the fat, which will have risen to the top. Reheat before serving.
Mrs. Walter G. Lohr

Spinaci

ITALIAN SPINACH

4 servings

1/2 cup consommé (homemade or canned)
2 pounds spinach
1 clove garlic, stuck on a toothpick
1 tablespoon olive oil
2 tablespoons butter
Pepper and salt (consommé may be salty if canned, so be careful)
Nutmeg

Bring the consommé to a boil; add the garlic and spinach, well washed and picked over. Simmer about 10 minutes. Remove the garlic and drain the spinach well. Chop the spinach; add the seasoning to taste. Heat the oil and butter in a skillet until it stops foaming but not until it browns. Stir in the spinach and heat thoroughly.

Watery spinach is horrid, but dry, carefully seasoned spinach is just lovely. To achieve that much to be desired state of grace, put it, after boiling and before chopping, in the potato ricer and really bear down on it. It's like magic. *Edward L. Brewster*

Spinach and Ricotta Balls

2 servings

1 pound spinach or 1 package frozen spinach
3/4 pound ricotta
1/2 teaspoon salt
4 tablespoons grated Parmesan cheese
2 egg yolks
2 teaspoons flour
1/4 cup melted butter

Boil the spinach for about 5 minutes. Squeeze dry and chop fine. Mix thoroughly the spinach, ricotta, salt, 2 tablespoons of the Parmesan cheese, and the egg yolks. When well mixed, form into balls about 1-1/4-inch in diameter and roll in the flour. Drop, a few at a time, into a large pot of simmering water and cook about 4 to 5 minutes. Keep warm until all are done. Sprinkle with the butter and the rest of the cheese before serving.

Edward L. Brewster

Spinach with Sour Cream Topping

350° / 4 servings

2 pounds fresh spinach
Salt
Butter
Nutmeg
1 cup sour cream
4 teaspoons prepared horseradish
1/4 teaspoon salt
1/4 teaspoon prepared mustard

Cook and chop the fresh spinach. Drain it well, using a potato ricer for the job. Season it well with the salt and nutmeg. Put it in an ovenproof dish, dot with butter and spread with the sour cream mixed with the horseradish, salt, and mustard. Heat it for about 30 minutes. This may be prepared early in the day to be heated at serving time. *Mrs. Thomas Schweizer*

Jannson's Temptation

400° / 6 servings

15 anchovy fillets
2 large onions
5 potatoes
4 tablespoons butter
1 pint heavy cream

Soak the anchovies in cold running water for a few minutes. Peel the onions and slice thinly. Peel the potatoes and cut into somewhat larger than match-stick size. Sauté the onions in 2 tablespoons butter. Arrange half of the potatoes in a shallow casserole, put the onions and drained anchovies on top, and add the rest of the potatoes. Pour half the cream and a little oil from the anchovy can over this. Dot with 2 tablespoons of butter. Bake until the potatoes are golden brown; add the rest of the cream and bake until the potatoes are tender, about 50 minutes altogether. Serve piping hot.

Another version from Denmark uses grated potatoes and herring instead of the anchovies and the dish is finished off with a dusting of cheese.

Edward L. Brewster

Holiday Spinach Ring

350° / 6 servings

2 pounds fresh spinach or 2 packages frozen spinach
1 cup thick sour cream
1/4 cup medium-sweet sherry
3 eggs, well beaten
2 tablespoons grated onion
1/4 teaspoon nutmeg
Salt, pepper, and MSG to taste

Cook the spinach, squeeze dry, and chop. Combine the spinach with the other ingredients and mix well. Pour into a well buttered ring mold (1-1/4-quart size), set in a shallow pan of hot water, and bake 40 to 45 minutes until the old broom corn says it is done. Let it stand a few minutes before unmolding. Fill the center with little creamed white onions and garnish with paprika.

You can also fill the center with chicken à la king, shrimp Newburg or such and use it as the main course of a small luncheon.

Edward L. Brewster

Savory Chopped Spinach

350° / 3 servings

1 10-ounce package frozen chopped spinach
1 3-ounce package cream cheese, softened
3 slices bacon
1/2 cup sour cream
1 tablespoon minced green onion
1 tablespoon horseradish
Salt to taste

Cook the spinach according to package directions. Drain thoroughly, then add the cream cheese and stir until blended. Cook the bacon until crisp, drain on paper toweling, and crumble. In a greased 1-1/2-pint casserole combine the spinach mixture with the bacon and remaining ingredients. Bake for 20 to 30 minutes or until thoroughly heated.

Miss Addie Flipper

Spinach with Rich Cheese Sauce

6 servings

1/3 cup dry vermouth
2 tablespoons cornstarch
2 tablespoons milk
1-1/2 cups medium cream
1/4 teaspoon salt
White pepper
1/2 cup Swiss cheese, grated
2-1/2 pounds spinach, cooked and well drained

Reduce the vermouth by boiling to 1 tablespoon. Remove from the heat. Stir in the cornstarch blended with the milk, then add the cream and seasonings. Simmer for 2 minutes, stirring. Blend in the cheese and simmer for 1 minute more. Pour over the hot spinach and glaze briefly under the broiler until the cheese sauce browns and bubbles.

Mrs. Thomas Brown

Baked Winter Squash

350° / 6 servings

3 or 4 pounds winter squash (acorn, Hubbard, or butternut)
3 tablespoons brown sugar
3 tablespoons butter

Peel and dice squash in 1/2-inch cubes and place in a greased baking dish. Sprinkle with the brown sugar and dot with the butter. Bake for 1 hour. Mash the squash with a fork before serving.

Miss Sue McCoy, Mrs. Edward Stimpson

Baked Acorn Squash

400° / 4 servings

2 acorn squash
1/4 cup raisins
1/4 cup brown sugar
1-1/2 cups apple sauce
1 tablespoon chopped walnuts (optional)
1/4 cup Rose's lime juice
1 tablespoon Worcestershire sauce
Salt and pepper
Butter

Halve the squash and remove the seeds. Mix the remaining ingredients except the butter and fill the cavities of the squash. Dot with the butter, place in a baking dish with 1/2 inch of hot water, and bake for 45 to 60 minutes. *Edward L. Brewster*

Summer Squash with Onions

4 servings

6 cups diced squash
1-1/2 cups diced onions
1/4 cup butter
2 teaspoons salt
1/4 teaspoon pepper

In a saucepan melt 1/4 cup butter, add the onions, and sauté until light brown; add the squash, 2 teaspoons salt, and 1/4 teaspoon pepper. Cover the saucepan and cook slowly without stirring for 10 minutes; then remove the lid and cook the squash for 30 minutes, stirring frequently. This may also be baked in a buttered casserole, covered, at 400° for 1 hour. Serve the squash sprinkled with paprika.

Mrs. Norman P. Ramsey, T. Bolling Robertson

Stuffed Tomatoes

350° / 8 servings

16 medium-size tomatoes
1 large onion, chopped fine
1 tablespoon butter
1 pound ground beef
1/2 pound ground lamb
Pulp from tomatoes
Salt and pepper to taste
1 tablespoon sugar, or more to taste
1 teaspoon chopped parsley
2 tablespoons dried mint (thisosmo)
2/3 cup long grain rice

Slice tops from tomatoes, reserving the caps. Scoop out the pulp with a teaspoon. Discard the hard centers, but place the remaining tomato pulp and juice in a bowl to be used later. Fry the chopped onion in butter in a large skillet until golden brown. Add ground beef and lamb and stir constantly until brown. Then add the tomato pulp, salt, pepper, sugar, parsley, mint, and 3 cups of water. Bring to the boiling point, add the rice, and stir. Continue cooking on a low flame for about 15 minutes or until rice is half cooked and the mixture has absorbed most of the liquid. Spoon the mixture into the tomatoes, replace the caps, and arrange tomatoes closely in a metal or glass baking pan. Pour in enough boiling water to cover the bottom of the pan. Bake for 1 hour.

Mrs. James Cianos

Bessarabian Nightmare

350° / 4 to 6 servings

6 tomatoes, peeled and sliced
2 medium onions, peeled and sliced
1 red or green pepper, seeded and sliced
3/4 teaspoon salt
1/8 teaspoon cayenne pepper
1/4 cup cooking oil
1/4 teaspoon garlic powder

Arrange the vegetables in layers in a casserole. Combine the seasonings with the oil, pour over the vegetables, cover tightly and bake for 45 minutes. Serve with hot cooked noodles, rice, or grits.

Mrs. William T. Baker

Fried Baked Tomatoes

350°

Tomatoes
Flour
Bacon fat
Sugar

Wash and cut tomatoes in half; if they are large, cut them in thirds. Sprinkle flour over them and fry them in hot bacon fat about 15 minutes on each side, until they are very brown. They should be turned only once, if possible.

Rub a Pyrex dish with butter and sprinkle lightly with granulated sugar. Put tomatoes in this dish and sprinkle with sugar, salt, pepper, and paprika. They are baked for as long as an hour and can be prepared a day ahead of time.

Mrs. J. Richard Thomas

Italian Zucchini

4 servings

1 onion, sliced thin
2 tablespoons salad oil
1/4 cup water
1 pound zucchini, sliced
1/2 teaspoon salt
Pinch of oregano
Chopped Italian parsley
Parmesan cheese, grated

Cook the onion in the oil, and add the water, zucchini, salt and oregano. Simmer 5 minutes, or until tender, then raise the heat to evaporate the excess liquid. Sprinkle with chopped parsley and grated Parmesan cheese just before serving.

Mrs. Mary F. Barada

Zucchini in Sour Cream

4 servings

1 pound zucchini
1 tablespoon butter
1/2 teaspoon salt
1/4 teaspoon paprika
1 teaspoon sugar
1/2 cup commercial sour cream

Wash the zucchini, trim ends, and shred coarsely. Heat the butter in a large frying pan. Add salt, paprika, and zucchini. Sauté over medium heat for about 5 minutes, stirring. Add sugar, cover the pan, and simmer 5 more minutes or until the zucchini is just tender. Do not overcook. Stir in the sour cream and heat through.   *Mrs. Lee Johnson, II*

Stuffed Zucchini

350° / 2 servings

1 large zucchini or yellow summer squash
1 large egg, well beaten
1/3 cup cottage cheese
1 cup sharp Cheddar cheese, shredded
Chopped parsley and chives
Salt, pepper, and MSG

Boil the squash whole for about 15 minutes, or until tender. Split in half lengthwise and scoop out the seeds. Mix the other ingredients and fill the cavities. Bake 15 to 20 minutes at 350° and then turn up the heat to 450° for 5 to 10 minutes to brown the filling.

This dish can serve as a main course for 2 as given above. By using 3 small squash it makes a nice first course or a vegetable for 6.

Edward L. Brewster

Stuffed Zucchini Gondolas

350° / 8 servings

4 medium-size zucchini
4 tablespoons butter, or less
1/2 pound sausage or ground or canned ham spread
1 clove garlic, finely minced
1/2 teaspoon finely chopped fresh or dried rosemary
2 tablespoons heavy cream or buttermilk
3 tablespoons finely minced parsley, preferably Italian
1/2 cup toasted bread crumbs
1/4 cup freshly grated Parmesan cheese
1 egg, lightly beaten
Salt and freshly ground black pepper
1/2 cup dry white wine or chicken stock
1/2 cup tomato purée or sauce

Trim the ends off the zucchini and split them in half. Using a melon-ball cutter or a small spoon, scoop out and reserve the center pulp of each half, leaving a shell for stuffing. Heat half the butter in a saucepan and cook the scooped-out pulp until wilted.

Meanwhile, cook the sausage, crumbling with a spoon, until done. Pour off all the excess fat. Add the sausage to the pulp, then add the garlic, rosemary, cream, parsley, crumbs, and half the cheese. Stir in the egg and salt and pepper to taste and, when blended, use the mixture to fill the zucchini halves. Sprinkle with the remaining cheese and dot with the remaining butter. Arrange the stuffed halves on a greased shallow baking dish. Pour the wine or chicken stock and tomato purée around the zucchini halves and stir. Bake 30 minutes, or until the zucchini are tender and the filling is golden brown.

Mrs. John H. Rice, Jr.

Bakerpatch Turnips or Parsnips

6 servings

12 yellow turnips (or parsnips), peeled and quartered
2 onions, peeled and quartered
1 cup bouillon
3 cups water
12 mushroom caps
1 tablespoon lemon juice
Salt
Pepper
Parsley
Paprika
2 tablespoons butter
1-1/2 tablespoons flour
1/2 cup cream
1/2 cup beef stock

Peel turnips (or parsnips); boil with onions in bouillon and water, covered, until tender, adding mushroom caps for the last 5 minutes. Drain the vegetables, reserving the liquid. Keep warm. Make

A traveling case, in red leather stamped with gold fleurs-de-lys, for a covered pewter soup dish. Such cases were made for important and fragile tableware which was carried on trips. The case is French, early 18th century.

a roux of butter and flour. When blended, add cream, 3/4 cup hot vegetable liquid, beef stock, lemon juice, salt, and pepper to taste. Mix in the vegetables. Top with chopped parsley and a sprinkle of paprika. *Mrs. W. Boulton Kelly*

Turnips and Onions

4 to 6 servings
16 small turnips, peeled
1 medium onion, minced
4 tablespoons butter
1-1/2 teaspoons sugar
Salt
White pepper
1/4 cup chicken stock

Parboil the turnips in salted water for 15 minutes. Drain and put in a frying pan with the minced onion and butter. Sprinkle with sugar, salt, and white pepper. Sauté until brown, shaking from time to time over a bright flame, about 20 minutes. Deglaze the pan with the chicken stock and pour over the turnips. *Edward L. Brewster*

RICE, PASTA & BEANS

Slow-Cooking Baked Beans

350° / 12 servings

2 20-ounce cans Campbell's baked beans
2 tablespoons Brer Rabbit molasses, mixed with 1/2 cup water
1 large and 1 small onion, cut up
1/4 pound fat back, cut up
1 cup dark brown sugar
3 heaping teaspoons Gulden's dark mustard
1/2 teaspoon Worcestershire sauce

Mix all the ingredients and place in a large casserole with a lid. Bake for 3-1/3 hours. Don't allow the beans to dry out; add hot water, if necessary.

Mrs. T. Garland Tinsley

Delicious Beans

275° / 8 to 10 servings

2 cups dried Navy beans or pea beans
1 onion
2 celery stalks
1 carrot
Parsley
Pinch of soda

Soak the beans overnight in cold water. Next day, drain them; tie onion, celery, carrot, and parsley in cheesecloth and add to the beans with a pinch of soda. Cover beans with boiling water and cook until tender and mealy but not broken. Strain off most of the water (saving this), leaving a cupful on the beans, and discard the cheesecloth bag of vegetables.

Sauce:

1 onion, finely minced
1 clove garlic, finely minced
2 tablespoons butter
2 tablespoons olive oil
2 fresh tomatoes, peeled and cut up
Pinch each of basil and thyme, fresh if possible
Salt and pepper
Paprika
Pinch of dry mustard
1/4 cup white wine

Cook the onion and garlic in butter and oil until tender. Add all the other ingredients; stir, then add the beans and cook a few minutes. If there is not enough liquid to cook the beans without scorching, add some of the reserved bean liquid. Turn into an earthen beanpot, cover, and bake for 2 hours.

Mrs. Alfred Himmelrich

Tabboula

4 to 6 servings

2 cups coarse cracked wheat
1 teaspoon salt
1/2 cup parsley, minced
1/4 cup mint, minced
1/2 cup chopped scallions, both white and green parts
2 tomatoes, peeled, seeded, and chopped
3/4 cup lemon juice
1 cup olive oil, or half olive and sesame oil, or half Wesson oil
Salt and pepper

In a large earthenware casserole with a lid, put the cracked wheat and salt. Cover with boiling water and put the lid on while you prepare the other ingredients; leave covered for 3/4 of an hour. Drain off the excess water and toss the wheat with the other well prepared ingredients. Leave it to marinate for a while. This is especially good with lamb or other grilled meat.   *Mrs. Henry Hays*

Ascanni Italian Spaghetti Sauce

8 servings

1/2 cup Wesson oil
6 cloves garlic
2 onions
4 tablespoons chopped parsley
1 large can tomatoes
2 cans tomato paste
2 teaspoons Worcestershire sauce
1/2 teaspoon Tabasco sauce
Salt and pepper
1-1/2 pounds ground beef
1/2 cup Parmesan cheese
2 eggs, beaten
1 teaspoon basil
1/4 cup milk

Heat 1/4 cup of the oil in a Dutch oven. Add 2 cloves of garlic, cut in thirds, and the onions, cut in large pieces. Cook until soft. Add half the parsley, the tomatoes and tomato paste, Worcestershire sauce and Tabasco, and salt and pepper to taste.

In a large skillet heat the rest of the oil. Add 4 cloves of garlic, minced, and a mixture of the meat, cheese, eggs, chopped parsley, basil, and milk. Cook until the meat loses its pink color; then put it in the Dutch oven. Allow it to boil up once and then simmer it for several hours. Serve with spaghetti which has been cooked al dente. The sauce freezes well in large or small quantities.

Mrs. Richard Lansburgh

Spaghetti Sauce of Three Meats

12 servings

1 pound each of stewing meat: beef, pork, and chicken, cut in large pieces
1 onion
4 garlic cloves, crushed
1 can (16 ounces) tomato paste
1 No. 2-1/2 can Italian tomatoes
3 bay leaves
1 tablespoon basil
1 cup chopped parsley
Juice of 1/2 lemon
1-1/2 pounds small Italian meat balls (or any meat ball recipe)
1 pound spaghetti or pasta shells

Brown the meat pieces in hot fat with the sliced onion and garlic. Add the strained tomatoes and paste. Stir in the seasoning and simmer for 1-1/2 to 2 hours. Add the lemon juice and correct the seasoning.

Have the meat balls and pasta hot; slice the meat, which you have lifted from the sauce and combine it all for a hearty buffet meal. The sauce, reheated, is even better than when it is first made. You will have sauce left over to freeze.

Mrs. Douglas Frost, Mrs. Charles Laidlaw

A red clay jug decorated with storks, Roman, 1st century A.D. The ware was called barbotine; the crisp decoration was applied with a funnel as is the decoration on a cake.

Fettucelli with Green Sauce

8 servings

1 pound fettucelli (a narrow version of fettucine noodles)
1/2 cup parsley, minced
1/2 cup basil, minced
1/2 clove garlic, minced
1/2 cup olive oil
1 cup ricotta
Dash cayenne
Ground black pepper

Cook fettucelli as directed. Keep hot. Crush parsley, basil, and garlic in a mortar with a pestle. Work in the oil, then the cheese. Season with cayenne and lots of freshly ground black pepper. Mix the sauce and fettucelli together and serve immediately. *Mrs. Curran Harvey*

Spaghetti Soufflé

350° / 6 servings

2 tablespoons butter
2 tablespoons flour
2 cups milk
8 tablespoons Parmesan cheese
1 teaspoon mustard
Cayenne
Salt and pepper
1/4 pound spaghetti
5 eggs
Tomato sauce (optional)

Melt the butter, add the flour, cook together a minute, and then add the milk. Stir it until it is quite thick and then add the cheese and stir until the sauce is thick and smooth. Season it well with mustard, cayenne, salt, and pepper. Cook the spaghetti al dente and drain well. Separate the eggs and stir the yolks into the cheese sauce one by one. Add the spaghetti and stir it up well. This may be done well before using it.

A half hour before the meal, beat the whites with a pinch of salt until stiff but not dry. Fold the spaghetti mixture gently into the beaten egg whites and spoon the mixture into a buttered soufflé dish. Bake in a preheated oven for about 25 minutes.

Sliced ham goes well with this soufflé, although a well flavored tomato sauce poured over the portions tastes good too. *Miss Alice Newman*

Spaghetti with Clam Sauce

6 servings

1 pound spaghetti
4 tablespoons olive oil
4 tablespoons butter
2 cloves garlic, minced
4 tablespoons shallots, finely chopped
1-1/2 cups clam juice
2 cups minced clams
1/2 cup chopped parsley
Grated Parmesan cheese

In a saucepan heat the olive oil and butter, add the garlic and the shallots, and sauté over a low fire until the shallots begin to color. Add the clam juice and simmer for 5 minutes. Stir in the clams and the finely chopped parsley. Bring this to a boil, then mix the sauce with the spaghetti (cooked al dente), and serve with grated Parmesan cheese.
Mrs. Jon Alan Wurtzburger

Spaghetti with Meatless Sauce

2 or 3 servings

1/4 cup olive oil
1/2 cup chopped onion
1 pound fresh mushrooms, sliced
1 clove garlic, minced
1 cup condensed consommé
1 cup tomato paste
2/3 cup water
1 teaspoon salt
1/4 teaspoon pepper
1/8 teaspoon ground cloves
Dash cayenne
Bay leaf
1/2 pound spaghetti

Heat the olive oil in a heavy skillet. Add the onion, mushrooms, and garlic. Cook 10 minutes or until the onions start to brown. Add the consommé, tomato paste, water, and seasonings. Simmer over low heat, uncovered, for about 1 hour. Cook the spaghetti al dente, drain, and pour the sauce over it. *Mrs. Arthur Stern*

Spaghetti alla Carbonara

8 servings

1/2 cup diced ham
1/2 cup sliced mushrooms
1/2 cup fried bacon, chopped
4 tablespoons olive oil
2 tablespoons butter
1 pound spaghetti
2 eggs, well beaten
3 tablespoons Parmesan, grated

Sauté the ham, mushrooms, and cooked bacon in olive oil and butter without allowing them to brown. Meanwhile, cook the spaghetti al dente. Beat the eggs and stir in the Parmesan cheese. When the spaghetti has cooked and been drained, quickly add the egg-cheese mixture to the meat and mushrooms and pour over the spaghetti. Toss lightly until the spaghetti is coated and serve immediately. *Mrs. John Eager*

Spaghetti with Pesto Genovese

6 servings

3 cups fresh basil
1 clove garlic
1/4 cup Italian olive oil
3/4 cup pine nuts
4 tablespoons butter
1/2 cup Parmesan cheese
Salt to taste
2 pounds spaghetti

Wash and dry the basil and remove the stems. Place it in a blender with the garlic, olive oil, pine nuts, butter and cheese. Purée. Cook the spaghetti al dente in boiling salted water. Drain and toss at once with the sauce. Add salt, if necessary. Sprinkle with additional cheese.

Malvina C. Kinard

Baked Noodles Parmesan

350°/6 servings

1 8-ounce package noodles
1 clove garlic, minced
1/2 pint sour cream
1/4 teaspoon Tabasco
1-1/2 cups cottage cheese
1 teaspoon Worcestershire
1/2 bunch green onions, finely chopped
1/2 cup Parmesan cheese, grated

Cook noodles according to package directions. Drain. Combine with all but the Parmesan cheese in a buttered casserole. Sprinkle Parmesan cheese on the top. Bake for 1/2 hour or until bubbly. One-half pound ground beef, browned in butter, can be added to this recipe. It can be made the day before and refrigerated; it can even be frozen before baking.

Mrs. John Lalley

Risotto Milanese

4 to 6 servings

4 tablespoons butter
1 cup long grain rice
1 medium onion, finely chopped
3-1/2 cups chicken stock
1/2 teaspoon saffron
3 tablespoons dry white wine or Madeira
1/2 cup sliced mushrooms or dried Italian mushrooms soaked in water (optional)
Additional butter
1/2 cup Parmesan cheese, grated

Melt the butter in a heavy saucepan. When hot, stir in the rice. Continue stirring until pale gold in color, then add 1 chopped onion. Cook a brief moment and add 1 cup of chicken stock, preferably freshly made. Cover the pan and cook slowly over low heat until the liquid is absorbed; then add saffron that has been dissolved in white wine or Madeira. Add 2-1/2 cups hot chicken stock. If desired, add the mushrooms at this point. Cover and continue cooking until all the liquid is absorbed and the rice is fluffy. Add a lump of butter and the Parmesan cheese. Stir very lightly and serve at once. This is usually served with chicken or veal.

Mrs. Thomas Brown, Mrs. G. Cheston Carey, Jr.

Sour Cream Rice

350° / 4 to 6 servings

2 tablespoons sugar
2 cups sour cream
2 cups cooked rice, salted
1 pound sharp cheese, grated
Red pepper, crushed

Combine sugar and sour cream. In a not-too-deep casserole put a layer of rice, then the sour cream, then the cheese. Sprinkle with red pepper (not too much!) Repeat the layers. Bake for 30 minutes, turn off the oven, and let it sit for 10 to 15 minutes. *Miss Juli Alderman*

Risotto with Chicken Livers

20 servings

5 onions
1 cup olive oil
5 cups of rice
2 quarts chicken broth
1 teaspoon Spanish saffron
1 pound mushrooms
3/4 cup butter
1-1/4 pounds chicken livers
1/2 cup flour
Salt and pepper
Parmesan or Romano cheese, grated

Chop the onions very fine and let them cook in the oil until transparent. Wash the rice and put it with the onions, stirring as you do so. Add a little broth and as it is absorbed add a little more until the rice is just cooked and the grains are quite separate. Season and add the saffron, which has been soaked in a little broth. (The saffron is certainly not an essential to the dish.)

Brown the mushrooms lightly in the butter. Roll the chicken livers in the flour and sauté them along with the mushrooms. Add 1 quart of chicken broth, salt, and pepper and cook until the chicken livers are just done, about 10 minutes.

At serving time, put a helping of the rice on a plate, making a depression on top. Put a spoonful of the chicken livers in it and sprinkle the cheese over the top, or pass it separately. If you have only one receptacle, you might combine the two, but it is not so pretty nor is the texture so good. *Mrs. Robert A. Milch*

Mexican Rice

6 servings

1-1/4 cups uncooked brown rice
2 large tomatoes, peeled and sliced
1 small onion, sliced
1 clove garlic, sliced
1/2 cup butter
1 cup cold water
2 teaspoons salt
2 cups beef broth

Soak rice for 15 minutes in hot water to cover. Rinse in cold water, drain thoroughly. Combine tomatoes, onions, and garlic in a blender. Blend until puréed. Melt the butter; fry the rice in it until golden. Add the tomato purée and simmer until dry. Add 1 cup cold water and salt. Cook until the water is absorbed. Heat the broth until boiling, add to the rice, cover, and simmer until the rice is dry. *Mrs. James Grieves*

Mock Ravioli Sauce

350° / 6 to 8 servings

1 onion, chopped
1/2 clove garlic, minced
1 pound ground beef
1 3-ounce can sliced mushrooms
3 cans tomato sauce
1 can tomato paste
1 cup water
3/4 teaspoon each basil, oregano, and rosemary
Salt and pepper to taste

Sauté the onion and minced garlic together until limp; add the ground beef, stir briefly, add the other ingredients, and simmer it all for about 2 hours. You may need to add some water to this as it cooks down. Meanwhile, mix together the following ingredients and set aside.

1/4 cup salad oil
1 package frozen chopped spinach, thawed
1/4 cup minced parsley
1/2 cup bread crumbs
1/4 cup Parmesan cheese
1/2 teaspoon sage
1/2 teaspoon salt

Mock Ravioli Casserole:

1/2 pound butterfly noodles, cooked al dente and drained
Mock ravioli sauce
Spinach mixture
8 ounces cottage cheese

In a greased casserole, build layers of the above ingredients, beginning and ending with the noodles. Bake for 30 or 40 minutes. While this is planned for the younger generation, thanks to the spices it appeals to more sophisticated tastes as well.

Mrs. Cynthia Hopkins

Gougère with Ham and Sour Cream

375° / 4 servings

1 cup milk
1/4 cup butter or margarine
Salt and pepper
1 cup flour
4 eggs
1/3 cup shredded Swiss cheese
2 tablespoons diced Swiss cheese

Spread:

2 cups ground ham
3/4 cup sour cream
Onion juice
Salt and pepper

Put the milk and butter into a heavy pan with the salt and pepper. As soon as the butter has melted, add the flour all at once and stir vigorously until the dough is smooth and has left the sides of the pan. This is a cream-puff dough. Remove from the heat, and beat in the eggs one at a time. Add the shredded cheese and put it all in a 10-inch pie plate which has been greased and floured. Sprinkle the diced cheese on top and put it in a 375° oven for 5 minutes, turn the heat down, and bake for 25 minutes more at 350° or until puffed and lightly browned.

Serve this hot, spread with the ham and sour cream mixture, as a luncheon dish, or you might like to roll the gougère with the ham inside it and then slice it like a jelly roll. *Mrs. Charles Bang*

Cheese Crêpes

4 servings

12 crêpes
1 pint cottage cheese
1 can Campbell's cheese soup
Grated Parmesan cheese

Make the crêpes from any good recipe and put a large tablespoon of highly seasoned cottage cheese in each. Fold over and place, folded side down, in a buttered baking dish. Pour over them the cheese soup or, less simply, a thick cheese sauce, and sprinkle with lots of grated Parmesan cheese. Put the dish under the broiler to brown.

Mrs. John T. King, Jr.

Gnocchi with Cheese

350° / 6 servings

1 quart milk
1/2 cup butter
1 cup hominy grits
1 teaspoon salt
1/8 teaspoon pepper

1/3 cup butter, melted
3/4 cup grated Gruyère cheese
1/2 cup grated Parmesan cheese

Scald the milk, add the butter, and then stir in the hominy grits, salt, and pepper. Cook, stirring often, until it is quite thick. Pour it evenly into a 9 x 12 x 2-inch pan and cool it. When it is quite cold, cut it into even rectangular pieces. Grease a flat ovenproof dish with butter and put in the pieces, overlapping each other. Pour the melted butter and the grated cheeses over the gnocchi and heat about 30 minutes. Put under the broiler then until the surface is bubbly.

Mrs. Charles M. Buchanan

Sardi's Restaurant Cannelloni

350°

Crêpes:

3 eggs
1 cup flour
Salt to taste
2 tablespoons melted butter
1-1/2 cups milk, approximately
2 tablespoons Cognac

Beat the eggs slightly, add the flour, salt, butter, and enough milk to make a thin batter the consistency of cream. Add the Cognac and blend it all in a blender at high speed for a few seconds. Refrigerate the batter for 2 hours. Pour by spoonfuls on a lightly greased griddle and brown the crepes lightly on both sides. This makes about 16 crêpes.

Cannelloni Meat Sauce:

1 pound ground beef
1/4 pound ground veal
1/4 teaspoon ground sage
1/4 teaspoon oregano
1 tablespoon salt
1/2 teaspoon pepper
1 onion, grated
1/4 pound mushrooms, chopped fine
3 cloves garlic, minced
4 cups canned tomatoes
1 cup tomato purée
1/2 cup tomato paste

Mix the beef and veal together, spread it in a pan, and cook for 20 minutes in the oven. Then stir it and continue cooking it for another 10 minutes. Meanwhile, in a saucepan, combine the herbs, salt, pepper, onion, mushrooms, and garlic; heat them while stirring on top of the stove. Spread the mixture over the meat in the oven and cook it for another 15 minutes. Remove the mixture from the oven, put it in a large saucepan, add the tomato ingredients, and after stirring them all together, simmer it for 1-1/4 hours. Correct the seasoning and cool. (This makes 6 cups; it may be frozen, and used for things other than cannelloni, such as spaghetti and lasagne.)

Cannelloni Filling

2 cups ground or finely chopped cooked chicken
1/2 cup cooked spinach, finely chopped
1/4 cup grated Parmesan cheese
3/4 cup chicken stock

Combine the first 3 ingredients, add the chicken stock and cook over a low flame for 20 minutes, stirring occasionally. Cool.

Cannelloni Sauce — A Velouté and Meat Sauce

4 tablespoons butter
4 tablespoons flour
1-1/2 cups chicken stock
White pepper and salt to taste
3/4 cup grated Cheddar cheese
1 cup cannelloni meat sauce
1/2 cup or slightly more heavy cream
Freshly grated Parmesan cheese

A parcel-gilt silver *kovsh*, presented to a citizen of Moscow by the Empress Elizabeth I of Russia sometime after 1752. It bears the imperial double eagle of Russia and is typical of the honorary drinking cups of this form that were used to reward deserving subjects.

In a saucepan melt the butter, stir in the flour, then the chicken stock, stirring it rapidly with a wire whisk until the sauce is smooth and thick. Cook for about 5 minutes over low heat, then season it with salt and pepper and stir in the cheese until it melts, and finally add the meat sauce and cream.

Preheat the oven to 450°. Spread each crêpe with a little of the chicken-spinach mixture and roll up. Put the rolled crêpes side by side in a casserole dish, mask with the cannelloni sauce, sprinkle with the freshly grated Parmesan cheese, dot with bits of butter, and bake in a hot oven for 10 minutes, until brown and bubbling. Serve immediately.

Mrs. Donald Brown

Lentil Casserole

350° / 6 to 8 servings

1 pound lentils
2 small onions, peeled
Bouquet garni of 1 bay leaf, 1 teaspoon thyme, 8-10 peppercorns
Salt and freshly ground pepper
1 pound Polish sausage, thinly sliced
1 small onion, peeled and minced
2 tablespoons butter
2 tablespoons flour
1-1/2 cups lentil liquid
1/2 cup tomato catsup

Wash the lentils and drain them. Pour them into a large pot and bury the 2 whole onions and the bouquet garni. Add boiling water to cover, bring to the boil, reduce the heat to a simmer, cover, and cook 30 minutes. Remove the onions and the bouquet garni. Drain, reserving liquid, and add seasoning. Mix the cooked lentils with sliced sausage and minced onion, and put them into a buttered casserole.

Melt the butter in a saucepan, add the flour, and stir until smooth. Gradually add 1-1/2 cups lentil liquid and stir until it thickens slightly. Add 1/2 cup catsup. Pour over the lentils in the casserole. Bake for 40 minutes.

Mrs. Bertram Bernheim, Jr.

Hominy Soufflé

350° / 6 servings

3/4 cup hominy grits
1 cup boiling water
2 cups milk
1/4 cup melted butter
3 eggs, separated
Salt

In the top part of a double boiler over direct heat pour hominy grits into the rapidly boiling water. Cook rapidly for a few minutes and then stir in 1 cup of the milk. Put over the bottom of the double boiler containing hot water and cook, covered, for 30 minutes. Remove from the heat; stir in the other cup of milk and the melted butter. Return to the double boiler to smooth it, then, off the heat, stir in the well beaten egg yolks. Cool thoroughly. Do this any time during the day.

Forty-five minutes before serving time, beat the whites until stiff and fold into the grits mixture. Taste for saltiness. Spoon soufflé into a buttered baking dish and bake for 45 minutes, or until it is golden on top. Dot with a little extra butter before serving.
Miss Joan Chetne

In a heavy saucepan cook the onions and garlic in butter and olive oil. When limp but not brown, add the beef and cook, stirring frequently, until well done. Add the wine; cover tightly and steam for 5 minutes. Add the basil, tomato paste, purée, and juice. Add the green pepper, celery, salt, pepper, and nutmeg and cook for 10 minutes. Boil lasagne in salted water for 20 minutes. Plunge in cold water for ease in handling, then drain.

Place 1/4 of the sauce in a shallow 3-quart baking dish. Place 1/3 of the mozzarella, sliced, on top of the sauce, interspersed with spoonfuls of ricotta. Sprinkle with Parmesan cheese. Over this put 4 ribbons of lasagne, overlapping. Repeat layer of sauce and cheese, making 3 layers of lasagne. On the top layer of sauce, omit the ricotta, adding only mozzarella cheese and Parmesan. Bake for 3/4 of an hour. Serve with additional Parmesan, red wine, and a salad.
Mrs. Henry T. Rowell, Mrs. Jon Alan Wurtzburger

Lasagne

350° / 6 servings

3 medium onions, chopped
2 garlic cloves, chopped
2 tablespoons butter
2 tablespoons olive oil
1 pound lean chopped beef
4 ounces red wine
1 teaspoon basil
1 cup tomato paste
1 cup tomato purée
2 cups tomato juice
1 green pepper, chopped
2 stalks celery, chopped
1 teaspoon salt
Pepper to taste
1 teaspoon freshly ground nutmeg
12 ribbons of lasagne
1/2 pound mozzarella cheese
8 ounces ricotta or cottage cheese
Freshly grated Parmesan cheese

SALADS

Cauliflower and Broccoli Salad

8 servings

1 head cauliflower in flowerets
1 head broccoli in flowerets
Vinaigrette dressing
A bowl about the size of a cauliflower head
Chopped parsley
Chopped hard-cooked egg

  Cook the broccoli and the cauliflower for 5 minutes in lots of boiling salted water. Drain well on paper towels. Stack the flowerets, alternating colors in the bowl, so that when the bowl is reversed onto a plate, the mound will look like a big parti-colored head. Place 1/2 cup of vinaigrette dressing over the vegetables while they are in the bowl, press down lightly (so it will hold its shape when turned out), and refrigerate for a couple of hours. Unmold and sprinkle with chopped parsley and egg before serving. This may be passed as an hors d'oeuvre with curried mayonnaise or served as a salad.

Mrs. Benjamin Griswold, IV

Cole Slaw with Beans

4 servings

1/2 teaspoon ground pepper
1 teaspoon salt
1/2 cup sugar
1 teaspoon prepared mustard
1/2 cup vinegar
2 beaten eggs
1 tablespoon butter
1/2 teaspoon celery seed
1 chopped onion
1 cup cooked kidney beans
2 cups coarsely chopped cabbage
2 or 3 chopped dill pickles

  Dissolve the pepper, salt, sugar, and mustard in the vinegar. Put this in the top of a double boiler with the beaten eggs and cook, stirring, over simmering water until it is thick and smooth. Off the fire, add the butter and then cool the dressing. Mix it with the celery seed, chopped onion, kidney beans, coarsely chopped cabbage, and pickles. Serve it well chilled.

Mrs. Victor Sulin

Marinated Tomatoes

6 servings

6 medium tomatoes
1 cup pitted ripe olives
2 cups chopped onion
1/4 cup fresh chopped parsley

1 teaspoon salt
2 teaspoons sugar
1/8 teaspoon turmeric
3/4 teaspoon cumin
1/4 teaspoon pepper
6 tablespoons olive oil
4 tablespoons lemon juice

Slice the tomatoes and mix with the olives, onion, and parsley. Marinate for at least 2 hours in a dressing made with the other ingredients. Serve cold.

Mrs. Edgar Sweren

Lentil Salad

4 servings

1 cup dried lentils
1 cup olive oil
1/4 cup tarragon vinegar
1/2 teaspoon salt
1/2 teaspoon dry mustard
1 teaspoon paprika
1/4 teaspoon pepper
1/2 cup sweet pickle relish
1/4 cup chopped shallots

Cook the lentils until just done in 1 quart water. If you overcook them, throw them away and begin again, for these must be tender, but firm. Make a dressing of the other ingredients, pour it over the lentils, and let it stand for a while before serving. Present the salad platter with plenty of chopped parsley and chives, a border of thinly sliced and seeded tomatoes, and perhaps a little riced egg in the very center for color. *Mrs. Alan Wurtzburger*

White Bean Salad

6 servings

1-1/2 cups pea beans
2 quarts boiling water
1 teaspoon basil
1/2 teaspoon thyme
2 teaspoons salt
1/4 teaspoon pepper
Bouquet garni
Bay leaf
Celery tops

Soak the beans overnight, drain, cover with 2 quarts boiling water and seasoning. Cook slowly 1 to 2 hours or until tender but firm. Chill.

Dressing for White Bean Salad

3 tablespoons olive oil
3 tablespoons lemon juice
1-1/2 teaspoons salt
1/4 teaspoon pepper
1/4 cup chopped chives
1/4 cup chopped parsley

Make the dressing and pour over the beans an hour before using. *Mrs. Bertram Bernheim, Jr.*

An Irish Salad Dressing

1 can Campbell's tomato soup
1/4 cup water
1/2 cup cider vinegar
1/3 cup sugar
2 teaspoons salt
2 teaspoons mustard
1 tablespoon Worcestershire sauce
1 large clove garlic
1-1/2 cups olive oil

Put all but the olive oil in a blender at medium speed to mix thoroughly, and then at high speed slowly add the olive oil so that the mixture thickens and homogenizes. In a tightly covered glass jar this dressing will keep for weeks at room temperature. If it separates slightly it is because it was not blended enough, but don't worry about it; just shake it up and use it anyhow. Don't keep this invention of an Irish cook in the refrigerator; it congeals then and looks messy. *Edward L. Brewster*

Tomato and Pepper Salad

6 servings

4 green peppers
6 firm tomatoes
2 tablespoons lemon juice
6 tablespoons oil
Salt and pepper
1/2 clove garlic, minced
Capers

Put the peppers under a hot broiler and roast them until the skin is charred black. Cool and skin them, remove the seeds and membranes, and chop them. Skin the tomatoes and remove the seeds and liquid by cutting them in half and squeezing gently. Chop these too, and drain. Combine the lemon, oil, salt, pepper, and garlic. Mix with the vegetables and strew some washed capers over the salad.

Or, if peppers do not appeal to you, make a salad in the same way but add either oregano or dill to the marinade. The tomatoes can be peeled but left whole, with chopped onion or a bouquet of dill in the cavities.

Mrs. Douglas N. Sharretts, Mrs. Edward Simpson, Mrs. Henry Wyman

Bermuda Salad

6 to 8 servings

1 small cauliflower, broken into flowerets
2 heads romaine, broken up
14 large stuffed olives, sliced
1/4 cup Roquefort cheese, crumbled
2 eggs well beaten
2 cups vegetable salad oil
3 tablespoons powdered sugar
1-1/2 teaspoons salt
1/4 teaspoon pepper
6-1/2 tablespoons vinegar
2 teaspoons granulated sugar
1-1/2 teaspoons prepared mustard
1 tablespoon paprika

Crisp the cauliflower in ice water. At serving time, put the romaine, olives, cauliflower, and cheese into a large bowl. Beat eggs until thick, slowly add oil, seasoning, and then vinegar. Add the remaining ingredients and beat until very thick. Pour over the salad and toss well.

Mrs. William Little

Tomato Aspic

6 servings

2 envelopes gelatin
1/2 cup cold water
Bouquet garni of 2 bay leaves, 3 whole cloves, 6 whole peppers
2 cups V-8 juice
1 small onion, chopped
1 stalk celery, chopped
Lemon juice
1 teaspoon salt
1 teaspoon Worcestershire sauce
Dash of cayenne
1 8-ounce carton cottage cheese
3 tablespoons mayonnaise
1/2 cup chopped stuffed olives

Soak the gelatin in the water. Add the bouquet garni to the V-8 juice and simmer with the onion and celery until flavorful. Strain, reserve the onion and celery, and add the gelatin. Stir until the gelatin is dissolved; add the lemon juice and the other seasoning and cool. Pour half the mixture with the cooked onion and celery into a mold and chill it until firm.

Mix the mayonnaise into the cottage cheese, beat until smooth, and spread over the stiff aspic. If the remaining half of the aspic has become too firm it will have to be melted again before adding the chopped olives to it. Pour this over the cottage cheese and chill the whole mold again. Turn out on a platter large enough to hold salad greens around the aspic and serve with additional mayonnaise.

Instead of the cottage cheese, hard-boiled eggs, the yolks combined with caviar, or a layer of cooked vegetables, may be used.

Miss Eleanor Holliday Cross

Sauerkraut Salad

6 to 8 servings

2-1/2 cups or 1 can (1 pound 4 ounces) sauerkraut
1/2 cup vinegar
1 cup sugar
3/4 cup chopped celery
3/4 cup chopped onion
1/2 cup chopped green pepper
1 small can pimientos, drained and finely chopped

Drain the sauerkraut and squeeze it dry. Boil the vinegar and sugar together until the sugar is completely dissolved. Mix with the other vegetables and chill. This will keep very well for several weeks.

Mrs. Roger A. Clapp, Mrs. Victor Sulin

Marinated Cucumbers

4 to 6 servings

1 cup oil
1/2 cup vinegar
1 tablespoon sugar
Salt and pepper
1 medium onion, peeled and sliced
2 cucumbers, peeled and sliced

Stir together in a quart jar the oil, vinegar, sugar, salt, and pepper. Then alternate the onions and cucumbers, adding a pinch of salt and pepper after each layer. When the jar is filled, cover with the top and shake hard. Refrigerate at least 12 hours before using them. They will hold their flavor and consistency 10 days to 2 weeks.

Mrs. Edward Stimpson, Mrs. Jack B. Wasserman

An ivory mortar and pestle for crushing herbs. It is a German work of the late 17th century.

Cold Spinach Mold with Tart Cream Dressing

8 servings

3 pounds spinach
Salt and pepper
Nutmeg to taste
2 tablespoons French dressing
2 tablespoons cream
2 tablespoons homemade mayonnaise
1 hard-boiled egg

Cook, drain, and chop the spinach well and season it highly. Add the dressing, cream, mayonnaise, and the mashed egg yolks to the spinach. Use the egg white, chopped, as a decoration in the bottom of a 4-cup mold. Spoon the spinach mixture into the mold and chill well. Turn out and serve with the following sauce.

Tart Cream Dressing

2 egg yolks, well beaten
1 tablespoon white wine vinegar
1 tablespoon prepared mustard
1/2 teaspoon pepper
1 tablespoon lemon juice
1 tablespoon sugar
1/2 teaspoon salt
1/2 teaspoon paprika
1 tablespoon butter
1 cup cream, whipped

Combine all the ingredients but the butter and whipped cream in the top of a double boiler and cook over simmering water, stirring constantly, until smooth and thick. Off the heat, add the butter. When the dressing is well chilled, fold in the cream, whipped and lightly salted.

Mrs. Frank N. Weller

Still life of utensils and food in a Dutch kitchen, detail from a kitchen scene of the 17th century.

DESSERTS

Almond Torte

350°

9 eggs
1 cup sugar
1/2 pound blanched almonds, grated
1 teaspoon vanilla
1/2 pint whipping cream
Instant coffee
Chocolate icing

    Separate the eggs and beat the yolks until light; add the sugar and beat until very creamy. Grate the almonds but do not grind them. (It must be remembered that the nuts take the place of flour in tortes and they cannot be oily, as they will be if you mistakenly and hurriedly put them in a blender.) Add the nuts and the vanilla to the egg yolks and sugar.
    Beat the whites until stiff but not dry and fold them in, then pour the mass into 2 buttered and floured 9-inch cake pans and bake for 30 minutes. Put the layers on a wire rack to cool. Finally, beat whipping cream and flavor it with instant coffee to put between the layers. Ice this rich dessert with a chocolate icing.

Mrs. Jerome Gelfand

Chocolate Torte

450°

3/4 pound sweet butter
3/4 pound powdered sugar
12 eggs, separated
3/4 pound grated almonds
1 pound Maillard's sweet chocolate
1-1/2 tablespoons bread crumbs

    Cream the butter well, add the powdered sugar, and beat it again until puffy. Add the egg yolks one at a time. Grate the almonds in a nut grater. Do not grind them nor put them in a blender; they are to be light and fluffy. Melt the chocolate over hot water. Now add the chocolate to the butter mixture, then fold in the almonds and bread crumbs. Finally beat the whites of the eggs until stiff and fold them in gently. Put three-quarters of this mixture in 3 ungreased layer cake pans (the ones with removable bottoms are the most convenient) and bake for 12 to 15 minutes. When the layers are cold, spread them with the remaining batter. Then ice the cake with the following icing.

Chocolate Torte Icing

1 8-ounce bar German Sweet Chocolate
1 cup brown sugar
10 tablespoons cream
1 tablespoon butter
1 teaspoon vanilla
Some whole blanched almonds

Melt the chocolate in a double boiler; stir in the brown sugar and cream, then the butter. Cook it all until it is thick, stirring occasionally. Off the fire, add the vanilla. When the mixture is cool, ice the torte and then decorate the top with the almonds.
Mrs. Walter Rosenbaum

Chocolate Orange Torte

325°

8 eggs, separated
1 pound granulated sugar
1/4 pound bitter chocolate, melted
1/2 pound grated pecans
3 tablespoons bread crumbs
Juice and grated rind of 1 orange
1 teaspoon vanilla
1/4 teaspoon ground cloves
1/4 teaspoon cinnamon
1 teaspoon allspice
1/2 teaspoon baking powder

Beat the yolks until very light; add all the other ingredients, and lastly fold in the stiffly beaten egg whites. Pour the batter into a well buttered deep funnel pan and bake for about 1 hour. The torte should be done but still moist inside. Let it shrink in the pan until it cools, and then it is ready to be turned out of the pan and iced with the following icing.

Chocolate Orange Icing

1 pound confectioner's sugar
5 tablespoons butter, at room temperature
3-1/2 ounces bitter chocolate, melted
Dash of salt
1 heaping tablespoon grated orange rind
7-8 tablespoons orange juice

Cream half the sugar with the butter. Add the melted chocolate, the salt, and the orange rind. Mix thoroughly again. Now gradually add more sugar and some orange juice, watching always that it is becoming the right consistency to spread. You may not use all the juice but do use all the sugar.
Mrs. Howard L. Schloss

Mocha Torte

325°

6 eggs, separated
1 cup sugar
1 cup flour
1 teaspoon baking powder
1 cup strong black coffee

Reduce the coffee to 1/4 cup, which will make enough coffee extract for both the torte and the filling. Beat the egg yolks and sugar together until light and fluffy and a ribbon is formed. Sift the flour and baking powder together and fold into the egg-and-sugar mixture. Add 2 tablespoons of the coffee extract. Beat the egg whites until stiff but not dry and fold them into the batter. Bake in 2 9-inch buttered and floured cake pans for 35 minutes. Cool before filling and icing with the following:

Filling for Mocha Torte

1-1/2 cups whipping cream
6 tablespoons confectioner's sugar
2 remaining tablespoons coffee extract
2 ounces grated semi-sweet chocolate

Whip the cream, stir in the confectioner's sugar, then fold in the coffee extract and chocolate.

Icing for Mocha Torte

2 egg whites, unbeaten

1-1/2 cups sugar
1/8 teaspoon salt
1/3 cup water
2 teaspoons light corn syrup
2 tablespoons instant coffee
1 teaspoon vanilla
2 ounces semi-sweet chocolate, grated

Combine the egg whites, sugar, salt, water, corn syrup, and coffee in the top of a double boiler. Beat with a rotary or electric beater about 1 minute, until completely mixed. Cook over rapidly boiling water, beating constantly until the frosting will stand up in peaks. Remove from the heat and add the vanilla. After frosting the cake, sprinkle chocolate over the top. *Mrs. J. Leo Levy*

Cocoa Torte

325°

8 eggs, separated
2 cups granulated sugar
1 cup cocoa
1 cup flour
2 teaspoons baking powder
2 teaspoons vanilla
1 cup cold water

Beat the egg yolks until light, then add the sugar and beat until they form a ribbon. Sift together the cocoa, flour, and baking powder. Add the vanilla to the water. Now combine these, the liquid alternating with the flour, into the egg mixture. When thoroughly folded in, beat the egg whites until stiff and fold them in gently as one does for a sponge cake.

Pour into 2 9-1/2-inch cake tins, the bottoms of which have been lined with waxed paper. Bake the layers for 35 minutes and invert on racks. Loosen the sides when cool, and spread each layer with whipped cream to which you have added a little vanilla. *Mrs. Louis B. Kohn*

Walnut Torte

350°

3 egg whites
1 scant cup of sugar
1 teaspoon baking powder
1/2 teaspoon salt
1/2 cup walnuts
20 Ritz crackers
3/4 teaspoon vanilla

Beat the whites stiff, then fold into them the sugar, baking powder, and salt. Grate the walnuts and combine them with the Ritz crackers, which have been made into crumbs in the blender. Fold these into the whites with the vanilla. Bake the torte in a greased 9-inch pie pan for 1/2 hour. Top it with whipped cream and some chocolate curls if you like. *Mrs. Arthur Waxter*

Nut Torte

350°

2 cups grated pecans
4 eggs, separated
1 cup sugar
2 tablespoons flour
1/2 teaspoon salt
1/2 teaspoon baking powder
1 tablespoon orange juice or Jamaica rum
1 cup whipping cream
1 teaspoon grated orange rind
6 ounces semi-sweet chocolate pieces
1/2 cup commercial sour cream

With a rotary grater and not a blender, grate 2 cups of pecans. A blender makes the nuts too oily. Beat the egg yolks until thick and light, then beat in the sugar. When it forms a ribbon, stir in the flour, salt, baking powder, orange juice or rum, and the grated nuts. Beat the egg whites stiff and fold them in. Pour into 2 8-inch layer cake pans which have been greased and lined with greased waxed paper. Bake for 25 minutes or until a slight poke leaves no mark. Cool.

Remove from the pans. One or two hours before serving, put the layers together with whipped cream flavored with the grated orange rind. Frost with the following mixture; melt the chocolate pieces over hot water; stir in the sour cream and a speck of salt. When well mixed, spread it over the torte. Garnish with a few grated nuts.

Mrs. Robert A. Milch

Woodford Pudding

350°

1/2 cup butter or margarine
1 cup sugar
3 eggs
1 cup flour (sifted)
1 teaspoon cinnamon
1/2 teaspoon cloves
1/4 teaspoon salt
1/2 teaspoon nutmeg
1 teaspoon soda
1 cup blackberry jam (the kind with seeds)
1/2 cup buttermilk or thick sour milk

Mix as for a cake: cream the butter, add sugar gradually, then when fluffy add the well beaten eggs in thirds. When the mixture is light and smooth, add 1/4 of the sifted dry ingredients, then the jam, then the flour mixture alternately with the buttermilk or sour milk, beginning and ending with flour. Pour it into a greased and floured 9 x 9 x 2-1/2-inch pan. Bake about 30 to 35 minutes or until the pudding tests done. Serve warm, cut in squares, with whipped cream or with one of the following sauces:

Brown Sugar Sauce

1 cup light brown sugar
2 scant tablespoons flour
1 cup water
1/4 cup butter
1 teaspoon vanilla
1 cup whipping cream, beaten stiff

Mix the sugar and flour, then add the water and stir it over the fire until it becomes hot and thick. When it is cool enough to melt the butter slowly, stir it in bit by bit and keep warm. Serve with the whipped cream, flavored with vanilla.

Sunshine Sauce

1 egg, separated
1/2 cup confectioner's sugar
1 tablespoon bourbon whiskey
1/2 cup whipping cream
Salt to taste
Nutmeg

Beat the egg yolk; add the sugar and beat until fluffy; add whiskey; fold in the cream, whipped to a custard consistency; then fold in the softly beaten egg white to which a pinch of salt has been added. A little nutmeg is good in it as the sauce is rather like eggnog.

Mrs. James D. Atkinson

Lemon Fluff Pudding

350°

1 cup sugar
2 tablespoons melted butter
Grated rind of 1 lemon
1/8 teaspoon salt
3 egg yolks, well beaten
4 tablespoons flour
1-1/2 cups milk
5 tablespoons lemon juice
3 egg whites, beaten stiff
Thick cream

Cream the sugar, butter, lemon rind, and salt together, then add the beaten yolks. Stir in alternately the flour with the milk and lemon juice.

A French strawberry dish in glazed earthenware (faience), from the shop of Bernard Palissy. These extraordinary mannerist pieces were made for the court at Fontainebleau. About 1570-1580.

Fold in the beaten whites and place in buttered custard cups set in a pan with 1 inch of hot water. Bake for about 45 minutes or until set. Serve very hot or very cold with either heavy cream or a fruit sauce. *Mrs. LeBaron S. Willard, Jr.*

Baked Orange Pudding

350° / 6 servings

3 eggs, separated
8 tablespoons sugar
3 tablespoons flour
2 tablespoons melted butter
1/2 cup evaporated milk
1 tablespoon grated orange rind
1 cup orange juice
1/4 teaspoon salt
Orange sections, peeled

Beat the egg yolks with 2 tablespoons of the sugar. Stir in the flour and melted butter. Gradually add the evaporated milk, orange rind, and orange juice; stir well until smooth. Beat the egg whites and salt until stiff but not dry. Gradually add the remaining 6 tablespoons sugar and beat until very stiff. Fold in the egg-yolk mixture. Pour into greased custard cups and place in a shallow baking pan in boiling water. Bake 30 to 35 minutes. Cool; then turn out onto dessert dishes and garnish with orange sections. *Mrs. Richard W. Emory*

Burnt Almond Mousse

12 servings

1 cup sugar
5 egg yolks
1 cup maple syrup
1/8 teaspoon salt
Vanilla
1 quart whipping cream
1 cup chopped roasted almonds

Caramelize the sugar over a very slow fire; cool it on a buttered surface and then pound it into fine bits. Beat the egg yolks until they are light, add the maple syrup and salt, and cook in a double boiler until it is thick, taking care that the bottom of the pan does not touch the water. Whip the cream stiff, and when the egg mixture has cooled, fold them all together: custard, nuts, vanilla, caramelized sugar, and whipped cream. Freeze without stirring in ice trays or in a large handsome mold in a deep freeze. *Mrs. Jerome Kidder*

Coffee Intrigue

4 to 6 servings

3 tablespoons of instant coffee dissolved in 1 cup of boiling water
32 marshmallows
1/2 pint heavy cream
1 teaspoon vanilla

Heat the coffee and marshmallows over boiling water until dissolved, stirring occasionally. Set aside until cool. Beat with a rotary beater for 4 or 5 minutes. Beat the cream until it is thick but not too stiff; add the vanilla and fold in the coffee mixture. Chill for at least 5 hours. Serve with frozen strawberries.

Another way: line a mold with lady fingers, pour in the coffee mixture, and freeze or just chill. Sprinkle with grated chocolate.

And for another flavor, replace the coffee and water with cream sherry. Add 1/8 teaspoon almond extract. Spoon the dessert into individual paper cups and mound it into peaks. Put the small cups on baking sheets for ease in handling and freeze until firm, several hours. Sprinkle with slivered almonds. This version makes a good buffet dessert because it is so easy to handle.

Miss Sylvia Betts Dodd, Mrs. Robert A. Milch

Cold Lemon Soufflé

8 servings

6 large eggs, separated
1-1/2 cups sugar
2/3 cup lemon juice
Grated lemon rind
2 cups heavy cream
2 tablespoons gelatin in 1/2 cup cold water
1 extra egg white

Decoration
Macaroon crumbs
Almonds
Whipped cream
Pistachio nuts

Put the egg yolks, 1 cup of the sugar, the lemon juice, and rind in a large saucepan and whisk over low heat until mousse-like. Taste to see if the additional 1/2 cup of sugar is needed. Remove from heat and beat until cool. Add the cream, whipped softly so that it barely holds its shape. Melt the gelatin over low heat and add it. Stir the mousse over ice until thickened, and then fold in the egg whites, beaten stiff but not dry. Turn into a collared soufflé case and put in the refrigerator. When it is firm, press crumbs on upstanding edge and decorate with whipped cream and nuts.

Mrs. Charles Parkhurst

Lemon Sherbet

5 to 6 servings

1 tablespoon unflavored gelatin
1/2 cup cold milk
1 cup sugar
6 tablespoons lemon juice
1 teaspoon grated lemon rind
1-1/2 cups milk, half-and-half, or cream
2 egg whites

Soak the gelatin in the half cup of milk and then dissolve it over hot water. Dissolve the sugar in the lemon juice, a rather long process made simpler if the bowl is put in a larger one containing hot water. When both gelatin and sugar are dissolved combine them, add the grated lemon rind, and then slowly add the milk or cream and chill in a freezing tray until almost firm. Put the mixture in a chilled bowl, add the unbeaten egg whites, and beat until light and fluffy. Spoon the fluffy mixture back into a freezing tray and freeze again until firm. Using cream, one has a smoother richer dessert, but milk, lower in calories, is almost as welcome.

Mrs. James D. Atkinson

Blender Lemon Ice

4 to 6 servings

1 cup sugar
2 cups water
1 lemon, thin yellow portion of peel and fruit only
1/2 teaspoon ginger or large piece candied ginger
1/8 teaspoon salt
Few drops yellow food coloring

Boil sugar and water 5 minutes. Remove from the heat and set aside. Put the lemon peel and fruit in the blender and whirl for 20 seconds or until finely chopped. Add the ginger, salt, and food coloring; turn on the motor again (to "stir" if you have a multi-speed blender) and gradually add the hot sugar syrup through the opening in the top while the motor is running. Pour into a refrigerator tray and freeze about 2 hours or until slightly firm. Empty into the blender container; turn on the motor (to "crush," if your blender so indicates) for 20 seconds. Return to the refrigerator tray and freeze until firm.

Robert Zimmerman

French Vanilla Ice Cream

1-1/2 quarts

6 or 7 egg yolks
4 cups heavy cream
1/4 teaspoon salt
1 cup sugar
1-1/2 inch piece of vanilla bean

In the top part of a double boiler, beat the egg yolks and 2 cups cream. Add the salt, sugar, vanilla bean; cook, stirring constantly, over hot, not boiling, water until thick enough to coat a metal spoon. Remove from the heat and lift out the vanilla bean. Split the bean in half lengthwise and, with the tip of a small knife, scrape the seeds into the cream mixture. Let it cool, then add the 2 remaining cups of cream. Freeze and cure according to the directions of your ice cream freezer.

Three crushed bananas can be added, in which case, halve the amount of vanilla.

Mrs. Thomas Schweizer

Macaroons in Sherry

Soak macaroons in sherry. Put vanilla ice cream in balls on top of the macaroons and add whipped cream flavored with sherry. *Mrs. James Weil*

Grapefruit and Meringue Ice Cream

2 pints whipping cream
3/4 cup granulated sugar
Juice and grated peel of 1 grapefruit
10 small meringues

Whip the cream until soft peaks are formed; add the sugar, grapefruit juice, grated rind, and the crumbled meringues. The mixture should be firm but not stiff. Put it in the freezer for several hours in a fancy mold. Unmold and surround with citrus fruit slices.

Mrs. Frank Dawson Griffith

Apricot Mousse

8 servings

1 pound apricots
1 cup granulated sugar
Few drops lemon or orange extract
1 tablespoon gelatin
3 tablespoons cold water
3 tablespoons milk
1 pint heavy cream

Purée the apricots after they have been soaked and cooked according to the package directions; add the sugar and extract. Soak the gelatin in the cold water, add the hot milk, and stir over hot water until the gelatin is dissolved. Add this to the purée. Whip the cream, and fold it into the purée. Spoon it into a wet mold and chill it in the freezing unit for about 3 hours. This may be unmolded or served directly from the mold.

If you prefer, combine less whipped cream with the fruit; the extra whipped cream can be put over the middle of the dessert. Prunes, raspberries, or strawberries, puréed, are just as agreeable as the apricots. *Mrs. Sara D. Redmond*

Frozen Cheesecake

2 icebox trays lined with graham-cracker crusts
7 ounces cream cheese
3/4 cup sugar
2 egg yolks
3/4 cup whipping cream
Juice of 1 lemon
2 egg whites

Soften the cream cheese and mix in the sugar, then the egg yolks, one at a time. Beat well; add the cream, the lemon juice, and finally fold in the stiffly beaten egg whites. Freeze at least 2 hours, although it will keep indefinitely.

Mrs. Curran W. Harvey

Frozen Grand Marnier Mold

4 servings

2 egg whites
6 tablespoons sugar
1 cup heavy cream
1/4 cup or less Grand Marnier

Beat the whites with a pinch of salt until softly peaked. Then gradually beat in 1/4 cup of the sugar and continue beating until the meringue is stiff and shiny. With the same beater, whip the cream stiff; then beat in the rest of the sugar. Gently blend in the Grand Marnier: fold in the whites. Turn into a 1-quart or individual molds and freeze until firm, at least several hours. Unmold and serve with Berry Sauce.

Berry Sauce

1 10-ounce package frozen strawberries
1 10-ounce package frozen raspberries
Grand Marnier

Defrost the strawberries and raspberries long enough to drain off the excess juices. Purée in a blender until smooth. Strain and add the Grand Marnier to taste.

All sorts of liqueurs work out well with this dessert—curaçao, framboise, crème de menthe—and up to half a pound of fruit purée can be incorporated into the meringue, as well. It needn't be frozen hard.

Lady Penrose

Frozen Grand Marnier Soufflé

8 to 10 servings

1/2 gallon vanilla ice cream
8 macaroons, dried and crumbled
8 tablespoons Grand Marnier
1 cup heavy cream, whipped

Soften the ice cream and add the macaroons and the Grand Marnier; fold in the whipped cream. Pour the mixture into a 3-quart mold or bowl suitable for freezing. Cover it with foil and freeze 4 to 5 hours or overnight. Unmold onto a serving dish and serve with the following sauce:

Grand Marnier Strawberry Sauce

2 pints strawberries
Sugar
6 tablespoons Grand Marnier

Wash and hull the berries, sugar them, and heat until soft but not mushy. Add the Grand Marnier and serve hot.

Mrs. Martin F. Knott, Mrs. William G. Speed, III

Coffee Almond Mousse with Tia Maria

4 to 6 servings

1 egg white
1 tablespoon instant coffee
1/8 teaspoon salt
2 tablespoons sugar
1 cup whipping cream
1/4 cup sugar
1 teaspoon vanilla
1/8 teaspoon almond extract
1/4 cup toasted chopped almonds
Tia Maria or crème de cacao

Beat the egg white until stiff; add the coffee and the salt and then add the sugar slowly, beating it all until it is stiff and shiny. Whip the cream

with the flavorings and set it aside while you fold the nuts into the egg mixture and then add the whipped cream. Pour it into individual pots and either freeze it or refrigerate it for a few hours.
    When served, pour a bit of the liqueur on each one.
Mrs. Jeanne Kaufman

Coffee Flummery

6 servings

1-1/2 cups strong coffee
1 cup table cream
1/2 cup sugar
Pinch salt
2 egg yolks, well beaten
1 level tablespoon gelatin
Vanilla to taste
2 egg whites, well beaten

    Mix together the coffee, cream, sugar, salt, and beaten egg yolks. Stir in a double boiler until the mixture coats a spoon. Remove from the stove. Add the gelatin, which has been soaked in 1/4 cup water, and stir until it is dissolved; then add the vanilla and fold in the egg whites, beaten stiff. Pour in a mold and serve ice cold.
Mrs. Jerome Kidder

Chocolate Ice Cream

2 servings

1 beaten egg
3/4 cup Hershey's chocolate syrup
1/2 pint cream whipped
Vanilla
Crème de menthe

    Beat the egg well and stir into the chocolate syrup. Then fold in the whipped cream and the vanilla and freeze in an ice tray for at least 3 hours. Serve with a topping of crème de menthe.
Milton H. Blake

French Silk

400°

Crust:

1/2 cup dark brown sugar, loosely packed
1 cup flour
1/2 cup chopped pecans
1/4 pound butter, softened

    Mix the ingredients together, pat them down in a 9 x 13-inch pan and bake for 15 minutes. Then break up the crust until crumbly, pat it down again, and chill it.

Filling:

1/2 pound sweet butter
1-1/2 cups sugar
2 teaspoons vanilla
1/2 teaspoon almond extract
3 ounces bitter chocolate, melted
4 eggs
A pinch of salt

    Cream the butter and sugar well in an electric mixer, then add the flavoring and the melted chocolate. Continue beating and add the eggs one at a time. Add a pinch of salt. Fill the crust and chill several hours at least.
    This freezes very well, and because of the chocolate it needs very little time to thaw before serving. This may be cut into squares or, using a fluted cutter, presented in rounds. Garnish with whipped cream and candied violets.
Mrs. Frank T. Gray

U. S. Mint Mousse

6 servings

1-1/2 cups boiling water
2 packages (3 ounces) lime-flavored gelatin dessert

1 cup cold water
1/2 cup green crème de menthe
1 cup heavy cream

Add boiling water to the gelatin; stir until dissolved. Add the cold water and crème de menthe and chill until slightly thick. Whip the cream until it is stiff and fold it into the gelatin. Pour the mixture into a 10 x 4-1/2 x 3-inch loaf pan or metal mold and refrigerate until set.

To remove the mousse from the pan, immerse the bottom and sides of the pan in hot water for 5 seconds. Decorate the unmolded mousse with rosettes of whipped cream and chocolate shavings.

Miss Amelia C. Stukes

Maple Mousse

4 servings

1 cup hot maple syrup
4 egg yolks, lightly beaten
1 pint cream whipped
4 egg whites, well beaten

Pour the hot maple syrup slowly over the yolks, beating constantly. Cook in a double boiler until the mixture coats the spoon. Chill, then fold in the whipped cream and the whites, well beaten. Place in a mousse mold and chill for 4 hours or freeze.

Miss Sara Andrews

Chocolate Ice Box Pudding

8 to 10 servings

3 bars (whole) German sweet chocolate
3 tablespoons sugar
2 tablespoons hot water or coffee
8 eggs, separated
1 teaspoon vanilla, Grand Marnier or brandy
2 packages lady fingers

Melt the chocolate with the sugar and water in a double boiler. Off the stove beat in the yolks, one at a time; add the vanilla. Beat the egg whites with a pinch of salt until stiff and fold into the chocolate mixture. Line a dessert bowl with half of the lady fingers. Alternate layers of lady fingers with the chocolate mixture. Let them stand in the refrigerator at least 3 hours. Serve with whipped cream.

Or, this can be called chocolate pie by turning the mixture into a 9-inch baked pie shell with the whipped cream spread decoratively on top. Still another and much richer version replaces the egg whites with whipped cream and suggests Cognac rather than vanilla. (See Biscuit Glacé.)

Mrs. Harry Dillehunt, Mrs. Curran W. Harvey, Mrs. John Lalley

Biscuit Glacé

8 servings

1-1/2 packages lady fingers
8 egg yolks
1/2 cup sugar
1 cup heavy cream
1/4 cup sugar
1/4 cup Grand Marnier
2 tablespoons Cognac
1/4 cup grated semi-sweet chocolate
1/2 cup heavy cream

Split the lady fingers and line the bottom and sides of a 3-inch-deep 1-1/2-quart mold with them. Beat the egg yolks with 1/2 cup of sugar until it is very thick and light. Beat the heavy cream stiff with 1/4 cup of sugar. Add the Grand Marnier, Cognac, and chocolate to the yolks and fold into the whipped cream. Pour into the lined mold and place in the freezer for at least 3 hours. When ready to serve, unmold and decorate with 1/2 cup cream beaten until stiff. Use a pastry tube for the decoration. This recipe should be tripled for 24, using 1 large and 1 small mold.

Mrs. Herbert Davis

Chocolate Rum Charlotte

6 servings

3/4 cup sugar
1/4 cup water
1/8 teaspoon cream of tartar
5 egg yolks, beaten
1 cup sweet butter
3 ounces semi-sweet chocolate
1 tablespoon water or coffee
A sponge cake
Golden rum

Melt the chocolate in the water or coffee. In a saucepan combine the sugar, water, and cream of tartar and boil without stirring until it spins a thread at 238°. In the meantime, beat the yolks until very light, and the minute the sugar is at the right temperature pour it in a thin stream on top of the yolks while continuing to beat them. Beat in the butter bit by tiny bit. When slightly cooled, add the melted chocolate.

Slice the cake in thin horizontal layers and sprinkle each slice liberally with golden rum. Rinse a charlotte mold in cold water. Trim the pieces, using half of them to line the bottom and sides of the mold, filling in all the spaces carefully. Spread the remaining slices generously with the soft butter cream and fit, spread side down, into the charlotte mold in layers. Press each slice down so that the mold is solidly packed with the butter cream and cake. Press down with a plate; chill for several hours.

To unmold, run a thin knife around the inside of the mold and invert on a serving plate.

Mrs. William Garvey

Peach Cream

8 to 10 servings

2 envelopes unflavored gelatin
1 cup light cream
6 3-ounce packages cream cheese
2 cups heavy cream
1 cup sugar
1 package (10 ounces) frozen sliced peaches (fresh are better when available)
Red and yellow food coloring

Soften the gelatin in 1/3 cup cold water. Scald 1 cup light cream and add the gelatin, stirring until it is dissolved. Cool. Soften the cream cheese; then beat until it is light. Slowly add the heavy cream, beating constantly until the mixture is smooth. Add the sugar. Purée the peaches (if frozen, thaw them first) in a blender or a food mill. Add to the cheese mixture. Mix well and stir in a few drops of red and yellow food coloring for a more pronounced "peach" color. Combine both mixtures. Pour into a lightly oiled 6-cup mold. Refrigerate several hours, until set. Unmold and decorate with additional sliced peaches.

Mrs. Howard Benedict

Charlotte Russe

8 servings

1/2 cup milk
2 eggs, separated
2-1/2 tablespoons sugar
Salt
1 tablespoon gelatin
2 tablespoons sherry
1 pint whipping cream
Lady fingers
Candied citron
Candied cherries
Blanched almonds

Scald the milk and beat together the sugar, egg yolks, and a pinch of salt. Cook these together until thickened into a custard. Soak the gelatin in 1/4 cup of water, then dissolve it in the hot custard. Cool slightly; add the sherry, then the whipped cream and the whites of eggs, which have been beaten stiff.

Traditionally, this dessert is presented in a mold lined with ladyfingers into which the creamy filling is poured, then chilled and unmolded. It may also be served from a pretty bowl, surrounded with lady fingers. If a richer dessert is wanted, candied citron and cherries and blanched slivered almonds may be added to the filling.

Mrs. Jerome Kidder

Orange Charlotte

6 servings

1 envelope gelatin
1 cup sugar
1-1/2 cups orange juice
4 tablespoons lemon juice
3 egg whites
1/2 pint whipping cream
1 package lady fingers
Grand Marnier

Soak the gelatin in some of the fruit juice. Heat the rest with the sugar and dissolve the gelatin in it. Cool. When it has become thick, fold in the beaten whites of the eggs and the whipped cream. Dip the lady fingers quickly into Grand Marnier or orange juice to take the "bought" taste from them. Line a mold or a pretty glass dish with them and pour in the gelatin mixture. This can be unmolded or served from the dish. In each case, decorate with grated orange rind and orange sections.

Mrs. Henry Wyman

Raspberries Frangipane

10 servings

6 egg yolks
1/2 cup sugar
Pinch of salt
1/3 cup flour
2-1/2 cups milk
2-inch vanilla bean or 1 teaspoon vanilla
2 tablespoons butter
6 or 8 almond macaroons
5 pints of raspberries
2 cups heavy cream, whipped
3 tablespoons sugar
1/4 cup kirsch

Make a Crème Anglaise: Beat the yolks with the sugar and salt until light; add the flour. Scald the milk, pour it onto the egg mixture, and blend thoroughly. Add the vanilla or vanilla bean. Cook and stir until thick. Remove from the heat and stir in the butter and crumbled macaroons. Cover well and chill. At serving time, put the custard into a bowl, the raspberries on top, and then the whipped cream, which you have flavored with sugar and kirsch. A little almond extract in the custard may appeal to you.

G.O.K.

Blender Strawberry Bavarian Cream

6 servings

1 package (10 ounces) frozen strawberries, thawed
2 envelopes unflavored gelatin
1/4 cup cold milk
1/4 cup sugar
2 egg yolks
1 heaping cup cracked ice
1 cup heavy cream

Drain the berries, reserving 1/2 cup of the syrup. Heat the syrup to simmering. Mix in the blender for 40 seconds the hot syrup and the gelatin, which has been soaked in the cold milk. Add the sugar, berries, and egg yolks and blend for 15 seconds. If your blender is multi-speed, turn it to "grind" or the highest speed for 20 seconds, adding the ice and cream through the opening in the top. Turn into a 1-quart mold and chill until set. Unmold to serve.

Robert Zimmerman

Lemon Soufflé with Custard Sauce

350° / 8 servings

5 tablespoons softened sweet butter
8 tablespoons granulated sugar
2/3 cup sifted flour
1 cup milk
6 eggs, separated
6 tablespoons lemon juice
2 tablespoons grated lemon rind
Pinch of salt

Prepare a 2-quart ring mold by buttering it with 1 tablespoon of butter and sprinkling with 2 tablespoons sugar. Knock the excess sugar out.

Make a roux by melting 4 tablespoons butter, adding 2/3 cup of flour, and mixing to a smooth paste. Then add all at once 1 cup of milk, stirring it as it comes to a boil. Lower the heat and beat until it is dough-like and does not cling to the sides of the pan. While it is still hot, beat in the 6 egg yolks one at a time. Beat very well and then add 5 tablespoons of sugar, one at a time; 6 tablespoons of lemon juice, slowly; and 2 tablespoons grated rind.

Add a pinch of salt to the egg whites and beat vigorously until they are stiff. Sprinkle 1 tablespoon of sugar over them and beat some more. Stir a few mounds of the egg whites into the soufflé base and then fold in the rest. Spoon, do not pour, the soufflé into the ring mold, using enough only to fill the mold 3/4 full. Put the mold in a shallow pan and pour boiling water halfway up the mold. Bake until dry when tested, about 45 minutes.

If the soufflé is to be eaten immediately, loosen the sides with a sharp knife and invert over a serving platter. Pour the sauce around it and dust with nutmeg. If, however, you plan to reheat it, do not unmold it. Let it cool, not in the refrigerator. Bake it in a preheated oven as before, but for 1/2 hour. To prevent its browning too much, cover it with aluminum foil.

Vanilla Custard Sauce

3 egg yolks
1/4 cup granulated sugar
1-1/3 cups milk
1 teaspoon vanilla or a 2-inch vanilla bean
Freshly grated nutmeg

Beat the egg yolks until slightly thickened. Pour in, as you beat, 1/4 cup granulated sugar and beat until they form a ribbon. Heat the milk with the vanilla and when it is at the boiling point, pour into it the yolks, beating all the while. When combined, put the sauce over direct heat and cook carefully until thick enough to coat a spoon. Remove the vanilla bean or stir in the extract and strain the sauce into a small bowl.

Michael Field

Chocolate Soufflé with Grand Marnier Sauce

325° / 5 or 6 servings

3 tablespoons butter or margarine
1/4 cup flour
1/4 teaspoon salt
1 cup milk
2 squares unsweetened chocolate, cut up
4 egg yolks
1/2 cup sugar
4 egg whites
1/4 teaspoon cream of tartar

In a saucepan melt the butter or margarine; blend in the flour and salt. Add the milk all at once; cook and stir until the mixture is thickened and bubbly. Remove from the heat, add the chocolate, and stir until melted. Beat the egg yolks until they are thick and lemon-colored. Beat the sugar into the yolks gradually and then add to the chocolate mixture. Beat the egg whites and cream of tartar until stiff. Carefully fold the egg whites into the chocolate mixture. Pour the batter into an ungreased 5-cup soufflé dish with a 2-inch foil collar, buttered and sprinkled with granulated sugar, wrapped around the dish. Secure the collar to the dish with tape. Bake about 1 hour and 10 minutes and serve with the following Grand Marnier Sauce.

Lacking the time and inclination for the Grand Marnier sauce, merely melt some vanilla ice cream to serve with the soufflé.

Grand Marnier Sauce

Makes 1 cup.

1/4 cup sugar
1 tablespoon cornstarch
3/4 cup orange juice
1/4 cup Grand Marnier
1/4 cup slivered almonds

In a small saucepan combine the sugar and the cornstarch. Stir in the orange juice and heat, stirring, to the boiling point. Add the Grand Marnier liqueur and the slivered almonds.

Miss Helen Flynn, Mrs. Duncan MacKenzie

Tangerine Soufflé

6 servings

3 eggs and 2 yolks
3 tablespoons sugar
4 small sugar cubes
4 tangerines (or enough to make 3/4 cup juice, strained)
3/4 packet gelatin
1/4 cup lemon juice
1 tablespoon Marsala
1/2 teaspoon vanilla
Orange food coloring
1/4 cup whipped cream or 2 egg whites beaten to a soft peak with a pinch each of salt and cream of tartar

Break the eggs and yolks into a large bowl and add the sugar. Rub the tangerine rinds with the sugar cubes to extract the oil. Crush the sugar cubes and add to the eggs. Beat over simmering water until 4 or 5 times in bulk and a mass of tiny bubbles—10 to 15 minutes. Remove from heat and beat 5 minutes more. Soften the gelatin in the lemon juice. Heat the juice of the tangerines and dissolve the gelatin. Add to the mousse with the Marsala, vanilla, and food coloring. Fold in the whipped cream or the egg whites. Pour into a 6-cup soufflé dish with a paper collar. Mixture should rise 1/2 inch above dish rim.

Chill to set; remove the paper. Serve plain if made with cream; serve with a heavy custard sauce if made with egg whites. This is a very light dessert, like a cold zabaglione.

Miss Anne Barlow

Germknödel

YEAST DUMPLINGS

1 ounce yeast
1/2 cup water
2 tablespoons flour
1 teaspoon sugar

Dissolve the yeast in warm water. Stir in the flour and sugar. Cover, place in a warm spot and let rise to double quantity.

Have the following ingredients at room temperature.

1 whole egg and 1 yolk
2 tablespoons sugar
2/3 cup milk
1 teaspoon grated lemon rind
1/2 cup melted butter
1/2 teaspoon salt
4 cups sifted flour
1 cup apricot jam

Beat the eggs; add the sugar, milk, lemon rind, and melted butter. Add the salt to the flour. Make a well in the flour; pour in the egg mixture and the yeast mixture. Beat the dough until large bubbles form. Sprinkle the top with flour, cover with a towel, and let rise in a warm place to double, about 1 hour. Remove the dough by large spoonfuls to a floured board and pat each spoonful flat. Place 1 teaspoon jam in the center of each disc and, with floured hands, form into a round ball. Set aside on a large floured tin or board, keeping well apart, to rise again in a warm, draft-free place, about 3/4 to 1 hour. When the dumplings are nearly double in size, bring a large pot of salted water to a boil. Turn down the flame to a gentle boil. Keeping the filling-side down, put the dumplings gently in the water, not more than 4 or 6 to a pot, depending on the size of the pot. They should not be crowded as they will swell somewhat in cooking. *Cover* and cook for 3 minutes. Turn the dumplings over with a wooden spoon and cook *uncovered* for 5 minutes. Remove with a slotted spoon and drain carefully. Prick in 3 or 4 places with a knitting needle so that the steam can escape. Transfer the dumplings, as cooked, to a buttered Pyrex dish kept over hot water.

Serve in one of these ways.

Place in a single layer on a heated platter and pour over the dumplings one of the following: **1 cup melted butter combined with 3 tablespoons rum and 1/3 cup poppy seeds; or 2/3 cup ground filberts; or 1 cup sifted powdered sugar.**

Or, more traditionally, pass the melted butter, sugar, poppy seeds, and ground nuts separately so that each guest may top his dumplings to suit his own taste. *Mrs. H. Morris Whitehurst*

Powidltascherl

POCKETS WITH PRUNE JAM

1/2 pound prunes
1/2 cup sugar
1 cup water
Lemon peel
2 pounds unpeeled potatoes
2 tablespoons butter
1/2 teaspoon salt
2 cups sifted flour
1 egg white

Soak the prunes overnight. Drain and remove the pits. Cook them in sugar water with a curl of lemon peel until thick. Remove the lemon peel and mash the prunes to the consistency of jam; then cool. Boil the potatoes in their jackets until tender. Skin and mash them. While they are still warm, work in the butter, salt, and flour. With floured hands, knead into a smooth dough.

Roll out the dough 1/4 inch thick and cut into 2-1/2-inch squares or circles with a pastry wheel. Place a rounded teaspoon of the prune jam in the center of each pocket. Brush the edges with egg white, fold over, and press the edges together tightly with your fingers. Bring a large pot of salted water to a boil; turn down to a simmer and place the dough pockets in the water to cook 10 to 15 minutes. Do not crowd them. When they are cooked, remove them with a slotted spoon and place them on a dish to keep warm over hot water. Sprinkle with the following coating:

Coating

1 cup coarsely grated fresh bread crumbs
3/4 cup butter
1/4 cup powdered sugar

Melt 3/4 cup of butter and brown the crumbs in the butter. To serve, sprinkle the buttered crumbs over the warm jam pockets and powder with sugar. *Mrs. H. Morris Whitehurst*

Waschermadeln

APRICOT BEIGNETS

6 servings

2 large eggs, separated
1 tablespoon sugar
1/2 cup white wine
1 cup sifted flour
1/4 teaspoon salt
1 teaspoon grated lemon peel
1/2 cup milk
18 ripe apricots
1/2 cup sugar
2 tablespoons water
1/2 cup rum
4 strips bacon
2 cups peanut oil
1/2 cup slivered almonds

If fresh apricots are not in season, well drained canned apricot halves may be used, or dried halves which have been soaked overnight and drained.

Make a batter of the 2 egg yolks, 1 tablespoon sugar, wine, flour, salt, and lemon peel. Let it rest for 2 hours. Stir in the milk, then fold in the stiffly beaten egg whites. Peel and pit the ripe apricots and marinate them in 1/2 cup of sugar, water, and rum for 1 hour; then drain. In a heavy skillet, cook the strips of bacon until they are crisp and then remove. (Use the bacon for another dish.) Pour the bacon fat and the peanut oil in a pan suitable for deep-fat frying.

Dust the drained apricots lightly with flour; dip into the batter and fry in the bacon-flavored oil, which has been heated to 370°. When golden brown, remove with a slotted spoon and drain on absorbent paper. Place in the oven to keep warm. Place the slivered almonds in a sieve and lower into the hot oil to crisp. Drain. To serve, place 3 apricot beignets on a warm plate, cover with the following custard sauce, and sprinkle with almonds.

Custard Sauce

1 cup milk
3 small egg yolks
1 teaspoon cornstarch
1/4 cup sugar
1 teaspoon vanilla

Beat all the ingredients until smooth and cook in the top of a double boiler until creamy. Remove from the heat and beat for 5 minutes or until smooth. *Mrs. H. Morris Whitehurst*

Budapest Babka

350° / 8 servings

3 ounces cream cheese
1/4 pound butter
1 egg
3/4 cup sugar
1 cup flour
1/4 teaspoon salt
1 teaspoon baking powder
3 apples, peeled and sliced
1/4 cup cinnamon and sugar

A Feast for a King, a woodcut from the *Schatzbehalter*, printed in Nuremberg in 1491 by Anton Koberger. The king eats from a wooden trencher and is served by a page (left) using a presentoir. The covered cup was a symbol of honor, and the king has only a knife as a utensil. At the right a servant brings hot dishes from the kitchen.

Combine the cream cheese and butter and beat until light and creamy. Add the egg and sugar. Sift the flour, salt, and baking powder together and add gradually to the first mixture. Butter a springform pan, fill with the batter, and smooth it evenly. Arrange the apple slices vertically in the pan spaced 1/8 inch apart and gently pushed down into the batter so that only the edge of each apple slice is above the batter. Sprinkle with cinnamon and sugar. Bake for 1 hour. *Miss Theresa Marks*

Kaiserschmarren

EMPEROR'S OMELET

350° / 6 servings

2/3 cup raisins
2 ounces brandy
4 large egg yolks
1/2 cup sugar
1 cup light cream
2 cups sifted flour
4 egg whites
1/4 pound butter
1/2 cup confectioner's sugar

Put raisins to soak in brandy. Beat the egg yolks and stir in 1/4 cup of the sugar and the cream. Slowly add the flour and stir until smooth. Beat the egg whites until stiff and fold them into the batter. Butter 2 large Pyrex pie plates. Pour the batter into the 2 pie plates and bake until puffed and golden brown. Turn out on a large wooden board, and with 2 forks tear the omelets into pieces about 1/2 x 2 inches. Melt butter in a skillet; add the omelet pieces, the remaining 1/4 cup of sugar, and the drained raisins. Sauté the pieces until all are coated with the butter and sugar and are golden brown. Turn out on a warmed plate, dust with confectioner's sugar, and serve at once.

Mrs. H. Morris Whitehurst

Salzburger Nockerln

SALZBURG OMELET

250° / 3 servings

5 egg whites
3 egg yolks
3 tablespoons butter
3 tablespoons milk
1 tablespoon sifted flour
3 tablespoons vanilla sugar
Powdered sugar

Eggs must be very fresh and at room temperature. Place fireproof pan with the butter and milk in the oven to heat. Beat the egg yolks until very light and sprinkle in the flour, beating all the while. In a separate bowl, beat the egg whites, adding the 3 tablespoons vanilla sugar bit by bit. Bring the pan out of the oven onto a low burner and turn the oven to 300°. The pan should be very hot, the butter melted and simmering with the milk. Quickly fold the egg whites and yolks together. Divide into fourths with a spatula and place the mounds in the hot milk mixture. Sauté for a minute or two on top of the stove, then place in the oven, and bake until the top is golden, about 10 minutes. Sprinkle with powdered sugar and serve hot. *Mrs. H. Morris Whitehurst*

Baklava

325°

2 pounds filo (uncooked pastry leaves)
1-1/2 pounds sweet butter
4 pounds chopped nuts
1 teaspoon cinnamon

Butter a 12 x 17-inch pan lightly. Cut the filo dough the size of the pan and keep it covered with a damp cloth as you work. It must not get dry, for it breaks when brittle. Mix the nuts and cinnamon together and melt the butter.

Each layer of pastry in Baklava is made of 5 buttered leaves, so place 1 filo leaf on top of the other, buttering as you do so, until you have 5; add a layer of nuts, then 5 more buttered leaves until they are used up. Bake in the center of the oven for 2 hours. When it is finished, add hot syrup (recipe follows), spooning it carefully and slowly over all, and let the pastry stand several hours before cutting in small portions with a sharp knife and serving.

Filo is obtainable in shops specializing in Greek and Middle Eastern foods.

Baklava Syrup

7 cups sugar
5 cups water
Juice of 1/2 lemon
1 stick cinnamon

Boil all ingredients together for about 15 minutes.
Miss Mary Elizabeth Cianos

Kastanien Reis

RICED CHESTNUT DESSERT

350°

1 pound chestnuts
1/2 cup sugar
1/2 cup water
1 tablespoon brandy
1 tablespoon maraschino liqueur
1 pint whipped cream, sweetened

Wash the chestnuts, score an incision on the round side, place on a tin sheet and roast until they puff open. Peel, skin, and cook them in boiling water for 1/2 hour. Drain and then purée through a food mill or sieve.

While the chestnuts are cooking, make a syrup of the sugar and water until it forms a thread at 230°. Combine the riced nuts with the syrup, adding only enough of the syrup to have a mixture which resembles rather dry mashed potatoes. Press the mixture through a ricer into a shallow serving bowl; the strands of the chestnuts should be firm and separate. Decorate with a fluted ring of whipped cream around the mound of the chestnuts and serve cold.   *Mrs. H. Morris Whitehurst*

Paskha

A RUSSIAN POT CHEESE DESSERT

16 to 18 servings

1 pound cream cheese, softened
1/2 pint creamed cottage cheese
1/4 pound butter, softened
3/4 cup fine granulated sugar
1/2 cup chopped almonds
1/3 cup chopped cherries
1/3 cup candied orange, lemon, and citron peels, chopped
1/4 cup seedless raisins, cut in pieces

Mix the cheeses, butter, and sugar; beat in a mixer until smooth. Mix the nuts and fruits into the blended mixture. Line a 2-quart perforated mold with damp cheesecloth. (A sieve or a freezer container which has had holes punched in the bottom is quite acceptable. The holes are necessary to drain the extra moisture from the cheese.) Spoon the mixture into the container and place in the refrigerator to drain overnight. Turn out the molded Paskha and decorate with a cross designed of almonds and fruits. This is a companion food to Kulich.   *Mrs. Charles T. Hanson*

Topfenpalatschinken

COTTAGE CHEESE PANCAKES

350° / 4 servings

1 cup milk
1-1/4 cups flour

1/4 teaspoon salt
2 large eggs and 1 yolk
1/8 pound butter

Stir the milk into the flour and salt until smooth. Add the eggs and beat well. Let the batter rest for 1/2 hour. Melt enough butter in an 8-inch skillet or omelet pan to coat it. Pour in enough batter at a time to make 8 large thin pancakes, not as thin as crêpes. Cook each pancake until bubbles appear, turn once, and brown on the other side. Add butter to the pan as needed. Slide out of the pan onto a buttered Pyrex plate to keep warm in the oven.

Filling:

3/4 cup raisins
1/4 cup rum or brandy
1/2 cup butter
2/3 cup sugar
1/2 teaspoon salt
1/4 teaspoon grated lemon rind
3 large eggs
1 cup fine-grained cottage cheese
3/4 cup sour cream

Put the raisins in the liquor to plump them up. Cream the butter with sugar, salt, and lemon rind. Beat in the eggs one at a time. When creamy, add the cottage cheese, sour cream, and drained raisins. Stir until well blended.

Sauce:

2-1/2 cups milk
1/2 cup sugar
1 teaspoon vanilla
2 large eggs

Combine the above ingredients and beat until smooth. Spread the cottage cheese mixture onto the pancakes, roll them up (the ends may remain open) and lay the 8 rolls, seam side down, in a row in a long buttered baking dish. Pour the sauce over the pancakes and bake until browned, 25 to 30 minutes. Serve hot. *Mrs. H. Morris Whitehurst*

Orange Cake

350°

5 egg yolks
1-1/2 cups sugar
1/2 cup orange juice
Grated rind
1-3/4 cups sifted flour
1 teaspoon baking powder
3 egg whites

Beat the yolks with the sugar until a ribbon is formed. Add the orange juice and rind, but grate enough extra to use some in the frosting. Sift the baking powder and flour together and fold into the egg mixture. Beat the whites until stiff, incorporate a little into the flour-egg mixture to balance the thickness of the two, and then fold in the remaining whites. Pour into an angel-cake pan, and bake 1 hour or until a tester comes out clean. *Miss Gretchen Sieglaff*

Orange Cake Icing

1-1/4 cups sugar
1/4 cup water
1/4 cup light corn syrup
1 egg white
1/8 teaspoon cream of tartar
Orange and lemon rind, grated

Bring the sugar, water, and corn syrup to a rolling boil. Cook to 238° using a candy thermometer, or until a small amount of the syrup dropped in ice water forms a soft ball. Immediately begin pouring the syrup into the egg white, which has been stiffly beaten with the cream of tartar. Continue beating (preferably with an electric mixer) as you pour in the syrup slowly. When the icing is quite stiff, beat in the grated rinds.

Miss Gretchen Sieglaff

Carrot Nut Cake

A DARK MOIST FRUIT CAKE TYPE

300°

3 cups flour
2 teaspoons baking soda
2 teaspoons baking powder
3/4 teaspoon salt
4 eggs
1-1/2 cups salad oil
2 cups sugar
2 cups grated carrots
1 cup chopped pecans
1/2 cup raisins
2 teaspoons cinnamon

Put the flour, baking soda, baking powder, and salt in a bowl; make a well in the center and add the eggs, beaten, the salad oil, and the sugar. Beat them all together, then add the carrots, nuts, raisins (floured to keep them from sinking), and cinnamon. Pour this into a buttered tube or bundt pan to bake 1 hour and 10 to 15 minutes. Sprinkle powdered sugar on top at serving time.

Mrs. Benjamin Griswold, IV.
Mrs. Charles Parkhurst

Fresh Coconut Cake

350°

1-3/4 cups granulated sugar
1/2 cup butter
3 cups cake flour
3 teaspoons baking powder
3/4 cup sweet milk
1/2 cup coconut milk
1 teaspoon vanilla
4 egg whites
White boiled icing
Freshly grated coconut

Cream the sugar and butter until puffy. Sift the flour and baking powder together twice. Combine the milk, coconut milk drained from the coconut, and vanilla. Add the flour and milk alternately into the sugar and butter mixture; when they are thoroughly but lightly mixed, fold in the whites of the eggs which you have beaten stiff. Bake in 2 9-inch layers for 30 minutes.

Use any good boiled icing for both filling and topping and use grated coconut very generously between the layers and on top of the cake.

Mrs. Arthur Waxter

Cassata Siciliana

A freshly made pound cake
1 pound ricotta cheese
2 tablespoons heavy cream
A scant 1/4 cup sugar
2 ounces Strega
3 ounces semi-sweet chocolate, coarsely chopped

Cut the pound cake horizontally into 1/2 or 3/4-inch slices. Put the cheese in the electric mixer bowl, and while beating it, add the cream, sugar, and Strega. When it is smooth fold in the chopped chocolate. Spread each layer of cake save the top one with the ricotta mixture, wrap it in polyethylene or aluminum foil, pressing the layers together, and refrigerate for several hours, until it is firm and ready to be frosted with Mocha Frosting (recipe follows).

Mocha Frosting

12 ounces semi-sweet chocolate
3/4 cup strong black coffee
1/2 pound chilled sweet butter, cut into small bits

Melt the chocolate and coffee together, cool slightly, and then beat in the ice-cold butter, small bit after small bit. Chill it until it is thick enough to spread and then frost the top and sides of the cake. To make it look like an Italian dish, you must swirl the chocolate fancifully. This is a do-the-day-before dish as the cake must ripen.

Mrs. Felix Leser

Black Bottom Cupcakes

350° / 24 medium-size cupcakes

**1/2 pound cream cheese
1 egg, beaten
1 tablespoon sugar
1/8 teaspoon salt
6 ounces chocolate bits**

Combine the cream cheese, egg, sugar, and salt and mix by hand. Then stir in the chocolate bits and set this mixture aside.

**3 cups flour, sifted
1/2 cup cocoa
2 cups sugar
1 tablespoon baking soda
1 teaspoon salt
2 cups water
2 tablespoons vinegar
2/3 cup salad oil
2 teaspoons vanilla**

Sift the flour, cocoa, sugar, soda, and salt together. Add the water, oil, vinegar, and vanilla, beating well. At first it will appear to be unmixable but just keep beating!

Use muffin tins and paper liners, filling 1/2 to 3/4 full with the dark mixture (flour and cocoa). Then drop one tablespoon of the cheese mixture on top of each one. Bake for about 20 minutes. These freeze successfully. *Miss Sylvia Betts Dodd*

White Fruit Cake

300° / 4 fruit cakes

**2 pounds white raisins
1/4 pound candied pineapple, diced
1/4 pound candied cherries, cut in half
1/8 pound candied angelica or, if unobtainable, increase cherries by 1/8 pound
1 pound walnut meats
12 eggs
1 pound butter
1 pound sugar
1 pound flour
1 teaspoon baking powder
1-1/2 ounces brandy**

Prepare 2 9-inch tube pans and 2 4-1/2 x 8-inch loaf pans by buttering them first and lining them with waxed paper. Then put the fruits and nuts in a bowl and flour them lightly to keep them from either sinking or sticking together.

Separate the eggs. Only then can you begin the fruit cake. Cream the butter and sugar until light and fluffy. Add the yolks, which have already been beaten together, and beat some more to form a ribbon. Sift the flour and baking powder together and fold it alternately with the fruit and the nuts and the brandy into the egg mixture. Finally fold in the stiffly beaten egg whites. Bake for 2-1/2 to 3 hours. Decorate with glazed fruits.

This cake keeps very well without the brandy aging process, but one can always add brandy from time to time. Store in a tightly covered container, and if you plan to keep the cakes a very long time, put an unpeeled apple in the tin, too.

Mrs. Ernest Wooden

Sunshine Cake

300°

**9 eggs, separated
1-1/2 cups sugar
1/2 cup water
1 teaspoon vanilla or almond extract
1/2 teaspoon lemon extract
1 cup cake flour
1 teaspoon cream of tartar
1/2 teaspoon salt**

A covered chocolate cup and saucer of Vincennes porcelain in a deep daffodil yellow. They were painted by the decorator Vieillard and bear the date letter for 1753.

Beat the egg yolks until lemon-colored and, while they are beating, cook the sugar and water to 238° or the soft ball stage. Keep beating the yolks as you pour the syrup into them. Add the flavorings.

Sift the flour 3 times and fold it into the egg yolks. Beat the whites stiff with the cream of tartar and salt, and lightly fold those in too. Spoon into a 10-inch angel-cake pan, put it into a 300° oven, then raise the heat to 350° and bake the cake about 45 minutes or an hour. Invert it to cool.

Miss Mary Lou White

Dacquaise

3-LAYERED MERINGUE

250°

**5 egg whites
1/8 teaspoon cream of tartar
1-1/4 cups granulated sugar
1 cup ground blanched almonds
1/2 cup zwieback crumbs
2 tablespoons sifted all-purpose flour
2 tablespoons sifted cornstarch
1/2 teaspoon vanilla**

Place the egg whites in mixing bowl. Add the cream of tartar and beat until frothy. Gradually add 3/4 cup of the sugar while beating and continue beating until stiff. Fold in the remaining sugar, almonds, zwieback, flour, cornstarch, and vanilla. Cut 3 8-inch circles of wax paper. Place on baking sheets. Spoon meringue onto circles and smooth with a knife. Bake for 45 to 60 minutes. When cool, spread each layer with the following Coffee Butter Cream, and serve with sweetened whipped cream. This freezes beautifully.

Coffee Butter Cream

**1 cup sugar
1/3 cup water
1/8 teaspoon cream of tartar
5 egg yolks
1 cup sweet butter, softened
2 tablespoons instant coffee
2 tablespoons Grand Marnier**

Combine sugar, water, and cream of tartar in saucepan. Stir over low heat until dissolved. Raise the heat and boil until it reaches 240° on a candy thermometer or forms a soft ball in ice water. While this cooks, beat egg yolks until they become pale yellow and double in volume. Pour the sugar syrup very slowly into egg yolks, beating constantly. Set aside to cool. When cool, beat in softened butter bit by bit. Stir in instant coffee and Grand Marnier to taste.

Mrs. Donald Brown

Vacherin Norma

275°

Meringue

**5 egg whites
1-1/4 cups sugar**

Filling

**1-1/2 cups heavy cream, stiffly whipped
Sugar and instant coffee to flavor
1 small jar preserved ginger in syrup**

Decoration

**Confectioner's sugar
1/2 cup heavy cream, stiffly whipped**

Line 3 baking sheets with silicone or baking paper. Beat the whites until they hold stiff peaks, add 1-1/2 tablespoons of sugar, and beat for 1/2 minute or until the mixture is glossy. Gradually fold in the remaining sugar with a large metal spoon. Divide the mixture among the three sheets in careful circles, 7-1/2 inches in diameter or, using a pastry bag and 1/2 inch tube, pipe the meringue in a spiral pattern. Bake the circles for 60 to 70 minutes until they are dried out and light colored. Cool on a wire rack and, when almost cold, peel off the paper.

Flavor the stiff cream with the instant coffee, about 1 teaspoonful dissolved in a speck of water, and sweeten slightly. Cut the glacéd ginger into fine shreds. Place the first meringue circle in an 8-inch spring form spread with half the whipped cream and cover with a layer of ginger. Place a second circle on top and spread with the remainder of the cream and ginger. Cover with the third circle. Cover with foil and chill in the refrigerator or freezer for 1 hour. At serving time remove the vacherin from the tin, sprinkle the top with confectioner's sugar, and with a star tube and pastry bag make some effective rosettes around the border using the remaining plain whipped cream.

Muriel Downes

Prune Soufflé

6 servings

25 large prunes
3/4 cup sugar
1 cup chopped nut meats
1 teaspoon vanilla or some brandy
4 beaten egg whites

Cook the prunes in water and purée, discarding the pits. Add the sugar, chopped nuts, and flavoring. Fold in the stiffly beaten egg whites. Put this mixture in the top of a buttered double boiler and cook for 1-1/2 hours without lifting the lid. Invert on a platter and mask with the following brandy sauce.

Brandy Sauce

4 egg yolks
1 cup milk
3/4 cup sugar
1 tablespoon brandy

Beat the yolks, milk, and sugar together and then stir until thick in a double boiler, taking care that the simmering water in the lower part of the double boiler does not reach the pan. Stir in the brandy.

Miss Grace Hatchett

Candied Orange Souflle

350° / 8 servings

12 candied orange slices
16 tablespoons sugar
Juice of 1 orange
Zest of 1/2 orange, chopped fine
2 tablespoons Raffetto Nesselrode sauce
12 egg whites

Cook the candied orange slices in a little water until soft, about 20 minutes. Chop the orange slices coarsely, add 4 tablespoons of sugar, and beat in the electric mixer only until well blended, not puréed. Add the orange juice, the zest, and the Nesselrode sauce.

Beat the egg whites until very stiff and add the rest of the sugar slowly, beating it the entire time. Fold the orange mixture into the whites carefully. Put a 3-inch collar around a 10-inch soufflé dish and spoon the soufflé into the ungreased dish. Put the dish in a pan in which there is 1 inch of hot water and set it in the oven for 40 minutes. Serve with the following custard sauce.

Brandy Custard

2 cups evaporated milk
1 cup sugar
12 egg yolks, well beaten
1-inch piece of vanilla bean
Brandy to taste

Beat the canned milk in a double boiler. Beat the sugar into the egg yolks and add it to the heated milk with the vanilla bean and the brandy, stirring it all over the fire until it has thickened slightly. Remove the vanilla bean at serving time.

Mrs. Stanford Z. Rothschild

Apricot Soufflé

400° / 4 servings

1 cup good quality apricot jam
2 egg yolks
2 soup spoons kirsch
6 egg whites
Ground almonds
Whipping cream
Sugar

If the jam is very thick, let it melt over a low flame in a saucepan. Off the heat add the egg yolks and the kirsch.

Butter a 1-quart soufflé mold and dust it with sugar. Beat the egg whites stiff but not dry and fold gently into the apricot mixture. Pour the apricot mixture into the mold and sprinkle the top with ground almonds. Put the mold into the oven. Immediately turn the temperature down to 375° and cook 20 to 25 minutes. Serve promptly with a sauce of fresh cream, lightly whipped and sweetened; or a soft custard sauce.   *Mrs. Edgar Sweren*

Apricot Chiffon Pie

1 tablespoon unflavored gelatin
1/4 cup cold water
5 eggs, separated
1-1/4 cups granulated sugar
3/4 cup apricot purée
1 cup heavy cream
1/4 teaspoon salt
1 baked 9-inch pie shell

Soak the gelatin in water 3 to 5 minutes. To the beaten egg yolks, add 3/4 cup sugar and the apricot purée and cook in a double boiler until the mixture coats a spoon. Add the softened gelatin and stir until the gelatin is dissolved. When the mixture begins to thicken, fold in the whipped cream and the stiffly beaten egg whites, to which the remaining sugar has been added, and the salt. Fill the pie shell and chill 2 to 3 hours.
Mrs. J. Jefferson Miller

Mocha Chiffon Pie

Vanilla wafers
1 cup semi-sweet chocolate morsels
1 8-ounce package cream cheese
6 tablespoons brown sugar
4 tablespoons sugar
2 tablespoons instant coffee
1/8 teaspoon salt
1 teaspoon vanilla
2 eggs, separated
1 cup heavy cream, whipped
Whipped cream for garnish
Grated unsweetened chocolate for garnish

Make a vanilla-wafer crust for a 9-inch pie shell. Melt the chocolate over hot water; remove from the heat and cool. Combine and mix in a bowl the softened cream cheese, brown sugar, coffee, salt, and vanilla. Beat in the 2 yolks, one at a time. Stir in the melted, cooled chocolate. Beat the egg whites stiff and fold them into the chocolate mixture. Fold in the whipped cream and turn into the cookie shell. Chill until firm. Garnish with whipped cream and grated chocolate.
Miss Sylvia Andrews

Grasshopper Pie

18 chocolate cookies
1/2 cup butter or margarine, melted
20-26 marshmallows
1/2 cup milk
1/2 pint heavy cream, whipped
1 to 1-1/2 ounces green crème de menthe
1 to 1-1/2 ounces white crème de cacao
Maraschino cherries (optional)

Crush the cookies into fine crumbs. Mix them with the butter or margarine and pat into the bottom and sides of a 9-inch pie pan. Chill. Combine the marshmallows and milk; heat slowly while folding the mixture over and over until the marshmallows are melted. Cool. Fold the liqueurs into the whipped cream. Fold in the marshmallow mixture and pour it into the chilled crust. Chill until firm. If desired, garnish with cherries.

Mrs. Robert Levi

Lemon Sour Cream Pie

1 cup sugar
3 tablespoons cornstarch
1/4 cup butter
1/4 cup lemon juice
3 egg yolks
Grated rind of 1 lemon
1 cup milk
1 cup sour cream
1 baked 9-inch pastry pie shell
1/2 cup heavy cream, whipped

Combine the sugar and cornstarch in a saucepan. Add the butter, lemon juice, egg yolks, lemon rind, and milk. Cook over medium heat, stirring constantly, until thickened and smooth. Chill. Fold the sour cream into the chilled mixture and spoon into the baked pie shell. Chill well. Serve topped with whipped cream, sweetened to taste, and decorate with grated lemon.

Mrs. Marvin Brown

Key Lime Pie

1 tablespoon unflavored gelatin
1/2 cup sugar
1/4 teaspoon salt
4 egg yolks
1/2 cup lime juice
1/4 cup water
1 teaspoon grated lime peel
Few drops green food coloring
4 egg whites
1/2 cup sugar
1 cup heavy cream, whipped
1 baked 9-inch pie shell, cooled

Thoroughly mix the gelatin, sugar, and salt in a saucepan. Beat together the egg yolks, lime juice, and water; stir into the gelatin mixture. Cook over medium heat, stirring constantly, just until the mixture comes to a boil. Remove from the heat; stir in the grated peel. Add the food coloring sparingly to give a pale green color. Chill, stirring occasionally, until the mixture mounds slightly when dropped from a spoon.

Beat the egg whites until soft peaks form; gradually add 1/2 cup sugar, beating to stiff peaks. Fold the gelatin mixture into the egg whites; fold in the whipped cream. Pile into the pastry shell. Chill until firm. Spread with additional whipped cream and edge with grated lime. Grated pistachio nuts are attractive in the center bordered by thin half circles of lime.

Mrs. Joseph D. Brown

Brandy Alexander Pie

1 envelope unflavored gelatin
1/4 cup cold water
2/3 cup sugar
1/8 teaspoon salt
3 eggs, separated
1/4 cup Cognac
1/4 cup crème de cacao
2 cups heavy cream
1 9-inch graham cracker crust
Chocolate curls or grated chocolate for garnish

Sprinkle gelatin over cold water in a saucepan. When it has softened add 1/3 cup of sugar, the salt, and the egg yolks; stir to blend them. Heat over simmering water, while stirring, until the gelatin dissolves and the mixture thickens. Remove from the heat and stir in the Cognac and the crème de cacao. Chill until the mixture starts to mound slightly when stirred. Beat the whites until stiff. Gradually beat in the remaining 1/3 cup of sugar and fold into the thickened mixture. Whip 1 cup of the cream and fold it in. Turn the filling into the crust and chill for several hours or overnight. Garnish with the remaining whipped cream and chocolate curls.

Mrs. Thomas Schweizer

Sour Cream Raisin Pie

450°

2 eggs, slightly beaten
1 cup sugar
1 cup sour cream
1 tablespoon flour
1/8 teaspoon salt
1/2 teaspoon cinnamon
1/2 teaspoon nutmeg
1 cup seedless raisins, chopped
1/2 cup chopped walnut meats (optional)
1 unbaked 9-inch pie shell

Beat together the eggs and sugar; gradually stir in the sour cream. Mix together the flour, salt, and spices; stir into the raisins and nuts. Add to the egg-cream mixture, then turn into a pastry-lined plate. Bake for 10 minutes at 450°, then lower the heat to 350° and bake for 25 to 30 minutes longer. It is done when a silver knife comes out clean.

Use a meringue made with 2 stiffly beaten egg whites and 3 tablespoons of sugar, gradually beaten into them. About 10 minutes before taking the pie out of the oven, add the meringue and bake until it is brown.

Mrs. Arthur R. Watson

Rose Hip and Raspberry Pie

450°

Rose hips, about 2 cups
Raspberries, about 2 cups
1/2 cup sugar
1/4 cup lemon juice
2 tablespoons cornstarch
Dashes of mace, nutmeg, and salt
2 drops red food coloring
2 tablespoons butter
1 9-inch unbaked pie crust, plus pastry for lattice or top crust

Slit the rose hips and remove the seeds. Simmer the rose hips in water until tender; drain. Combine them with the raspberries and put them in the uncooked pie crust. Sift the sugar over the fruit and mix in the cornstarch, which has been dissolved in lemon juice. Let it all blend together for 15 minutes or so with shakes of the seasonings, the red coloring, and dabs of butter. Cover the berries with either a lattice or a whole top crust and bake for 10 minutes; reduce the heat and bake 40 to 55 minutes more at 350°.

Mrs. Francis C. Rienhoff

A Rich Pecan Pie

300° / 2 pies

Dough for 2 single pie crusts
Pinch of salt
4 eggs
3/4 cup water
1 pound Domino light brown sugar
1/4 cup soft butter
1 teaspoon vanilla extract
4 ounces unbroken pecan halves

Line 2 9-inch pie plates with the rolled-out dough. Beat the eggs and salt in a small mixing bowl until thick and pale. Combine the sugar and water in a heavy 2-quart saucepan. Place it over

moderate heat, stirring, until the sugar dissolves; then bring it to a full boil and cook it for 3 minutes. Then, while beating the eggs again, pour the hot syrup slowly into the eggs. Add the softened butter and the vanilla. Turn the mixture into the pastry-lined plates, arrange the pecans over all attractively and bake until set, about 40 minutes.
Mrs. William Hazelhurst

Creamy Rhubarb Pie

425°

1 egg, beaten
1 cup commercial sour cream
1 cup sugar
1/2 teaspoon salt
3 tablespoons tapioca
3 cups finely cut fresh rhubarb
1 unbaked 9-inch pie shell

Combine the egg, sour cream, sugar, salt, and tapioca in a bowl. Fill the pie shell with the rhubarb. Pour the egg-and-cream mixture over the rhubarb. Bake in a 425° oven for 15 minutes; then reduce the heat to 350° and continue baking for 30 to 35 minutes.
Mrs. Vernon H. Norwood

Rum Cream Pie

1/2 envelope unflavored gelatin
1/4 cup water
1/2 cup sugar
1/8 teaspoon salt
3 egg yolks
1/4 cup dark rum
1 cup heavy whipping cream
Shaved chocolate
1 8-inch graham cracker crust

Sprinkle gelatin over water to soften, add the sugar, salt, and egg yolks, and stir over simmering water or low heat until the gelatin dissolves and the eggs thicken. Do not boil. Stir in the rum and cool until the mixture starts to thicken; then whip the cream, fold it into the mixture, and pour it all into the crust. Chill for 2 or 3 hours before serving. Garnish with whipped cream and shaved chocolate.
Mrs. William Hazelhurst

Transparent Pie

425° / 4 to 5 servings

1/3 cup butter
1 cup sugar
2 eggs, beaten thick and light
2 teaspoons white corn syrup and a pinch of salt
1 teaspoon vanilla
1 unbaked 8-inch pie crust

Cream the butter with the sugar, then beat in the other ingredients. Pour into the unbaked crust. Bake at 425° for 8 minutes, then reduce the heat to 325° and bake about 20 minutes longer or until the pie is golden brown.
Mrs. James Dallas Atkinson

Thanksgiving Chess Pie

350°

1 cup butter
3 cups sugar
2 tablespoons cornmeal
6 eggs, beaten
1 tablespoon vinegar
1 teaspoon vanilla
1 9-inch unbaked pie shell

Cream the butter, sugar, and cornmeal; add the beaten eggs and then the other ingredients. Fill the piecrust and bake for 1 hour. Makes 1 large pie, or 6 ramekins.
Mrs. Jerrie Cherry

Crystallized Grapefruit

250°

5 large or 6 small grapefruit
Salt
5 cups granulated sugar

Remove the pulp from the grapefruit, leaving some of the white membrane. Cut the peel into strips 2-1/2 x 1/2 inch, or into ovals 1-1/2 x 1 inch. Cover with salted water, allowing 1 tablespoon salt to each pint of water, and boil for 20 minutes. Drain, add fresh unsalted water to cover by at least 1/2 inch, and boil again for 20 minutes. Drain and repeat with fresh water another time. After pouring off the third water, add 5 cups of granulated sugar and simmer together until all the sugar is taken up and the grapefruit is clear, about 1 hour.

Now lift 5 or 6 pieces of peel out onto a plate which has been covered with granulated sugar. Roll the peel in the sugar until it is completely coated, then lay side by side on a cookie sheet; repeat with the rest of the peel.

When all the peel has been coated, heat the oven to 250°, then turn off the heat. Slide the cookie sheet of grapefruit peel into the oven and leave it there for 2 to 3 hours or overnight to dry out the peel. Then remove and store the peel in a cool, dry container. This makes about 2 pounds. It is dry on the outside, not sticky, and soft on the inside.
Miss Eleanor Holliday Cross

Coeur à la Crème

8 servings

1 pound creamed cottage cheese
1/2 pound cream cheese
2 tablespoons confectioner's sugar
1 cup heavy cream

Beat the cottage cheese until it is smooth, then add the cream cheese (warmed to room temperature) and the confectioner's sugar. Beat again until smooth; add the heavy cream and beat at high speed until blended. Now pack the mixture into a 7-inch heart mold with drain holes or a classic reed mold lined with cheesecloth. If there are no heart-shaped molds in your house, punch holes in a cottage cheese carton instead. Place over a dish into which the excess water can drain and refrigerate overnight. Unmold and serve with whole strawberries, raspberries, or crushed fruit. Rum sauce is good with this as well, as long as you're not in France.
Mrs. William Hazelhurst,
Mrs. LeBaron S. Willard, Jr.

Toffee Bread

White bread
Milk
Butter
Golden syrup
Brown sugar
Thick cream

Soak fat fingers of white bread in milk, fry until golden in butter, then add golden syrup and brown sugar and continue cooking to caramelize them. Serve with thick cream.

Naturally, there are no amounts given—who knows how many children are involved to eat this quick and easy dessert?
Mrs. Alan Campbell

Cornflake Ring

10 tablespoons butter
1-1/4 cups brown sugar
7 cups cornflakes

There is no exact recipe for this but the above ingredients are a good guide. Melt the butter in a heavy spider and add the brown sugar. Stir it all until it has melted, then add the cornflakes. Toss them around until they are well coated, then pack into an oiled 8-cup ring mold. Leave it only long enough to cool, then invert it over a serving dish. Don't take the form off then; wait until you are sure the ring is quite cold. Serve ice cream, strawberries, raspberries, or who-knows-what in the center.   *Miss Wendy Wurtzburger*

Wine Jelly

3 servings

1 package lemon Jell-o
1 cup water
1 cup medium-dry or sweet sherry, depending on your taste
Green grapes

Soften gelatin in 1/4 cup water. Heat the sherry and remaining water, add to the gelatin mix, and stir to dissolve. Pour in a mold and chill until set. Turn out and decorate with green grapes.
Mrs. Holland Mills

Lemon Cheese

4 eggs
2 egg yolks
2 cups granulated sugar
1/4 pound butter
3 lemons, both grated rind and juice
Dash of salt

Beat the eggs and egg yolks lightly and then put all the ingredients in the top of a double boiler. Cook slowly, stirring constantly, until the mixture is thick. Do not let the water in the bottom of the double boiler touch the upper pan at any time. Poured into sterile glasses, the lemon cheese will keep refrigerated for a long time. It may be used as a tart or cake filling or as a spread on English muffins.   *Mrs. Richard F. Cleveland*

Candied Violets
Candied Rose Petals

Rose petals or violets
1 egg white
1 tablespoon water
Granulated sugar

Violet blossoms are candied whole; rose petals are separated from the flower. Always snip the white base from the rose petals, as it tastes bitter.

Mix the egg white with 1 tablespoon water. Dip each blossom or petal in this mixture and drain on paper toweling. While still damp sprinkle the petals well with granulated sugar; then shake off the excess sugar. Place on waxed paper to dry for 12 hours. When thoroughly dry store in a covered container in the refrigerator.
Mrs. Francis C. Rienhoff

Crème Caramel

300° / 8 servings

1 cup sugar
1/3 cup water
1 quart milk
1 vanilla bean
1 cup sugar
8 eggs

In a 1-1/2-quart charlotte mold or baking dish place 1 cup sugar and 1/3 cup water and stir over low heat until dissolved. Turn up the flame and cook until the sugar has caramelized to a nut-brown. Remove from the heat and tilt the dish until it is coated with the caramel.

Meanwhile, in another saucepan, cook the milk, vanilla bean, and sugar just until the milk comes to a boil. In a bowl, beat the eggs vigorously and pour the boiled milk into the eggs a bit at a time, beating all the while. Pour the milk-and-egg mixture into the caramel-coated dish, then place the dish or charlotte mold in a large pan of hot water. Bake for about 1 hour. When the custard is firm and the top is brown, the caramel is ready to take out of the oven. Refrigerate overnight.

Mrs. Donald Brown

Bread and Butter Pudding

350° / 6 servings

8 slices raisin bread or brioche
Butter
Extra raisins
Rum
Candied orange peel (optional)
4 whole eggs
2 egg yolks
1 pint table cream
Light brown sugar

Butter the bread lightly and put half of it into a soufflé dish. Shake a few raisins in the dish; sprinkle the bread with rum. Add the rest of the buttered bread and sprinkle it, too, with rum and raisins and perhaps some candied orange peel.

Beat together the eggs and cream, add a little more rum if you like, pour it over the bread, and let it stand at least an hour. If this is not sweet enough, shake some light brown sugar over the top before baking. Put the pudding in a water bath and bake for an hour or until puffy and high.

Miss Margaret Masters

An Authentic English Trifle

8 servings

4 egg yolks
2 cups light cream
1/4 cup sugar
1 teaspoon vanilla extract
Pinch of salt
A sponge cake of the best materials
Raspberry jam
3/4 cup sherry wine
2 cups whipping cream
1/2 cup powdered sugar
1 tablespoon vanilla extract
1 dozen blanched almonds

Make a custard with the egg yolks beaten until light, the table cream, granulated sugar, vanilla, and salt. This is all put in a double boiler over simmering water and stirred until the custard coats a spoon. Put in a cool bowl and chill.

Have ready a sponge cake either of 2 layers or 1 layer cut in 2 horizontally. Cut the cake layers into finger-size pieces; spread each piece with the jam and sprinkle with the sherry. Whip 2 cups of whipping cream until stiff; flavor with powdered sugar and vanilla.

Now, put half the cake pieces in a bowl, add half the custard, then half the whipped cream. Repeat this and finally strew the almonds on top.

Some people add macaroons but then the name must be changed for a trifle is made only of sponge cake.

Mrs. Jose L. Hirsh

A pair of dessert pots with covers, ornamented with flowers. They were made at Sceaux-Penthièvre, mid-18th century.

Riz Imperatrice

8 servings

3/4 cup rice
1 quart milk
1/2 teaspoon salt
3/4 cup sugar
Vanilla to taste
2 envelopes gelatin
1 cup heavy cream, whipped
Strawberries
Cointreau or kirsch

Cook the rice in the milk to which the salt and sugar have been added. When it is cooked, force it through a sieve or food mill and add vanilla to taste. Soften the gelatin in 1/2 cup water and dissolve it in the hot rice. When the rice has cooled to lukewarm, fold in the whipped cream, beaten stiff. Turn into a wet ring mold and chill.

When it is firm turn out on a platter and fill the center with strawberries which have soaked for 1/2 hour in Cointreau or kirsch.

Mrs. Charles Parkhurst

Mystery Mocha Pudding

350°

1 ounce unsweetened chocolate
2 tablespoons butter
3/4 cup sugar
1 cup flour
2 teaspoons baking powder
1/4 teaspoon salt
1/2 cup milk
1 teaspoon vanilla
1/2 cup brown sugar
1/3 cup sugar
4 tablespoons cocoa
1 cup cold coffee

Melt the chocolate with the butter, then add the 3/4 cup of sugar. Sift the flour, baking powder, and salt together and add to the chocolate mixture alternately with the milk and vanilla. Pour the batter in a 9 x 9-inch buttered baking dish.

The cake gets its name because of the mysterious final step: combine the brown sugar, 1/4 cup granulated sugar, cocoa, and cold coffee together and pour it all over the top. Bake for 40 minutes and serve from the baking dish. You may add 1/2 cup chopped nuts to the mixture to make it richer.

Miss Gretchen Sieglaff

Brandied Chocolate Cups

6 servings

1 12-ounce package chocolate bits
2 tablespoons sweet butter
Small fluted paper muffin cups
3/4 tablespoon gelatin
1 cup hot milk
2 tablespoons sugar
Salt
1/2 pint whipping cream
Brandy to taste
Unsweetened chocolate, grated

Pour a package of chocolate bits into the top of a double boiler. Add 2 tablespoons sweet butter and set over hot, not boiling, water. Stir. As soon as the chocolate has melted and is thoroughly blended with the butter, completely coat the inside of 6 or more paper cups with the chocolate, using the back of a spoon to press the melted chocolate against the paper. Set them on a plate in the refrigerator for more than an hour. Then carefully peel the paper off, and if the chocolate chips a little, try not to care.

Soak the gelatin in a little cold water; dissolve in 1 cup hot milk. Add 2 tablespoons sugar and a grain of salt. When the mixture starts to set, fold in the whipped cream. Flavor well with brandy. Fill each cup nearly full and dust with grated bitter chocolate.

Mrs. Robert A. Milch

Pennsylvania Apple Cake

350° / 6 servings

1 cup salad oil
3 eggs
2 cups sugar
1 teaspoon vanilla
2 cups flour
1 teaspoon baking soda
1 teaspoon cinnamon
1/2 teaspoon salt
1 cup chopped nuts (any kind)
4 cups peeled apple slices

    Beat the salad oil and eggs until frothy, add the sugar and the vanilla, and beat again. Then add the flour, baking soda, cinnamon, and salt; stir until well blended. Finally fold in the chopped nuts and sliced apples. Bake in a buttered 9 x 13-inch pan for 1 hour. Spread the icing (recipe follows) on the cake as soon as it comes from the oven.

Pennsylvania Apple Cake Icing

1-1/2 tablespoons butter
3/4 cup confectioner's sugar
1 teaspoon vanilla
3 ounces cream cheese

  Make the icing by bringing the ingredients to room temperature and blending them all together well.

    This is a versatile cake which can be cut in small squares and decorated with crystallized violets, nuts, or fresh strawberries, or baked in large-size paper cups, which are excellent for buffets. It freezes well.
                                                  Mrs. Harry E. Foster

Baked Apples Post

400° / 6 servings

6 medium-sized baking apples
1/4 cup butter

A monkey eating fruit, shown in an English stained-glass roundel of the 15th century.

1/2 cup light brown sugar
1/4 cup raisins
1/2 teaspoon cinnamon
1/4 cup grape nuts cereal
1/3 cup bran flakes

    Wash and core the apples. Pare the top half. Set each apple in a square of foil and bring the wrap up over the lower half; place them in a baking dish. Melt the butter; add the brown sugar, raisins, cinnamon, and stir until well blended. Add the cereals to half of the butter-sugar mixture and use that to fill the centers of the apples, packing in well. Bake for 40 minutes. Reheat the remaining butter-sugar mixture, pour it over the apples and bake them for 10 minutes longer. The dessert can then be frozen if you wish.
                                                 Mrs. George F. Roll

The Children's Unbaked Apple Dessert

1/4 cup sugar
1 cup graham-cracker crumbs
1/3 stick butter
1 quart applesauce (homemade is best)
1/2 pint heavy cream, whipped
Currant jelly

Blend sugar and crumbs together. Melt the butter in a heavy skillet and add the sugar-crumb mixture. Stir until it becomes golden in color and set aside. Meanwhile, spoon some applesauce into a serving bowl to cover the bottom. Spoon some graham-cracker mix over the applesauce. Alternate the layers until the bowl is 3/4 full, ending with the applesauce. Cover with whipped cream and put dabs of currant jelly on top of it all.

Miss Pamela Milch

Apricots with Rum Sauce

4 servings

1 can large halved and pitted apricots
Chopped almonds
Butter

Fill the drained apricots with coarsely chopped almonds. Dot with butter and brown under a broiler. Serve with Rum Sauce (see following recipe).

Rum Sauce

2 eggs
4 scant tablespoons sugar
3 tablespoons rum
1/4 cup whipping cream

Beat the eggs well with the sugar, then add the rum and fold in the whipped cream.

Mrs. George L. Clarke

Blueberry Pudding

6 servings

4 cups blueberries
1 cup granulated sugar
2 tablespoons lemon juice
Thin buttered bread
Thin buttered toast

Stew the blueberries with the sugar and lemon juice for a few minutes, adding enough water just barely to cover the berries. Line a deep dish with the buttered bread and layer the blueberries and the bread, topping the last layer of blueberries with the pieces of toast. Be sure the bread is well saturated. Put it in the icebox to chill. If there is extra juice, use it to pour on later at serving time, although thick cream or sour cream both go well with this dish.

Mrs. Sara D. Redmond

Blueberry Tart

350°

1 quart blueberries
3/4 cup sugar
1 egg
1 tablespoon cornstarch
2 tablespoons water
Juice of 1 lemon

Wash over the blueberries and add the sugar. Beat the egg and mix it in, then add the cornstarch, which has been dissolved in the water and lemon juice. Put it all in a large saucepan and cook slowly until it is juicy.

Crust

1/2 pound butter
2 tablespoons sugar
2-1/2 cups flour
1 egg yolk

Sift the flour and sugar together, cut in the butter, and when it is well blended add the well beaten egg yolk. Roll it into a ball; chill it, then pat it into a 9-inch spring form pan. Add the berries and bake for 45 minutes.   *Mrs. Arthur P. Korach*

Cranberry Shortcake

375°

3/4 cup sugar
1 cup flour
1 teaspoon baking powder
1/8 teaspoon salt
2 tablespoons butter
1/2 cup milk
1-1/2 cups raw cranberries

Sift the dry ingredients together and cut in the butter, using a pastry blender, until it looks like coarse meal. Add the milk, stir lightly, then add the carefully washed and dried cranberries.

Bake in an 8-inch square pan, well buttered and floured, for 40 minutes. The cake should be golden brown on top and test done in the center. Serve warm with the following sauce.

Cranberry Shortcake Sauce

1/2 cup butter
1/2 cup brown sugar
1/2 cup white sugar
1/2 cup light cream or half-and-half

Mix ingredients together and cook over hot water for 20 to 30 minutes. Serve hot with shortcake.   *Mrs. William G. Speed, III*

Figs Royale

Fresh figs
Port
Whipping cream
Almonds

Prick each fresh fig with a fork and let stand in port to cover for at least 2 hours. Put the figs in a handsome bowl with the port, and cover them with lightly whipped cream. Cover the cream with shaved almonds.   *Mrs. Charles T. Albert*

Fruit Salad Kintail with Apricot Dressing

12 servings

1 pineapple
1 pint strawberries, halved
1 pint blueberries

Quarter the pineapple, remove the core and, cut the fruit loose from the skin; then slice in pieces. Combine with the strawberries and the blueberries and stir with 2 tablespoons sugar. Refrigerate for at least an hour and then serve with the following apricot dressing.

Apricot Dressing

1 cup creamed small-curd cottage cheese
1/2 cup apricot preserves
1/4 teaspoon ground ginger
1 teaspoon sherry

Blend all the ingredients together; cover and chill before using.   *Mrs. Duncan MacKenzie*

Fresh Fruit with Rum Sauce

1 jar guava jelly
1 pint vanilla ice cream
1 ounce Jamaica rum
1 teaspoon brown sugar
1 pint heavy cream
Any fresh fruit such as berries or peaches

Melt the guava jelly and the ice cream, add the rum and sugar, and finally stir in the cream, which

has been stiffly whipped. Taste to be sure there is enough rum, and serve over or with the fruit.
Mrs. Henry Hays

Easy Summer Fruit Tarts

8 servings

2 8-ounce packages cream cheese
4 tablespoons butter
4 tablespoons sugar
2 tablespoons cream
8 small tart shells
Whole small strawberries or raspberries
Currant jelly

Rice the cream cheese. Beat the butter and sugar until fluffy. Add the cream cheese and cream and beat again well. Spoon this into the little shells and put small berries over all. Melt the jelly and pour it over the top. Cool before serving.
Miss Margaret Masters

A figure from the margin of a page of a Gospels, Armenian, 1455. The manuscript was written at the Monastery of Gamaghiel at Khizan by Hohannes *vardapet* and illuminated by the priest Khatchatur.

Winter Fruit Compote

350° / 12 to 16 servings

1 16-ounce can sliced peaches
1 16-ounce can apricot halves
1 16-ounce can pitted bing cherries
1 16-ounce can pear halves
1 can pineapple chunks
1 can mandarin orange segments
1/2 box dried prunes
1/4 cup raisins or golden raisins
Lemon juice
Orange juice
1 cup brown sugar
1 cup either macaroon crumbs, gingersnap crumbs, graham-cracker crumbs, cookie crumbs, or (in desperation) crumbled cornflakes

Drain the fruits, mix them gently in a buttered casserole; squeeze the lemon and orange juice over the fruits. Combine the brown sugar and the crumbs and sprinkle them generously over the top of the casserole. Bake for 45 minutes or longer. Serve warm or cold, with or without brandy, crème fraîche, or whipped cream.
Miss Sylvia Betts Dodd, Mrs. Frank Holm, Mrs. Jose L. Hirsh, Mrs. Jerome Kidder, Mrs. Sidney Levyne, Mrs. Charles Parkhurst

Winter Cake

325°/6 servings

1 cup flour
1 teaspoon baking soda
1 cup sugar
1 egg
1/2 teaspoon salt
1 cup canned fruit, not drained

Thoroughly mix the above ingredients, adding the fruit last. Place the batter in a well greased 8 x 8-inch pan and sprinkle the top with the following.

1/2 cup brown sugar
1/2 cup chopped nuts

Bake for about 45 to 50 minutes until well done. When cool, cut into 2-inch squares.

Mrs. Victor Sulin

Plums with Apricot Sauce

350°/8 servings

1 cup dried apricots
4 tablespoons sugar
1 teaspoon grated lemon rind
2 pounds tinned greengage plums
8 slices stale cake or even buttered bread
4 tablespoons butter
4 tablespoons sugar

Soak the apricots for a few hours in water to cover, then cook until tender. Drain them and put through a sieve. Stir in the sugar and lemon rind. Cut the plums in half and take out the stones.

Put the cake slices in the bottom of a casserole, with the plum halves on top. Put a dot of butter in each half and sprinkle with a little sugar. Bake for about 1/2 hour. Reheat the apricot purée, taste for sweetness, and pour it over the plums at serving time.

Miss Margaret Masters

Plums and Figs

Drain plums and/or figs well. Cover them with a café-au-lait colored mixture of crème de cacao and sour cream. Don't add another thing to this.

Mrs. Alan Wurtzburger

Stuffed Baked Peaches

350°/6 servings

6 large firm peaches
2 tablespoons butter
1-1/2 tablespoons sugar
3/4 cup macaroon crumbs
1 egg yolk, beaten
1 tablespoon Cognac
4 tablespoons Marsala or sweet sherry
1/4 cup water

Peel the peaches, cut in halves, and remove the pits. Scoop out a little of the pulp to enlarge the hollow and mash this pulp. Cream the butter and sugar together; mix in the macaroon crumbs, peach pulp, egg yolk, and Cognac. Stuff the peaches. Arrange the peaches in a buttered baking dish, if possible one attractive to serve from too. Sprinkle 1 teaspoon of wine on each half. Pour the water into the dish and bake for 25 minutes or until the peaches are tender but still firm.

Canned cling peaches may be used when fresh ones are out of season. Bake them only 15 minutes.

Mrs. Arthur Stern

Candy Peach Crisp

350°/6 servings

6-8 large fresh peaches, pared and sliced
1 cup brown sugar
1 cup flour
1/3 cup butter, melted
1/2 cup ground nut meats

Place a layer of peaches in the bottom of a large pie plate and sprinkle them with 1/4 cup of brown sugar. Add the remaining peaches. Cover with a mixture of the flour, butter, remaining brown sugar, and nut meats, creamed together. Bake 45 to 60 minutes, checking at 30 minutes. Keep checking until the peaches are soft. Serve warm with cream.

This dessert can also be made using a partially baked pie shell.
Mrs. Edward Stimpson

Peaches with Sour Cream and Strawberries

8 servings

8 peach halves, fresh or canned
Brandy
Lemon juice
1 pint hulled strawberries
2 cups sour cream
Sugar to taste
2 tablespoons Grand Marnier
Macaroon crumbs

Sprinkle the peach halves with brandy and lemon juice and chill well. Fold the strawberries into the sour cream; add superfine sugar to taste and the Grand Marnier.

To serve, arrange peach halves in a large bowl, pour the strawberry-cream mixture over them, and sprinkle with finely crushed macaroon crumbs.
Mrs. Richard W. Emory

Orange Mélange

4 servings

1 quart orange sherbet
6 California oranges, peeled and sectioned
1 jar Dundee marmalade
Jamaica rum to taste
1/2 cup shaved almonds

Present the orange sherbet surrounded by the orange sections. Thin the marmalade to a sauce consistency with the rum, and add the shaved almonds to it. Serve with the sherbet or pour it over the orange sections. This tastes equally good with vanilla ice cream, but the other looks prettier.
Mrs. Charles T. Albert

Boodle's Orange Fool

8 servings

2 oranges and rind
1 lemon and rind
1 tablespoon heather honey
A little Cointreau (optional)
1/2 pint heavy cream
Sponge cake

Combine the juice of the oranges and the lemon, the grated rind of 1/2 lemon and 1 orange, the honey, and perhaps the Cointreau. Whip the cream and fold in the juices and honey. Put the sponge cake, cut in bite-sized pieces, in a bowl; pour the cream mixture over this. Let it chill in the refrigerator for 4 hours.
Miss Charlotte Walker

Oranges in Syrup

6 servings

6 navel oranges
1 cup sugar
Grand Marnier

Using a vegetable peeler, cut the rind off 2 of the oranges in long, very thin pieces, taking care not to pick up any of the white skin. With a small knife, cut the rind into long slivers. Combine in the saucepan with the sugar and 1/2 cup water. Bring to a boil slowly. Cook over moderate heat for about 8 minutes or until the syrup is about as thick as corn syrup. Remove from the heat.

Meanwhile, section the oranges and place in the bowl. Pour the hot syrup over the oranges and refrigerate. Just before serving, stir in about 2 tablespoons of Grand Marnier (or to taste). To peel, hold the fruit (orange, grapefruit, or lime), in your left hand. Cut off all the rind and the white skin, using a sharp, fairly large knife, working around and around over a bowl to catch any juices. Peel right down to the flesh, and if you miss any white skin, cut it off. To section, cut down on both sides of each section as close to the membrane as possible and push the section into the bowl. Remove seeds, if any.
Helen McCully

Caramelized Pears with Marrons Glacés

375° / 6 servings

3 large pears
6 tablespoons butter
6 tablespoons sugar
1 cup heavy cream
3 glazed chestnuts

Peel and halve the pears; scoop out the cores and cut away the stems. Cut a thin slice from the round side so that the halves will sit flat. Arrange them in a shallow baking dish (preferably one that can go over direct heat). Put 1 tablespoon butter and 1 tablespoon sugar on each half and bake, basting frequently, for 30 minutes or until tender. Arrange the pears in a deep serving dish or platter. Cook the remaining sugar-and-butter sauce over direct heat, stirring until it caramelizes and turns a deep golden brown. Remove from the heat and stir in the heavy cream to dissolve the caramel. Spoon the sauce around the pears. (There is enough sauce for 6 pears.) Garnish the center of each pear half with half a marron glacé. Serve hot or chilled.

Mrs. Alan Boyd, Mrs. Robert A. Milch

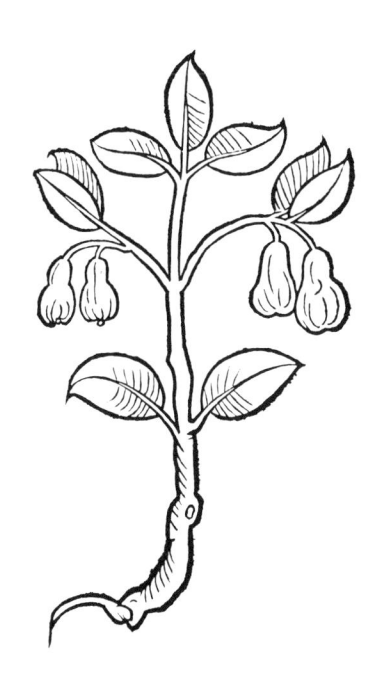

Poires à l'Orange

300° / 6 servings

6 ripe pears
1 cup orange juice
Grated peel of 1 orange
1/4 cup Cointreau
Juice of 1 lemon
3 to 4 tablespoons honey
Heavy cream

Cut the pears in half and core but do not skin them. Place the pear halves face down in a buttered shallow ovenproof dish. Mix together the orange juice and grated rind, Cointreau, lemon juice, and 3 to 4 tablespoons of honey. Pour over the pears. Cook until the pears are tender but still hold their shape. Baste from time to time. If the orange-juice-honey mixture is not thick enough, reduce it in a separate pot. Place pears on a serving dish; cover with the syrup. Serve very cold with heavy or whipped cream.

Mrs. Benjamin Griswold, IV

Pears with Chocolate

1 large can Bartlett pears
1/4 cup sugar
Pinch of salt
2-1/2 teaspoons instant coffee
1 teaspoon vanilla
Sour cream
Shaved sweet chocolate

Drain the pears, reserving the juice. Add the sugar, pinch of salt, and instant coffee to the juice. Boil for 5 minutes. Remove from the heat and add vanilla. Place the pears in a casserole and cover with the juice mixture. Just before serving, put them in a warm oven for long enough to maintain the heat. Serve with sour cream and chocolate.
Mrs. Lee Johnson, III

Old-Fashioned Strawberry Shortcake

425° / 6 servings

3 pints strawberries
1/2 cup plus 1 tablespoon sugar
2 cups flour
1 tablespoon baking powder
1/2 teaspoon salt
1/4 cup shortening
1/3 cup light cream
3 eggs
Butter or margarine
Heavy or whipping cream

Wash, hull, and slice the berries. Mash slightly with a fork. Sweeten to taste, using about 1/2 cup sugar. Let them stand at room temperature for an hour or so to draw out the juices. Sift the flour with the baking powder and salt and the remaining tablespoon of sugar. Cut in the shortening until it resembles coarse crumbs. Add the light cream mixed with the eggs. Stir the ingredients just until all the flour has been moistened. Turn out onto a slightly floured board and knead the dough for half a minute. Shape into a circle about 1/4 inch thick and 8 inches in diameter. Place on a baking sheet and bake until golden, 15 to 20 minutes. Split while hot, and spread the bottom layer generously with butter. Fill it with half the strawberries, replace the top layer, and cover with the remaining berries. Pass cream in a pitcher or serve it whipped if you like.
Miss Eleanor Holliday Cross, Mrs. W. C. Halbert

Rhubarb in Cream

6 to 8 servings

6 cups (about 2 pounds) fresh rhubarb, cubed
2 cups sugar
1 cup heavy cream, whipped

Put rhubarb and 2 cups sugar into top of a double boiler. Cook over rapidly boiling water until the rhubarb is just tender, not mushy, stirring once or twice. Add more sugar if needed. Let it cool to room temperature. Whip the cream; stir it into the rhubarb. Pile into a glass bowl and chill all day. It will separate into 2 layers again, but the cream will be rosy from the juice. *Mrs. John E. C. White*

Caramel Almond Roll

350° / 10 to 12 servings

7 ounces almonds
1/4 cup sifted flour
1 teaspoon double-action baking powder
1/4 teaspoon salt
4 egg whites
3/4 cup brown sugar, packed
6 egg yolks
1 teaspoon vanilla extract
1-1/2 cups heavy cream, whipped
Confectioner's sugar

Blanch and grate the almonds, which will yield 1-1/2 cups. Mix the almonds well with the flour, baking powder, and salt, and set aside. Place the rack in the lower quarter of the oven. Line a 15-1/2 x 10-1/2 x 1-inch jelly-roll pan with unglazed paper and grease the paper. Beat the egg whites until stiff, adding 1/4 cup of the brown sugar gradually. Continue beating until the meringue stands in stiff peaks. Set aside.

Beat the egg yolks until they are very thick. Add the remaining 1/2 cup sugar and beat again until thick. Add the vanilla extract. Fold the almond mixture into the egg yolks; then carefully fold in the meringue. Turn the batter into the prepared pan. Spread evenly and bake until browned, about 25 minutes. Allow the cake to cool in the pan, covered with a damp towel, and then chill.

When ready to serve, turn the cake out on a towel. Spread it with whipped cream which has been sweetened with sugar and flavored to taste with vanilla. Roll up from the narrow end and serve sprinkled with confectioner's sugar.

Mrs. Robert A. Milch

Marron Butter Cream Roll

400° / 6 servings

3/4 cup sifted cake flour
1 teaspoon baking powder
1/4 teaspoon salt
4 eggs
3/4 cup sugar
1 teaspoon vanilla extract
Confectioner's sugar
1/4 cup dark rum
Marron Butter Cream (see below)
12 chocolate almond leaves

Preheat the oven. Line the bottom of a jelly-roll pan 15 x 10 x 1 inches with waxed paper. Butter the bottom of the pan as well as the surface of the waxed paper. Sift the flour, baking powder, and salt together. Beat the eggs with a wire whisk until light and foamy. Continue beating, adding the sugar slowly, until the mixture is very thick and at least doubled in bulk. (If whisk beating is too difficult, a hand mixer may be used.) Sprinkle the sifted dry ingredients over the batter and fold them in gently. Fold in the vanilla. Pour the batter into the prepared pan and bake for 12 to 15 minutes or until the cake is delicately browned and the top springs back when touched lightly. Loosen the cake around the edges with a knife and turn it out on a large tea towel that has been sprinkled evenly with sifted confectioner's sugar. Working quickly while the cake is still warm, carefully remove the paper. Cut off the crisp edges of the cake with a sharp knife. Sprinkle the cake with the dark rum. Starting at the long side of the cake, gently roll up the cake right along with the towel. The towel will prevent the cake from sticking to itself. Place the rolled cake on a cake rack to cool.

When cool, unroll the cake and remove the tea towel. Spread the top of the cake with 1/2 the marron butter cream. Re-roll the cake. Place it on a long silver platter and frost the outside of the roll with the remaining butter cream. A pastry bag and tube will add an artistic touch. Decorate the log with chocolate curls. Garnish the platter with seasonal greens and chocolate leaves.

Marron Butter Cream

2 cans (6 ounces) marrons glacés
1/2 cup sugar
1/3 cup light corn syrup
3 egg yolks
1/2 pound sweet butter, softened
1/4 cup dark rum

Finely chop the marrons. Combine the sugar and corn syrup in a small saucepan and cook over medium heat, stirring constantly, until the mixture comes to a full bubbling boil; then remove it from the heat. Beat the egg yolks with a wire whisk until foamy and lemon-colored; add the hot syrup gradually and continuing beating until the mixture is cool. Beat in the butter a little at a time. Stir in the rum and marrons.

Mrs. Irwin J. Nudelman

Chocolate Roll with Sherry-Flavored Whipped Cream

375°

6 eggs, separated
1/2 cup sugar
6 ounces semi-sweet chocolate
2 or 3 tablespoons coffee
Powdered sugar
Unsweetened cocoa
Heavy Cream
Cream sherry

   Beat the egg yolks until light and lemon-colored. Gradually beat in the sugar. Melt the chocolate with 2 or 3 tablespoons coffee and blend with the beaten egg yolks. Beat the whites of the eggs until stiff but not dry, and fold into the egg-chocolate mixture. Pour into an 11 x 14-inch pan which has been buttered, lined with wax paper, and buttered again. Bake for about 15 minutes, or until it is light and puffy and breaks away from the sides of the pan. Remove from the oven and cover with a damp cloth for about 10 to 12 minutes to make the souffle fall!

   Sprinkle waxed paper with powdered sugar and cocoa; turn the cake out on the mixture and remove the waxed paper which adheres to the chocolate roll. Let it cool; then spread with whipped cream which has been well laced with cream sherry. Roll carefully so as not to break the tender cake. If you want further richness, serve sherry-flavored whipped cream in a separate bowl to top the slices.

Mrs. Francis Kennedy

Rum or Brandy Sauce

1/2 cup butter
1 cup sugar
3 tablespoons rum or brandy
2 egg yolks
1 cup heavy cream

   Cream the butter and sugar, then add the rum or brandy. Beat again and add, one at a time, the 2 egg yolks. Pour in the cream, put it all in a double boiler and cook slowly until slightly thick. Serve hot.

Mrs. LeBaron S. Willard, Jr.

Sauce à l'Abricot et à l'Orange

1/2 pound dried apricots
1/2 cup sugar
Pinch of salt
Grated rind of 1/2 orange
Cognac or kirsch

   Wash the apricots and cook them according to the package directions. Purée in a blender, a little at a time. Add a little orange juice if it is too thick to blend. Add the sugar, salt, and orange rind. Cook to dissolve the sugar; then add Cognac or kirsch to taste.

Mrs. Frank Weller

Thick Cherry Dance

6 servings

1 can (2 cups) pitted Bing cherries
1/8 cup sugar
Juice and rind of 1/2 lemon
1/2 cup (or less) brandy

   The day before using, drain the cherries and put the juice into a pan with the sugar, lemon juice, and rind. Cook to thicken and reduce to 1 cup. Add the brandy off the stove. Pour over the cherries and refrigerate overnight. Serve on French vanilla ice cream.

Mrs. Edward A. Griffith

BREADS

Old-Fashioned White Bread

375°
    At 100°, melt
1/4 cup lard in
1-1/2 cups buttermilk
    In a large bowl, put
1/4 cup sugar
1 teaspoon salt
1/2 teaspoon baking soda
1 package dry yeast

    Add the warm lard-buttermilk mixture and beat well with a rotary beater. Sift in 1 cup of unbleached flour at a time, stirring to make a soft but still moist dough. This will require about **4 cups of flour or perhaps a little more,** measured unsifted. Knead thoroughly for at least 10 minutes, adding a sprinkle of flour from time to time to prevent sticking.

    Put the ball of dough in a larded bowl, rolling the ball to coat it lightly with the lard. Cover it with a towel and let it rise to double bulk in a warm (90°-100°) place, about 45 minutes to 1 hour. Punch the dough down and let it rise again to double bulk, about 1/2 hour.

    Punch the dough down and knead it again a little bit. Form it to fit a greased 9-1/4 x 5-1/4 x 2-3/4-inch loaf pan, or better still, cut it in half and put in two 7-1/8 x 3-1/2 x 2-1/4-inch pans. The pans will be about 2/3 full. Let the dough rise again until it is well above the rim of the pans and then bake it until it is nicely browned. Small loaves will take about 1/2 hour, the large loaf somewhat longer.

    If you have a Kitchen Aid mixer the whole thing can be done in its bowl, using first the whisk and then the dough hook. It makes better bread and makes it ever so much easier.

    An oven with the pilot light on but with no burners lighted is just about the right temperature for proofing any yeast breads. The dough will rise rapidly, so check it frequently until you know your own oven's habits. The rapid rising tends to produce a bread with open texture and fairly large bubbles. If you prefer a finer texture with tiny bubbles, proof the dough at about 75°-80°. This can be done by propping open the oven door. Experience and a thermometer will teach you how far open it should be. Of course, at the lower temperature the proofing time will be much longer, perhaps as long as 2 hours for the first raising.

    A loaf of bread is done when it has just shrunk away from the side of the pan and when it makes a hollow "klunk" when lightly tapped with a fingernail. Let loaves cool on a wire cake rack as soon as you take them from the oven. *Edward L. Brewster*

Super-Duper Health Bread

350° / 2 loaves

This recipe should not be attempted by an amateur. Read the *Notes* thoroughly before attempting the recipe.

3/4 cups milk
2 packages active dry yeast or 2 fresh yeast cakes
Pinch of sugar
2-1/4 cups boiling water
2 cups quick-cooking oats
3-1/2 cups whole wheat flour (100% whole graham wheat!)
3/4 cup dark molasses
1-1/2 tablespoons butter or margarine
2-1/4 teaspoons salt
2-1/2 cups all-purpose flour

Warm a glass container, a small bowl, with hot tap water and then dry it. Add the milk which has been warmed to body temperature (98°) to the warmed glass bowl; then add the yeast and a pinch of sugar. Stir until dissolved. If you use yeast cakes, flake the yeast into the milk. Pour boiling water over the oats, and over the whole wheat if you are using your own home-ground coarse wheat flour. Otherwise, add commercial whole wheat flour at the end with the all-purpose flour and add boiling water to the oats in a large mixing bowl. Stir the oats-and-water mixture and let it cool to body temperature.

Warm the molasses, butter, and salt together in a saucepan and add them to the oats mixture. Then add the milk and yeast mixture to the ingredients in the large bowl and stir with a strong spoon. Now add the flour gradually. If you are using commercial 100% whole wheat flour, add it now. Be sure to save about 1 cup of all-purpose flour for kneading. Mix the flour in with your hands, since the dough is very heavy. Cover the dough with a clean cloth and place it out of drafts in a warm room. If the room is chilly, place the bowl on a rack over hot water. The dough should rise in 1 hour.

Turn the dough out on a floured board and knead it lightly for 3 minutes. Divide the dough into 2 balls and shape them into loaves. Place the loaves in 2 greased bread pans, cover, and let stand in a warm place until they are double in bulk. Bake them for about 1 hour. Remove the pans and let them cool slightly and then remove the bread from the pans and cool it completely on a rack. This bread keeps very well.

Notes

Make this bread on days you expect to be home all day and use a timer to remind you to look at the dough while it is rising.

Temperatures are vitally important! Follow the temperature directions carefully.

If the final ball of dough is too sticky, add a little all-purpose flour.

If you want to make your own whole wheat flour, find a reputable feed store, ask for "re-cleaned wheat" for human consumption, and then grind the wheat to the texture of yellow cornmeal. This can be done either with a small hand mill or an electric blender.

Mrs. George Wells

Cardamon Seed Bread

SWEDISH COFFEE BREAD

375°

Dissolve
2 yeast cakes in
1 tablespoon sugar
by crumbling the yeast and stirring it into the sugar. In a saucepan mix
1 cup milk
1/2 cup sugar

1 teaspoon salt
1 tablespoon lard
1 tablespoon sweet butter
   Heat to 100°, melting the lard and the butter and dissolving the sugar and salt. Grind
10 cardamon seeds
   and add to the warm milk mixture. Add the dissolved yeast and beat all with a whisk. Stir in
1 cup all purpose flour. Add
2 eggs, lightly beaten
   and mix all thoroughly. Stir in
3 to 4 cups all-purpose flour to form a moist but workable dough. Knead until smooth and elastic, at least 10 minutes, adding sprinkles of flour to prevent sticking.
   Roll the ball of dough in a buttered bowl to coat it lightly, cover with a towel, and allow it to rise to double bulk at 75°-80°, 1-1/2 to 2 hours. Punch it down and allow it to double in bulk a second time, about 1 hour. Cut it down again and form it into small twists, rolls, or buns to suit your taste. Allow them to rise a third time on a greased cookie sheet.
   Brush a little egg beaten in water, saved for that purpose from the above and bake at 375° for about 1/2 hour until richly browned.
   See instructions for Old-Fashioned White Bread.
   Edward L. Brewster

Corn Pancakes

4 to 6 servings

1 can creamed corn (1-1/2 pounds)
2 egg yolks
1 tablespoon sugar
1/4 cup milk
2 tablespoons melted butter
Salt and pepper
4 tablespoons flour, sifted with 1/2 teaspoon baking powder
2 egg whites, stiffly beaten

   Combine all the ingredients except the egg whites and blend well. Fold in the egg whites. To fry them, drop by tablespoons on a hot griddle that has been wiped with a greased paper towel.
   Mrs. Bertram Bernheim, Jr.

Couronne of Whole Brie

400° / 20 to 30 portions

4 packages active dry yeast
2 cups tepid water
8 cups all-purpose flour
1-1/2 tablespoons salt
3 tablespoons sugar
3 tablespoons lightly salted butter
1 egg, lightly beaten
12-inch diameter whole ripe Brie, served at room temperature

   In a large bowl, sprinkle the yeast over water; stir until dissolved. Mix the flour, salt, and sugar together and add to make a stiff dough, then add the softened butter. Knead the dough in a lightly greased bowl; dust lightly with flour. Cover with a tea towel and let rise in a warm, draft-free place until it has doubled in bulk. Punch down and knead again briefly. Place again in the bowl, cover and let rise again until almost double in bulk.
   Grease a cookie sheet and place in the center of it an ovenproof object (such as a bowl or cake pan, open side down) which has the same diameter as the Brie with which you are going to serve the Couronne. Grease the bowl or pan on the outside rim. Form the dough into 3 round sausages, each one about an inch or so in diameter and long enough to encircle the pan. Braid the bread, blending the ends so that you have an unbroken circle. Fit to the pan and brush with beaten egg and bake for 30 to 35 minutes until golden brown. Cool on a rack. Serve the Couronne with

the Brie in the center. Decorate the top with a garland of green and Concord grapes and freshly salted pecan halves.

One-half of this recipe will yield an 8-inch circle to serve with an 8-inch Brie. This same recipe makes 2 loaves of bread (baked in 9 x 5 x 3-inch pans).

You may alter the garnishes of this classic to suit the seasons. The grapes suggested as a garnish in the recipe above are most abundant in late summer. In the late fall, dried fruits and nuts might be used and the Couronne surrounded with fresh floral greens and bittersweet. In the springtime, use fresh greens and baby's breath to surround the Brie, and large strawberries with grapes.

Mrs. Irwin J. Nudelman

Limpa

SWEDISH RYE BREAD

375°

Heat gently
1 cup water
1-1/2 tablespoons shortening
1/4 cup sugar
1 tablespoon salt
1/4 cup medium-dark molasses
   until all are melted and dissolved.
   In a large bowl, put
2 cups buttermilk
1/2 teaspoon baking soda
   Add the warm liquid mixture, and sift in and mix thoroughly
1 pound rye flour. Dissolve
1 package dry yeast in
1/4 cup warm water. Add
1/2 teaspoon sugar
   When it foams, add it to the rye-flour mixture. Now sift in
about 1 pound white flour, preferably unbleached.

Blend well to form a moist, soft dough, adjusting the amount of flour to the consistency of dough you want. Knead the dough for at least 10 minutes, adding a sprinkle of white flour from time to time to prevent sticking. Put the ball of dough in a greased bowl, rolling the ball to coat it lightly with the grease. Cover it with a towel and let it rise to double bulk in a warm place, 90°-100°, for about 1-1/4 hours.

Turn out on a floured board and knead thoroughly again. Shape into 3 oval loaves. Sprinkle a cookie sheet with **cornmeal** and place the loaves on it. Let them double in bulk and then bake them until they are crusty and nicely browned, 50 to 60 minutes. To get a glossy crust, mix **1 teaspoon salt** and **1/2 cup of water** and brush this on the loaves when you put them in to bake, again after about 15 to 20 minutes, and finally after about 30 to 35 minutes.

Edward L. Brewster

Nut Bread

350°

1/4 pound butter
1 cup sugar
3 egg yolks, beaten
1/2 cup milk
1 teaspoon vanilla extract
1 teaspoon lemon extract
2 cups flour
1/2 teaspoon salt
2 teaspoons baking powder
1/2 cup finely chopped nuts (pecans or walnuts)
3 egg whites, beaten stiff

Cream the butter and sugar. Mix the egg yolks with the milk and extracts. Sift the flour with the salt and baking powder. Add the egg-yolk mixture and flour alternately to the butter-sugar mixture. Add the nuts and then fold in the egg whites.

Put in a large greased loaf pan or 2 small 7 x 4-inch pans and bake for about 40 minutes. This is excellent for sandwiches, using cream cheese and butter.
Miss Emily King

Oatmeal Bread

375° / 4 5 x 9-inch loaves

2 packages active dry yeast
1 cup warm water
3-1/3 cups skim milk
1/4 cup butter
2 cups rolled oats
1/2 cup molasses
1 tablespoon salt
10-11 cups sifted flour

It should be noted immediately that this is a rather large recipe and if the cook just wishes to "try it once" it is easily divided in half.

Dissolve the yeast in warm water. Heat the milk and butter until bubbly; pour it over the oats to stand for about 1/2 hour. Add molasses, salt, and yeast. Add enough flour to make a stiff dough and work it until it leaves the side of the bowl or, more simply, put the whole thing in an electric mixer with a dough hook attachment and mix it all by current as you think of other things. In any case, when the dough is no longer sticky and is pliable, shape into a ball and put it into a buttered bowl with a cloth over it to protect against drafts and prevent a crust from forming. Leave it in a warm place until the dough doubles in bulk, which should be in about 1 hour. Punch the ball down and knead on a floured board for 10 minutes, more or less, adding flour if it appears to be necessary.

Divide into loaves; let it rest, covered with a cloth, for about 10 minutes, then put it into prepared 5 x 9-inch loaf pans, or any other size you prefer, and let it rise again until light. (Prepared pans are buttered ones, not oiled, as oil tends to make the dough soggy.) Bake the loaves for 40 to 50 minutes, or until they sound hollow when tapped. Cool on wire racks.
Mrs. Robert Myers

Old-Time Bread

325° / 3 loaves

In a large bowl put
1/2 cup uncooked Scotch oatmeal
1/3 cup Wheatena
Then mix the following ingredients together:
3 tablespoons cooking oil
2 tablespoons dark molasses
2 tablespoons honey
2 heaping tablespoons wheat germ meal
1 heaping tablespoon malted milk or dry milk
2 tablespoons salt

Combine all the ingredients in the large bowl; pour 2 cups of hot water over them and cool until lukewarm.

Dissolve 1 package dry yeast (or 1 cake yeast) in 1/2 cup of lukewarm water and add to the bowl mixture, blending thoroughly. This mixture will absorb between 6 and 7 cups of unbleached flour, which should be sifted in and blended as you go. Knead and place in a greased bowl. Cover with a cloth and place in a warm spot for about 2 hours, or until double in size. Grease 3 5 x 9-inch bread pans and divide the dough between them. Place in the oven, set at the lowest temperature possible, with the door open. Let the bread rise until it is just higher than the top edge of the pan; this takes about 1/2 hour. Shut the oven door. Bake at 325° for about 40 minutes. When done, the bread will be golden brown and will sound hollow when tapped on the bottom of the loaf. Remove from pans immediately and wait 1 day before eating, if you can.
Mrs. Austin Read

Sour Rye Bread

450 / 2 1-1/2 pound loaves

The Sour

**1/2 ounce or 4 teaspoons caraway seed
6 ounces or 1-1/2 cups white rye flour
1/2 ounce yeast
4 ounces or 1/2 cup warm water**

Mix all these together to "set the Sour"—ferment it overnight in a covered bowl in a warm place.

Basic Dough

**1 cup warm water
The Sour (above)
6 teaspoons salt
2 teaspoons salad oil
1-1/2 ounces yeast
1 cup warm water
1-3/4 cups white rye flour
3-3/4 cups clear (unbleached) flour**

Mix the Sour in 1 cup warm water, then add the salt and salad oil. Mix to a soft mass. Dissolve the yeast in 1 cup warm water and then add to the sour mix. Mix, then add white rye flour and clear flour. Mix by hand until a coherent mass is formed. Then turn out on a floured board and knead until a putty-like consistency is reached. Place in a covered bowl in a warm place. Let the dough rise approximately 1 hour, until nearly double in bulk.

Divide the dough into 2 pieces (about 1-1/2 pounds each), round up, and mold into loaves. Place lengthwise on a baking sheet covered with baking parchment paper and dusted with cornmeal. Let the loaves double in size while standing in a warm, moist place. Slash the tops of the loaves with a sharp knife; do not cut too deeply. Wash the loaves with 3/4 ounces cornstarch dissolved in 1 cup boiling water just prior to putting them in the oven.

Preheat the oven and bake about 45 minutes. To test for a proper bake, look for a golden brown color; turn the loaves over and thump the bottom with your fingers; they should have a hollow resonance, not a muffled sound, when hit.

"White rye" will probably not be found on a supermarket shelf; you will have to buy it from a baker. "Clear flour" can be replaced with all-purpose, but buy the "clear" from a baker if possible for best results.

Sam L. Silber

Grapenut Muffin Bread

**1 cup grapenuts
2 cups sour milk
4 cups flour
2 teaspoons soda
3/4 cup sugar
1/4 cup shortening
1 cup sweet milk**

Soak grapenuts in sour milk for an hour. Add the flour, soda, and sugar, sifted together. Melt the shortening and add with the sweet milk to the flour mixture. Bake in 2 well-greased small loaf pans for 1 hour. *Miss Avonia Read*

Cheese Loaf

375° / 2 loaves

2 cakes active yeast
1/2 cup lukewarm water
3/4 cup milk
3/4 cup water
1/3 cup sugar
1/4 cup butter
1/2 teaspoon ginger
1 tablespoon salt
1 egg
1-1/2 cups grated sharp cheese
5-6 cups white flour
Melted butter

Dissolve the yeast in the lukewarm water and leave it for a bit as you scald and then cool the milk and water. Add the sugar, butter, ginger, and salt to the cooled milk, and then the yeast. Beat the egg with the grated cheese, add to the yeast mixture, and then add 2 cups of the flour.

Cover the sponge and let it rise in a warm place for about 30 minutes. Punch it down and beat in the rest of the flour gradually, stirring and kneading until the dough leaves the sides of the bowl. It should take about 6 cups of flour in all, depending on the type of flour and the weather. Knead the dough until it is pliable, shiny, and smooth. Cover it with a cloth and put it in a warm place until it has doubled in bulk. Punch it down again, knead a few minutes more, shape into loaves, and leave it for 10 minutes to rest. Then put it into 2 greased loaf pans, 9 x 5 inches, and let it rise until it has doubled in bulk. Brush the loaves with melted butter and bake about 30 minutes, or until the loaves give off a hollow welcome sound when tapped. *Miss Elizabeth Amery*

Date Nut Loaf

325°

1/2 cup sifted flour
1/2 teaspoon salt
1 rounded teaspoon baking powder
1/2 cup sugar
1/2 pound pitted dates, cut up
1/2 pound walnut meats, broken
2 eggs, separated
1/2 teaspoon vanilla

Sift the flour, salt, baking powder, and sugar over the dates and nuts. Mix well. Beat the yolks, add the vanilla, and stir into the dry mixture. Beat the whites stiff and dry and fold them in. Turn into a small loaf pan lined with buttered or waxed paper. Bake one hour; turn out and peel the paper off at once. When cool, wrap the loaf in foil. (It will keep for weeks).

To serve, slice it very thin. It is easier to butter the end of the loaf before slicing. This is excellent for tea. *Mrs. S. Page Nelson, Jr.*

Butter Horns

375° / 4 dozen rolls

2 cakes active yeast
1/2 cup warm water
1/2 cup melted butter
2 eggs, well beaten
1 cup milk, lukewarm
1/4 cup sugar
1-1/2 teaspoon salt
4-5 cups bread flour
Some melted butter

Dissolve the yeast in warm water; then add the butter, eggs, milk, sugar, and salt. Beat them together thoroughly and then add flour, enough to clean the sides of the bowl and to make a fairly stiff dough. Let it rise, covered, in a buttered bowl in a warm place for about 1 hour.

Punch it down, then take enough dough to make a 12-inch circle when rolled out 1/4 inch thick. Spread the circle with melted butter and cut it into pie-shaped pieces. Roll each piece, starting with the wide bottom edge, to the point, making a horn. Place on a buttered sheet and let the horns rise to double their bulk again, which should take about 30 minutes. Bake for about 20 minutes.

This same dough may be used for coffee bread, Swedish rings, and the like.

Miss Elizabeth Amery

Cold Oven Popovers

10 to 12 popovers

2 eggs
1/2 teaspoon salt
1 teaspoon melted butter
1 cup milk
1 cup flour

Beat the eggs, salt, and butter into the milk, then add the flour, mixing it in with a spoon without being at all concerned about a little lumpiness. (Overbeating is the enemy of a popover.) Fill buttered custard cups about 2/3 full and place them on a cookie sheet, so they won't tip over, in a cold oven. Then set the oven at 425° and leave them for 40 minutes. Make a small slit in each popover after they are baked to allow the steam to escape.

Miss Eleanor Holliday Cross,
Mrs. Harry Dillehunt

Pulled Bread

Take the crusts off a large loaf of good unsliced bread and give them to the birds. Pull the rest of the loaf apart in a reckless fashion with 2 forks.

Toast in a slow oven until brown and crisp. Some people butter the bread before toasting, which the editors do not recommend.

Mrs. Alan Wurtzburger

Sour Cream Pancakes

2 servings

5 tablespoons unsifted flour
1 teaspoon baking powder
1/4 teaspoon salt
2 eggs, unbeaten
1/2 pint sour cream

Sift the flour, baking powder, and salt into a bowl. Beat the eggs with the sour cream and stir (but do not beat) into the dry ingredients. Bake on an ungreased griddle. These fluffy things are delicious with sautéed apple rings.

Mrs. C. Edwin Fitzell

Buttermilk Waffles

4 large waffles

1-1/2 cups flour
1 teaspoon baking powder
3/4 teaspoon baking soda
1/2 teaspoon salt
1-1/2 cups buttermilk
2 eggs
6 tablespoons melted butter

Put all the dry ingredients into a bowl, add the buttermilk, the well-beaten eggs, and the melted butter. This must be beaten thoroughly before making 4 large waffles. It is easier to use a blender, and those who like to use one may merely put all the ingredients into the jar at one time and turn the current on briefly.

Mrs. James D. Atkinson

Southern Puffy Spoon Bread

375° / 6 servings

3 egg yolks
2 cups buttermilk
1/2 cup white corn meal
1 teaspoon baking powder
1 teaspoon soda
1/2 teaspoon salt
2 tablespoons melted butter
3 egg whites, stiffly beaten

Butter the sides and bottom of a 1-1/2-quart baking dish, at least 2-1/2 inches deep. Put the dish in the oven while the spoon bread is being prepared. Beat the egg yolks well and stir in the buttermilk. Sift the dry ingredients and add them to the bowl. Add the melted butter and finally fold in the stiffly beaten egg whites. Spoon the batter into the hot baking dish and bake for about 30 minutes, until golden brown.

Mrs. James D. Atkinson

Crisp Corn Cakes with Lacy Edges

1 large egg
1 cup thick buttermilk
1 cup white corn meal
1/2 teaspoon soda
3/4 teaspoon salt
Pinch of sugar
2 teaspoons pork or bacon fat (optional)

Beat the egg thoroughly and add the buttermilk; stir well. Sift the dry ingredients together and incorporate the egg and buttermilk, beating the batter until it is smooth. Add the melted fat if you like its flavor. The batter may be baked in a very hot greased medium-sized skillet for 25 minutes in a 425° oven or it can be dropped by spoonfuls into the skillet and fried on top of the stove. Southerners are apt to bake the bread, and cut it into wedges, to serve with plenty of butter and boiled greens (cabbage or kale). A Northern version suggests fresh pork sausage and honey.

Mrs. James D. Atkinson, Mrs. Michael Sheehan

Spider Cake

CORNBREAD

350°

2 tablespoons unsalted butter
1-1/2 cups white stone-ground corn meal
1/4 cup sugar
1/2 cup flour
1 teaspoon salt
1-1/2 teaspoons baking powder
2 cups milk
2 eggs, beaten
1 cup heavy whipping cream

Put the butter in a 2-1/2-quart baking-serving dish or heavy iron skillet and place it in the oven until the butter has melted. Keep it warm but don't let the butter burn.

Mix the dry ingredients together, add the milk and beaten eggs, and beat well. Pour the batter into the hot buttered pan and bake for 10 minutes. Then pour the whipping cream into the center of the cornbread without stirring it and return it to the oven to bake another 20 minutes. The circumference will be like cornbread but the center will be almost liquid. This tastes very good with chicken, pork, or ham.

Mrs. Frank T. Gray

Indian Puffs

400° / 6-8 popover-like puffs

**3/4 cup water-ground corn meal
1 cup hot milk
3 eggs, well beaten
1/4 teaspoon salt**

Stir the cornmeal into the hot milk until it thickens. Add the beaten eggs and the salt. Fill greased popover pans 3/4 full and bake for 30 minutes. Serve immediately. The "puffs" resemble a popover, but are also something like crisp spoon bread. They are good served with roast beef instead of Yorkshire pudding.

A friend found this recipe in an old trunk in the loft of a barn. It dates from about 1830. The original recipe reads: "Take 3 eggs, half a pint of milk, 5 large tablespoons full of Indian meal. Bake them in tea cups in a bake pan."

Mrs. Bradford Jacobs

Quick Sally Lunn

350°

**2-1/2 cups sifted flour
3 teaspoons baking powder
3/4 teaspoon salt
1/2 cup butter
1/2 cup sugar
3 eggs
1 cup milk**

Sift the flour with the baking powder and salt. Cream butter, add sugar, and cream again. Add the eggs one at a time, beating between each addition; then fold in the flour alternately with the milk. Bake it in a buttered Turk's pan or a bundt pan, for 55 to 60 minutes. Serve it with plenty of butter.

Mrs. John Paul Troy

Crispy Biscuits

375° / 36 biscuits

**2-1/2 level teaspoons baking powder
6 cups flour
3/4 teaspoon salt
3 tablespoons shortening
1-1/2 to 2 cups cold milk**

Sift the baking powder, flour, and salt into a bowl. Mix in the shortening, add the cold milk (just enough to make a rather stiff dough), then work it with your hands until it is smooth and elastic. Roll the dough out on a lightly floured board and cut with a biscuit cutter. Bake on an ungreased baking sheet until golden brown, about 25 minutes.

Miss Rita St. Clair

Kulich and Braided Easter Loaves

350°

1 cup sugar
2 cakes yeast
1/2 cup warm water
1-1/2 teaspoons salt
4 eggs
2/3 cup soft shortening
1-1/2 cups lukewarm milk
1 tablespoon rum extract
6 drops yellow food coloring (optional)
7-1/2 to 8 cups sifted all-purpose flour
1-1/3 cups seedless raisins
1-1/3 cups finely chopped mixed peels
1/3 cup finely chopped blanched almonds
Melted shortening

Mix together the sugar and yeast in a large bowl; add the water and stir until the mixture dissolves. Add salt, eggs, shortening, milk, extract, and coloring; mix well. Beat the flour into the liquids until the dough is thick enough to handle. Mix together the raisins, peels, and almonds. Stir these into the dough. Turn the mixture out on a lightly floured board and knead until smooth and elastic. Place in a greased bowl; cover and allow to rise in a warm place until double in bulk, about 1 hour. Punch down and turn onto a floured board.

For small round loaves (representative of Byzantine domes of churches), divide the dough into 4 or 5 parts. Fill greased 1-pound coffee cans to within about 2 inches from the top. Allow the dough to rise 1 hour in a warm place or until light. Brush with melted shortening and bake in a preheated 350° oven for about 40 minutes, or until done. Remove to a cooling rack and brush with melted shortening. While warm, make the icing and pour or brush onto the loaves. Then decorate the iced loaves with candied fruit peel to form the Russian letters XB, meaning "Christ is Risen." (Omit letters if loaves are made for Christmas.)

For braided loaves, divide the dough in parts for 3 or 4 loaves. Roll the dough for each loaf about 3/4 of an inch thick. Cut three long strips and braid. Fasten the ends by tucking under and securing. Place the loaves on a greased baking sheet and allow them to rise for 1 hour in a warm place or until light. Brush with melted shortening and bake the braids in a preheated oven at 375° for 25 to 30 minutes. Remove to a cooling rack. Brush with melted shortening. Make the icing and pour or brush it onto the loaves while warm. Decorate with almonds, cherries, and citron.

Kulich and Braided Easter Loaves Icing

2 tablespoons butter
1/4 cup milk
1/4 teaspoon rum extract (optional)
1 pound confectioner's sugar
Toasted almond halves
Strips citron
Halves of candied cherries

Melt butter in milk and add rum extract. Stir confectioner's sugar into the mixture until a consistency that will pour or brush onto the loaves is reached. Decorate with almonds and candied fruit.

Mrs. Charles T. Hanson

COOKIES

Scotch Apricot Bars

350°

1 cup butter
2 cups flour (for the crust)
1/2 cup granulated sugar
1-1/3 cups dried apricots (1 box)
4 eggs, well beaten
2 cups light brown sugar
2/3 cup flour
1/2 teaspoon salt
1 teaspoon baking powder
1 cup chopped nuts (black walnuts are best)
1 teaspoon vanilla
Confectioner's sugar

  Mix with your hands the butter, 2 cups of flour, and the granulated sugar and pat the mixture into a buttered oblong pan, 9 x 13 inches. Bake for 25 minutes or until it is light brown. While it is baking, have ready the apricots, which have been boiled 10 minutes and drained, then chopped. Add the eggs and the light brown sugar. Sift the dry ingredients together and add those with the chopped nuts and vanilla. Spread this over the crust and bake 30 minutes more. Cut the bars when cool and sprinkle them with the confectioner's sugar.

Mrs. Arthur Stern

Butterscotch Brownies

325° / 36 brownies

1/2 cup melted butter
2 cups brown sugar
2 eggs, well beaten
1 cup sifted flour
2 teaspoons double-acting baking powder
1 teaspoon vanilla
1 cup coarsely chopped nuts

  Melt the butter over low heat and stir in the brown sugar until it is well blended. Cool it slightly, and then add the eggs. Sift the flour, salt, and baking powder together, and add to the sugar-and-egg mixture. Finally, add the nuts and vanilla. Spread this in a well greased 9 x 13-inch pan and bake for 30 minutes. These will appear soft, but the middle should be soft. A caramel glaze adds enormously to their appearance.

Caramel glaze

1/4 cup brown sugar
2 tablespoons heavy cream

  Add heavy cream to brown sugar. Boil until a small amount dropped in cold water forms a soft ball, then with a pastry brush glaze the brownies before cutting. While still warm, cut into 36 pieces.

Mrs. L. Wilson Davis, Mrs. LeBaron S. Willard Jr.

Almond Kuchen

425°

1/2 pound butter
1/2 pint sour cream
2 cups unsifted flour
Sugar
Blanched almonds

Soften the butter and then beat it with the sour cream. Stir in the unsifted flour until it cleans the side of the bowl. Refrigerate it at least a half a day, then roll it out into a large thin circle on a floured surface. Sprinkle it all with coarse sugar. Cut it into pie-shaped triangles, and beginning with the wide end, roll toward the tip. Put a sliver of almond at each tip. Put the pastries on an ungreased cookie sheet close together and bake for about 12 minutes, or until the kuchen are just touched with golden brown at the edge. Remove them from the sheets to cool. If not used immediately, freeze the pastries, bringing them to room temperature for use or warming them slightly.

Mrs. Tom Freudenheim

Bourbon or Rum Balls

24 balls

2 cups chocolate cake, white cake, yellow cake, or any cake as long as it is not fresh, or 2 cups vanilla or chocolate wafers
1/2 cup chopped nuts
2 tablespoons unsweetened cocoa
2 tablespoons white corn syrup
1/4 cup bourbon or rum
A little softened butter

Grind or crumble the cake or cookies, easily done in an electric blender. Mix with all the other ingredients very thoroughly. Take a teaspoon at a time and mold into balls. Roll in plain powdered sugar or, better still, a mixture of 1 teaspoon cocoa and 1/2 teaspoon cinnamon to every rounded tablespoon of sugar. Place the balls on a cookie sheet for 2 to 3 hours to dry. Roll once more in the sugar and store in a box with a tightly fitting lid.

A refinement of this is to add jam to the ingredients and, when the balls are set, to cover them with melted chocolate. In this case make them larger in size and serve as an entire dessert.

Mrs. LeBaron S. Willard, Jr.

Sugar Cookies

375°

1 pound butter
4 cups sugar
4 tablespoons milk
4 teaspoons vanilla
2 teaspoons lemon extract
1 teaspoon ground nutmeg
4 eggs
8 cups flour
4 teaspoons baking powder
1 teaspoon salt

Cream together the butter and sugar until light and fluffy; add the milk, vanilla, lemon extract, nutmeg, and eggs. Sift the flour, baking powder, and salt and add to the mixture, using an electric mixer, although if it gets too stiff you will have to finish by hand. Mix it well. Refrigerate the dough overnight. Remove just enough dough from the refrigerator for each rolling. Roll it very thin on a marble slab. Cut with cutters and place the cookies on well-oiled cookie sheets. Brush the tops with egg white, mixed with a little water and beaten up a bit. Decorate with red and green colored sugar and blanched almond halves. Bake until they are just done. They must be watched as they may get too brown. Remove from the cookie sheets when they have cooled slightly. Store in tins. This amount will make 500 cookies if rolled very thin.

Mrs. William G. Speed, Jr.

"V'la l'coco!" sang the chocolate vendor as he walked the Parisian streets selling his sweets—just so was he painted by Gavarni. French, 1855-1857.

Blond Brownies

375°

1/2 pound butter
2 cups light brown sugar
4 eggs, well beaten
2-1/2 cups sifted cake flour
2 teaspoons baking powder
2 teaspoons vanilla
2 packages miniature chocolate bits
1-1/2 cups pecans, broken

    Melt the butter, add the sugar, and stir until it has dissolved. Add the eggs. Sift the flour and baking powder together and add that, with the vanilla, to the batter. Coat the chocolate bits and the nuts lightly with flour, then fold into the cake dough. Butter a 9 x 12-1/2-inch pan and dust with flour. Bake the brownies for 1/2 hour and then leave the pan in the oven for another 15 minutes. Cut into squares while still warm. These keep well if they are wrapped in foil, once they are cooled. *Mrs. Isaac Hecht*

Christmas Butter Crescents

350°

1 cup butter
1/2 cup brown sugar
1/4 teaspoon salt
2 teaspoons pure vanilla
2-1/4 cups sifted flour
Confectioner's sugar for rolling

    Cream the butter, brown sugar, salt, and vanilla together. Then work in the flour. Chill until the dough is stiff enough to handle. Roll, shape into small crescents, and bake for 12 to 15 minutes or until lightly browned. Remove them from the cookie sheet and roll while warm in confectioner's sugar. When cool, roll them again in the sugar and store in tins. *Mrs. Harrison L. Winter*

Chinese Chews

300°

2 cups flour
1 cup butter
1 cup brown sugar

Mix to crumbs and put in a shallow pan (8 x 16 inches or smaller). Bake 10 minutes, then remove and spread with the following mixture:

1-1/2 cups brown sugar
2 tablespoons flour
1/4 teaspoon salt
1 cup chopped pecans
2 eggs
1 teaspoon vanilla
1/2 teaspoon baking powder

Beat together all the ingredients. Spread over the baked crust and bake slowly until light brown, about 40 minutes. The inside should be fairly moist when removed from the oven. Cool and cut into squares.

Mrs. Jon Alan Wurtzburger

Cornflake Macaroons

350°

2 egg whites
1 cup sugar
Pinch of salt
1/4 teaspoon almond extract
1/4 teaspoon vanilla extract
1 cup shredded coconut, frozen or fresh
1/2 cup chopped nuts, if you like
2 cups cornflakes

Beat the whites until stiff. Add the sugar gradually while continuing to beat. Fold in the other ingredients and drop by teaspoonfuls on a greased cookie sheet. Bake until done, 15 to 20 minutes.

Miss Pamela Milch

Date Nut Chews

325°

2/3 cup sweetened condensed milk
2 teaspoons vanilla
1/4 cup powdered milk
1/8 teaspoon salt
1/2 cup wheat germ
3/4 cup chopped dates
3/4 cup broken walnuts or pecans

Combine all the ingredients but the dates and nuts and blend together well. Stir in the dates and nuts and drop by teaspoonfuls on well greased cookie sheets. Bake for 12 to 15 minutes. Remove them while they are still hot.

Mrs. S. Page Nelson, Jr.

Rich Doughnuts

2 eggs
1 cup sugar
2/3 cup sour cream or buttermilk
1 teaspoon soda
1 teaspoon baking powder
3-1/2 cups flour
1 teaspoon salt
1/2 teaspoon nutmeg
1/2 teaspoon cinnamon
2 tablespoons melted shortening
2 pounds leaf lard or Crisco for frying

Beat the eggs well; add the sugar and the sour cream, to which you have added the soda. Sift the dry ingredients together and add those with the melted butter to the egg mixture. Chill the dough. Roll out to about 1/2-inch thickness on a floured pastry cloth and cut with a well-floured biscuit cutter. Heat the lard in a deep pan to 380°. Drop in the doughnuts, turning them constantly until they are golden brown. Drain them on paper towels.

Mrs. Maurine Hayter

Lemon Cheese Squares

350° / 16 squares

1/2 cup butter
1 cup sifted flour
1/4 cup powdered sugar
2 eggs
1/4 teaspoon salt
2 tablespoons flour
1 cup granulated sugar
3 tablespoons fresh lemon juice (or 2 tablespoons fresh lime juice)

Blend the butter, flour, and powdered sugar and spread it in a 9 x 9-inch ungreased pan. Bake for 10 minutes. Combine the other ingredients and pour over the baked mixture and bake 30 minutes longer. Sprinkle powdered sugar over the top when out of the oven. Loosen the sides with the sharp point of a knife. Let the cake cool and then cut it into squares. These can be refrigerated, but should be removed about 1/2 hour before serving.

Miss Hortense Reit

A Cookie Dough for Cheese Cake or Ice Cream Pie

400°

1 cup sifted all-purpose flour
1/4 cup sugar
1 teaspoon grated lemon rind
1/4 teaspoon vanilla
1 egg yolk
1/4 cup butter, melted

Combine the flour, sugar, lemon rind, and vanilla. Make a well in the center and add the egg yolk and butter. Work together quickly with hands until blended. Wrap the dough in waxed paper and chill it for about 1 hour. Roll out 1/8 of an inch thick and place it over the buttered bottom of a 9-inch spring form cake pan. Trim off the dough by running a knife around the edge. Bake until a light gold color, then cool.

Mrs. Arthur Stern

Old-Fashioned Gingerbread

375° / 6 servings

1 cup molasses
1 teaspoon baking soda
1 teaspoon ginger
2 cups sifted flour
5 tablespoons butter
1/2 cup boiling water

Stir together, then beat the molasses, baking soda, ginger, flour, and softened butter. Add the boiling water and bake in a buttered 9-inch square cake pan for about 20 minutes. Top with whipped cream, ice cream, applesauce, or fudge sauce.

Mrs. Mary F. Barada

Honey Jumbles

325°

1-1/2 cups sugar
1 cup lard or Crisco
4 eggs
1 cup honey
1/2 cup strong coffee
4 teaspoons soda
3 teaspoons vanilla
1/2 teaspoon nutmeg
3 drops anise
6 cups sifted flour

Cream the sugar with the lard or Crisco. Add the eggs, honey, the strong coffee in which the soda is dissolved, vanilla, nutmeg, 3 drops of anise, and about 6 cups of sifted flour. Drop by teaspoonfuls on buttered cookie sheets. Bake until brown, about 10 to 15 minutes.

Miss Gretchen Sieglaff

Chocolate Macaroons

300° / 70 small macaroons

4 egg whites
1/2 teaspoon salt
1/4 teaspoon cream of tartar
1-1/2 cups sugar
1/2 pound semi-sweet chocolate bits
1 cup broken walnuts
1 teaspoon vanilla

    Beat the egg whites until they are foamy. Add the salt and the cream of tartar. Continue beating until the whites are stiff enough to hold peaks but not dry. Add the sugar, 2 tablespoonfuls at a time, beating thoroughly after each addition. Fold in the chocolate, nuts, and vanilla. Drop by teaspoonfuls onto a baking sheet covered with greased heavy paper. Bake for 25 minutes. Remove the macaroons from the paper while they are still slightly warm.
    Mrs. Robert Berney

Stay Up All Night Meringues

375°

2 egg whites
2/3 cup granulated sugar
Salt
1/2 teaspoon vanilla or mint flavoring
1 package chocolate bits (plain, mint, or butterscotch)

    Beat the egg whites, at room temperature, into stiff peaks. Continue beating as you slowly add the granulated sugar to the egg whites. Add a pinch of salt and the vanilla or mint flavoring. Fold in the chocolate bits. Crushed nuts may also be added and food coloring may be used if desired.
    Drop by spoonfuls onto aluminum foil spread on a baking sheet. The cookies may be placed close together since they do not spread while baking. Place in the oven and immediately turn the oven off. Leave in the oven overnight or at least 4 to 6 hours.
    Mrs. W. Gibbs McKenney

Molasses Cookies

350°

1 cup butter
1 cup sugar
2 eggs
4-1/2 cups sifted flour
3 tablespoons ginger
1 teaspoon salt
1 teaspoon soda
1/2 cup black molasses

    Cream the butter; add the sugar, then the eggs, and beat until puffy and light. Sift together the dry ingredients and mix in alternately with the molasses. Form into a roll and chill for several hours, after dividing the dough into 5 or 6 pieces. Remove only 1 piece at a time so that the dough will keep well chilled as it is rolled. Use a marble slab if possible or keep the kitchen cool while working with the dough. Cut the cookies into any shapes you fancy and bake on a buttered cookie sheet for about 10 minutes.
    Mrs. Robert Levi

Oatmeal Cookies

400°

1/4 pound butter
1/2 cup sugar
1 cup flour
1/2 teaspoon salt
1/2 teaspoon baking powder
1/4 cup light cream
1/4 cup light corn syrup
1-1/2 cup oatmeal
1 teaspoon vanilla extract

    Cream the butter with the sugar until light.

Sift together the flour, salt, and baking powder and add gradually to the mixture. Pour in the cream and corn syrup, blending thoroughly. Add the oatmeal all at once with the vanilla and blend carefully but not heavily. Drop by 1/2 teaspoonfuls, 2 inches apart, on a well greased cookie sheet. Bake 4 to 5 minutes.

Ben Cooper, Mrs. Arthur Gompf

Lacy Oatmeal Cookies

350° / 5 dozen cookies

1/2 pound melted butter or half margarine and half butter
2-1/4 cups light brown sugar
2-1/4 cups regular oatmeal (not instant)
1 teaspoon vanilla
1 egg slightly beaten

Mix together the melted butter, sugar, oatmeal, vanilla, and egg. Drop by teaspoonfuls on an ungreased cookie sheet, allowing for a 3-inch spread. Bake until brown, around 5 to 7 minutes. Cool the cookies before removing with a wide spatula.

Mrs. Richard H. Randall, Jr.

Scotch Cones

300°

1/2 cup molasses
1/2 cup butter
1 cup flour
2/3 cup sugar
1 teaspoon ginger
1 tablespoon brandy

Heat the molasses to the boiling point and add the butter. Gradually add the sifted dry ingredients, stirring constantly. Add the brandy. Drop small portions from the tip of a spoon onto a greased baking sheet, 2 inches apart. Bake 12 minutes or until they stop bubbling. Cool slightly and roll over the handle of a wooden spoon into cornucopias. If they become too crisp, reheat in the oven for a few minutes. Fill with vanilla ice cream and serve with caramel sauce.

Mrs. Sol Kann

Serbian Pecan Strips

325°

1 pound ground pecans
1 cup sugar
1 tablespoon lemon juice
3 egg whites, unbeaten
2 egg whites, beaten
1-1/2 cup confectioner's sugar plus some for sprinkling

Mix the ground pecans and the sugar. Stir in the lemon juice and unbeaten egg whites, which will make a sticky mixture. Dust a marble slab or board thickly with confectioner's sugar and dust your hands with it as well. Pat the nut mixture out into a 6-inch square about 1/4 inch thick.

Beat the remaining egg whites until stiff, gradually adding the confectioner's sugar to make a thick meringue. Spread it over the pecans. Using a wet knife, cut the mixture into strips 1-1/2 inch x 3/4 inch and put them on a well greased cookie sheet. Use a paper towel or a wet flat knife to make the borders even before baking. Bake for 20 minutes.

Mrs. Frank T. Gray

Sugar Cookies

350°

2 cups of butter
2 cups of sugar
3 egg yolks
4 cups of flour
Vanilla to taste
Salt

Cinnamon sugar
1 whole egg, beaten

Cream the butter and sugar; add the egg yolks and beat until light and puffy. Add the flour, vanilla, and salt. Mix into a ball and chill for 3 or 4 hours. Roll out in a cool place or on a marble slab, getting the dough very thin. Brush with the beaten egg and sprinkle with cinnamon sugar and chopped nuts after cutting with fancy cookie cutters. Bake about 10 minutes or less on a buttered cookie sheet.
Mrs. David Hutzler

Scotch Shortbread

325°

**1 pound butter
1-1/4 cups granulated sugar
5 cups flour**

Cream the butter and sugar until light. Work the flour into the mixture and then knead until smooth on a floured board. Divide the dough into 8 equal balls and smooth them into rounds about 1/2 inch thick. Prick well with a fork and crimp edges in an ornamental fashion. Place on a cookie sheet on brown paper and bake until golden brown, about 20 to 30 minutes. Immediately cut each round into reasonable-sized wedges.
Mrs. Richard F. Cleveland

Walnut Wafers

350°

**1 cup chopped walnuts
1 cup brown sugar
2 tablespoons flour
1 teaspoon baking powder
1 egg, beaten**

Mix all the ingredients well and drop by teaspoonfuls on a greased baking sheet. Bake for 5 to 7 minutes.
John Turnquist

Snucker Doodles

350°

**1 cup butter
1-1/2 cups sugar
2 beaten eggs
2-1/2 cups sifted flour
1 teaspoon baking soda
1/2 teaspoon salt
1 teaspoon vanilla
1 teaspoon almond flavoring**

Cream the butter and sugar together. Add the eggs and beat well; then add the flour, soda, salt, and vanilla and almond flavorings. Drop by the teaspoonful on an ungreased cookie sheet and bake until lightly browned.
Mrs. L. Wilson Davis

A chocolate pot of silver with the handle at the side, by J.-T. Vancombert, Paris, 1774.

A NOTE ON WINE

The appearance of this rather special cook book coincides with a rather special moment in the history of the use of wine in this country. In the mysterious way of such things wine has caught on, and very abruptly too. For altogether too long the use of it was mainly by two sorts of people: those of fairly cosmopolitan and sophisticated background and outlook, and those whose ties with the wine-growing countries of Europe were not yet broken and for whom wine was a regular and necessary part of their daily fare.

All that is changed now. Wine isn't yet as American as apple pie, but it has ceased to be exotic. Millions have found and are finding what a glass of wine can do for the simplest meal.

When such a change takes place in the food habits of a nation as large as ours, the consequences in terms of supply are staggering. This is especially true of the most famous and distinguished wines such as the great classed growths of Bordeaux, the *grands crus* of the Burgundian Côte d'Or and Chablis and those from the most eminent vineyards of the valleys of the Rhine and its tributaries. There isn't nearly enough of these to meet the new demand. This means that from now on the use of these becomes the privilege of the exceedingly well-to-do. Except on very special occasions the rest of us must content ourselves with the next best.

Which is by no means so distressing as it sounds, for the law of diminishing returns applies conspicuously to wines. The difference in quality between Château Lafite and some of its neighbors —the lesser *crus classés*, the *crus bourgeois* and so on—is not nearly so great as the difference in price. Many a Côte du Rhone stands up very well indeed by comparison with the classic Chateauneuf du Pape. Wines from many secondary French and German districts, more familiar to Europeans than to us, begin to show up in our markets. The exploration of these can be fascinating.

We are learning, too, in this changing situation, that France and Germany have no monopoly of good and superior wines. Expanding demand has wrought its usual magic and brought us a tremendous assortment of wines, unfamiliar but often excellent, not only from Italy and Spain and Portugal, but from Austria, Yugoslavia, Hungary, Switzerland. These countries have a wine-making tradition extending back a thousand years and more.

Not least, the remarkable accomplishments of the past twenty years in American wine growing, most importantly in California but elsewhere as well, are coming to be realized.

Well, what to do about it?

To begin with, stop worrying about eminent names unless you know exactly what you want and can afford it.

Second, there is no substitute for tasting, *en famille* or in groups. The popularity of group wine tastings makes sense—for the knowing as well as for the inexperienced. After all, the professional wine taster is not a wizard: his equipment consists of a well-functioning sensory system, attention, a knowledge of what he is looking for, and a good sensory memory. He is looking for certain perfectly definite defects and virtues, for the characteristic aroma and bouquet that come from a certain grape or combination of grapes, for definite regional characteristics, for evidence of specific wine-making techniques. In learning what to look for, reading helps; but there is no substitute for repeated experience. And the way to begin is to begin, preferably with experienced friends.

Third, price is a sound though not infallible guide. In wines as in other things one usually gets what one pays for though there can be bargains, especially as one gains confidence in exploring the wines now coming in from the less familiar areas. Dollar for dollar you are likely to do better among the good red Spanish riojas and, say, the delicate white wines of Austria than among the more familiar growths of Bordeaux and the Rhineland —and wind up with wines of not dissimilar style.

Fourth, don't overdo the business of "building a cellar". Wine-making techniques have changed greatly during the past quarter century, and most wines today are ready by the time they reach the market. True, the big wines of Bordeaux and Burgundy gain much with bottle age, but even these now reach their peak much sooner than they used to. And on the other hand there are many wines such as the good red Beaujolais and white Muscadet which are never better than when very young. The importance of great age has been much exaggerated, especially by the "baroque" school of English writers on wine.

Finally, choose your wine according to the company it is going to keep. Save that bottle of Corton Charlemagne or Cheval Blanc for a half dozen people who can appreciate what they are about to receive. When the time does come for serving some particularly fine wines, then the menu is planned accordingly to flatter the wine by making it stand out, by taking care not to overwhelm it. But if the food is the thing, then let the wine take its proper place discreetly, in the background. Which isn't to say that superior wines will be inappropriate, only that they should not be unduly conspicuous. They will still make their important, some would say essential, contribution to the meal.

Philip Wagner

A bride's cup or trick cup with two capacities. The upper cup swivels away when one attempts to drink from it. Silver gilt, made by Tobias Volkhamer in Munich about 1640.

MENUS

A Buffet Hors d'Oeuvre Dinner

COLD HORS D'OEUVRE

Smoked Beef Sticks
Jarlsberg and Port du Salut Cheese
Steak Tartare with
capers and anchovies
Gravlaks with Mustard Sauce*
Raw Vegetables with Avocado Dip:
Zucchini Sticks,
Young Asparagus Tips,
Jerusalem Artichokes
Crab Fingers with Mustard Mayonnaise
Cucumber Sticks Wrapped
in Prosciutto
Brown Bread and Crackers

HOT FOOD

French-fried eggplant
Hot crab, cocktail-size lump, mixed
with mayonnaise and mustard
Grilled tiny lamb chops

*See index for page numbers of starred recipes.

DESSERTS

Orange Soufflé*
Crème Brulée
Coffee

Mrs. Stanford Rothschild

A Summer Menu

Chlodnick Soup
(Buttermilk Soup with Shrimp
and Cucumber)
Crisp Crackers

Vitello Tonnato*
Cold Rice and Peas in a Border
of Boston Lettuce

Homemade Raspberry Ice Cream
Brownies

Wine: Soave

Mrs. Robert A. Milch

After-Theatre Supper Menu

*Oysters in Champagne Sauce**

Pâté
Green Salad

*Hot Baked Peaches or Apples,
heavily laced with liqueur*

Wine: Champagne

Carol Cutler
Author, Food Columnist

Summer Menu

Melon with Prosciutto

*Alice's Gumbo**
served over rice

French Bread

Green Salad with Lemon Dressing

Fresh Fruit with Ginger Sauce

Wine: Pouilly Fumé

Mrs. Edwin A. Daniels, Jr.

A Dinner Menu from Michael Field

Chicken Liver Pâté

Broiled Leg of Lamb

Potatoes Anna

Spinach Salad

*Lemon Soufflé with Custard Sauce**

Wine: Pommard

Michael Field *(by permission)*
Author, Lecturer, Walters Art Gallery

Supper for Fifty

Cocktails
Dry Roasted Mixed Nuts
(6 8-ounce jars)
Olives
(4 10-ounce jars)
Carrot Sticks
(2 dozen carrots)
Celery Sticks
(2 large bunches)

*Lasagne**
(2 pans 12 x 20 x 3 inches deep)
Baked Ham
(15-20 pounds)
Salad
(enough to fill an 18-inch bowl twice—
lettuce, 10; avocado, 5; artichoke hearts,
3 cans; tomatoes, 15)
Italian Bread
(5 loaves)

*Apple Crisp**
2 pans 12 x 18 x 2 inches deep, or
applesauce, homemade, 3 gallons)
Oatmeal Cookies
(6 dozen)

Coffee

Mrs. Herbert Davis

Buffet Dinner for 24

*Egg and Caviar Mousse**
*Tongue in Aspic**
Buttered Biscuits Filled with Sliced Ham
Seafood Newburg

*Biscuit Glacé**

Wine: White Beaujolais

Mrs. Robert D. Myers

Late-Evening Supper

Smoked Scotch Salmon
*Brioches Brouillées**
*Sliced Broccoli, cooked but crisp
and lightly buttered*

Pears with Raspberry Sauce
Madeleines

Wine: Meursault

Mrs. Lawrence Bachman

Buffet Supper

*Hot Veal in White Wine Sauce**
Boeuf en Gelée
Crab and Lobster Salad
Smithfield Ham

Mixed Green Salad

French Bread, Small Rolls, and Crackers
Brie Cheese

*Chocolate Mousse**

Wine: Pouilly Fuissé

Mrs. Sol Kann

A Summer Luncheon Buffet

Fettuccine with White Truffles

Cold Roast Pork
A boned, trimmed loin, cooked with
celery, carrots, onions, white wine,
garlic, rosemary, and mace
Cold Broccoli Vinaigrette

*Coeur à la Crème with
Plump Strawberries**

Wine: Soave, well chilled

Mrs. Alan Wurtzburger

Dinner Menu

Celeriac Remoulade

*Braised Fresh Tongue**
Fried Potato Cake   Baby Lima Beans

*Oranges in Syrup**

Coffee

Wine: Pommard

Helen McCully
Food Editor, House Beautiful
Lecturer, Walters Art Gallery

A dinner parade—fish, fowl and flummery! Colored wood engraving by Grandville (French, 1803-1847) from *Un Autre Monde*, Paris, 1844.

A French Dinner for Six

Gougère

Coquilles Saint-Jacques
Romaine Soufflé*
Beet and Cauliflower Salad

Crême Renversée
Wine: Montrachet

Philip S. Brown
Author, Lecturer, Walters Art Gallery

Dinner for Six

Hors d'Oeuvre Variés:
Shredded Carrots,
Celery Root Remoulade,
Leeks Vinaigrette

Chicken Breasts and Oysters*
Brussels Sprouts and Walnuts

Pear Tart

Wine: White Burgundy

Dr. and Mrs. William Garvey

Buffet for 24 People

*Hors d'Oeuvre
(to be served with drinks):
Pickled Antipasto
Assorted Cheese Tray:
Brie/Gorgonzola/Jarlsbergost
Crackers*

Escabêche*

Cold Aspen Soup*
*(to be served in mugs as a last drink
before approaching buffet table for
main course)*

*Buffet Table:
Baked Canadian Bacon*
Lobster Mousse*
Spinach Pie*
Crispy Biscuits**

*Dessert:
Quick Chocolate Grand Marnier*
Espresso*

Preparation: This entire menu may be prepared 24 to 48 hours before serving. The Spinach Pie and Biscuits are best served hot. Miss Rita St. Clair

Before or After the Theater Menu

*Chicken Liver Pâté with
a Bowl of Chilled Puréed Peas*

*Crab Bisque
French Bread*

Green Salad served with Brie

*Peaches or Pears in Wine
Espresso*

Wine: Montagny

Mrs. Israel Rosen

A Special Summer Sunday

*Broiled Deviled Lobsters with
Lemon Butter**

Beaten Biscuits with Sweet Butter

*Salad of
Watercress, Hearts of Palm,
Artichoke Hearts, Belgian Endive and
Bibb Lettuce
Rich Vinaigrette Dressing*

*Frozen Raspberry Mousse Parfaits with
Miniature Palmiers*

Wine: Corton-Charlemagne

Mrs. Irwin Nudelman

A French Menu from England

Truites Farcis au Beurre Noisette

Ballotine de Canard
Pommes Nouvelles
Celeri au Jus

*Vacherin Norma**

Wine: Pommard

Muriel Downes
Cordon Bleu, London
Lecturer, Walters Art Gallery

A Festive Luncheon

Claret Consommé

*Sweet and Sour Chicken Breasts**
with Rice
Zucchini Stuffed with Purée of
Green Peas

*Pulled Bread**

Ginger Cake Roll

Wine: Beaujolais

Malvina Kinard
Author, Lecturer, Walters Art Gallery

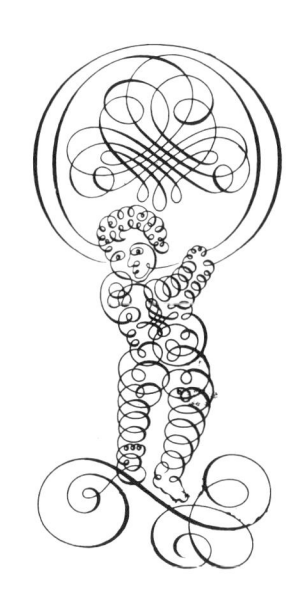

INDEX

A

Almond(s)
    burnt, mousse, 174
    chutney spread, 16
    glazed and salted, 15
    kuchen, 225
    roll, caramel, 210
    torte, 169
Anchovy bread, 55
Andaluçian soup, 46
Angels on horseback, 22
Antipasto, pickled, 15, 17
Appetizers
    almond(s)
        chutney spread, 16
        glazed and salted, 15
    antipasto, pickled, 15, 17
    artichoke
        first courses, 26
        hearts, in aspic, 27
    avocado(s)
        dip, guacamole, 16
        with vermouth, 27
    beans, green, dilled, 16
    broccoli, with green mayonnaise, 27
    Brussels sprouts, 16
    canapé rolls, hot, 20
    carrot
        pancakes, 28
        salad, 28
    cauliflower, with green mayonnaise, 27
    cheese
        balls, 17, 18
        bouchées, 18
    chick peas, Hummus, 20
    chicken
        bits, 17
        wings, little drums of, 16
    clam(s)
        and blini, 30
        dip, curried, 20
    crab
        dip, 18
        Lorenzo, 18
    eggplant, Caponata, 17
    gravlaks, pickled salmon, 25

Appetizers *(cont'd)*
    ham
        aspic, blender, 30
        and crab meat, 30
    Hawaiian delight, 34
    herring ring, 31
    knockwurst, in chafing dish, 20
    lettuce, pain de laitue, 32
    melon & shrimp, crème fraîche, 31
    mushroom(s)
        caviar, 21
        cheese-stuffed, 21
        piroshki, 24
        raw, filled, 21
        stuffed, 21
        under glass, 32
    olive(s)
        cheese puffs, 22
        marinated, 22
    open sandwich, prize, 32
    oysters, Angels on horseback, 22
    pâté
        chicken liver, 22
        of cod's roe, Taramasalata, 23
        English, 23
        in jelly, 23
    peach, filled with ham mousse, 31
    peanut butter, cocktail style, 24
    peperonata, 24
    piroshki, Russian, 24
    pizzas, ever-ready individual, 25
    potato-skin, hors d'oeuvre, 25
    sardine paste, 33
    scallops, broiled, 26
    Seviche in avocados, 27
    spinach and rice, 25
    tomato(es)
        with smoked salmon & cucumber, 34
        surprise, 34
    vegetables, marinated, 15, 17
Apple(s)
    baked, Post, 203
    cake, Pennsylvania, 203
    unbaked, dessert, 204
Apricot(s)
    bars, Scotch, 224
    beignets, Waschermadeln, 185

Apricot(s) *(cont'd)*
    chiffon pie, 195
    mousse, 176
    and orange sauce, 212
    salad dressing, 205
    sauce, for pheasant, 98
    with rum sauce, 204
    soufflé, 195
Artichoke(s)
    à la Constantinople, 136
    bottoms with asparagus tips, 135
    first courses, 26
    hearts, 135
        in aspic, 135
        sautéed, 135
Asparagus
    Syrian, 136
    tips, with artichoke bottoms, 135
    and tongue, in aspic, 67
Aspen soup, cold, 42
Aspic
    artichoke hearts in, 27
    eggs in, 127
    ham, blender, 30
    parslied ham in, Jambon persillé, 60
    tomato, 166
    tongue & asparagus in, 67
Avocado(s)
    dip, guacamole, 16
    Seviche in, 27
    with vermouth, 27

B

Bacon, Canadian, 66
Baklava, 187
Barcelona chicken breasts, 79
Barlovento duck, 95
Bass, rock, with lemon sauce, 100
Bavarian cream, strawberry, 181
Bean(s)
    baked, slow cooking, 154
    delicious, 154
    green
        casserole, 142
        in cream, 143
        dilled, 16
        piquant, 142
    lentil casserole, 162
    lima, casserole, 143

Bean(s) *(cont'd)*
    lima, lima, 143
    soup, New Jersey, 37
    white, salad, 165
Beef
    brisket, with chestnuts & prunes, 53
    hamburger(s)
        edible, 49
        pizzas, individual, 25
        Stroganoff, 50
    kebabs, 50
    kidney stew, 70
    meat balls, Russian, 48
    loaves, individual, 49
    roast
        rare, 53
        Spanish, 54
        vinaigrette, 48
    steak(s)
        baked, 52
        deviled, 52
        fillet Louis XV, 55
        fillet, with mushrooms & truffle sauce, 56
        fillet, niçoise, 54
        flank, marinated, 52
        sirloin, marinated, 51
        tartare, 48
        tournedos, Maria Pia, 55
        tournedos Rossini, 55
    stew, Greek, Stifado, 50
    tenderloin, roast Charentais, 53
    tongue
        and asparagus, in aspic, 67
        braised, 66
        piquant, 66
Beets
    with cheese, 137
    in orange sauce, 137
Beignets, apricot, Waschermadeln, 185
Bermuda salad, 166
Bessarabian nightmare, 151
Beurre blanc cottage sauce, 116
Biscuits, crispy, 222
Biscuit glacé, 179
Black bottom cupcakes, 191
Blini, and clams, 30
Blueberry
    pudding, 204
    tart, 204
Bluefish
    in gin, 99

Bluefish *(cont'd)*
    with sour cream topping, 99
Boodle's orange fool, 208
Borscht, 37
Bouillabaisse, New England, 35
Bourbon balls, 225
Brandied chocolate cups, 202
Brandy Alexander pie, 196
Brandy sauce, 194, 212
Bread and butter pudding, 201
Breads
    anchovy, 55
    biscuits, crispy, 222
    butter horns, 219
    cardamon seed, 214
    cheese loaf, 219
    corn cakes, crisp, 221
    corn pancakes, 215
    couronne of whole Brie, 215
    date nut loaf, 219
    Easter loaves, braided, 223
    grapenut muffin, 218
    health bread, super duper, 214
    Indian puffs, 222
    Kulich, 223
    nut, 216
    oatmeal, 217
    old-time, 217
    popovers, cold oven, 220
    pulled, 220
    rye, sour dough, 218
    rye, Swedish, 216
    Sally Lunn, quick, 222
    spider cake, corn bread, 221
    spoon, southern puffy, 221
    toffee, dessert, 199
    white, old-fashioned, 213
Brioche, filled with scrambled eggs, 129
Brisket, with chestnuts & prunes, 53
Broccoli
    with green mayonnaise, 27
    soup, cream of, 36
    spirited, 136
    whipped, 136
Brown flour soup, 37
Brownies
    blond, 226
    butterscotch, 224
Brussels sprouts
    hors d'oeuvre, 16
    in onion cream, 137

Budapest babka, 185

C

Cabbage
    cole slaw, with beans, 164
    with noodles, Holishes, 138
    red, Danish, 137
Cake(s)
    apple, Pennsylvania, 203
    caramel almond roll, 210
    carrot nut, 190
    Cassata Siciliana, 190
    chocolate roll, 212
    coconut, fresh, 190
    cup, black bottom, 191
    fruit, white, 191
    gingerbread, old-fashioned, 228
    marron butter cream roll, 211
    orange, 189
    shortcake
        cranberry, 205
        strawberry, 210
    sunshine, 191
    winter, 207
    see also Torte
Canadian bacon, 66
Canapé rolls, hot, 20
Candied violets & rose petals, 200
Cannelloni, Sardi's Restaurant, 161
Cantaloupe soup, chilled, 38
Caponata, 17
Caramel almond roll, 210
Cardamon seed bread, 214
Carrot(s)
    brandied, 138
    glazed, 138
    nut cake, 190
    pancakes, 28
    and potato casserole, 138
    salad, 28
    soufflé, 139
    tart, 139
    Vichyssoise soup, 39
Cassata Siciliana, 190
Casseroles
    bean, green, 142
    bean, lima, 143
    Bessarabian nightmare, 151
    cheese, 130

Casseroles *(cont'd)*
    chicken, 89
        and eggplant, 88
        and wild rice, 89
    crab, 112
    eggplant, 141
    eggs, scrambled, 129
    lentil, 162
    mock ravioli, 160
    mushroom, 145
    oyster, 126
    paysanne, 60
    pork chops & apple, 61
    potato & carrot, 138
    scallop & mushroom, 123
    shrimp & wild rice, 108
    veal, 73
Cauliflower
    and broccoli salad, 164
    with green mayonnaise, 27
Celery root, mashed, 139
Charlotte
    orange, 181
    chocolate rum, 180
    Russe, 180
Cheese
    balls, 17, 18
    bouchées, 18
    casserole, 130
    coeur à la crème, 199
    couronne of whole Brie, 215
    crêpes, 160
    loaf, bread, 219
    olive, puffs, 22
    pot cheese dessert, Russian paskha, 188
    soufflés, 131
Cheesecake, frozen, 176
Cherries, pickled sour, 57
Cherry dance sauce, 212
Chestnut dessert, Kastanien reis, 188
Chick peas, Hummus, 20
Chicken
    Andaluçian soup, 46
    baked marinated, 85
    bits for cocktails, 17
    with cabbage, 84
    casserole, 89
    with Champagne sauce, 86
    coq au vin, 88
    and crab meat rosemary, 91
    with creamed oysters, 91

Chicken *(cont'd)*
    in cucumber sauce, 87
    curry, buffet, 59
    with curry dumplings, 91
    and eggplant casserole, 88
    honey baked, 85
    Inigo Jones, 85
    livers, *see* Liver(s), chicken
    "Muddles Green" green, 84
    with mustard & pernod sauce, 84
    oven-baked, 90
    paella, 119
    picnic, 90
    poached with vegetables, 87
    and sweetbread salad, 89
    Tajin, with prunes & almonds, 87
    Tandoori, American Embassy, 92
    tarragon, 86, 90
    with tomatoes in cream, 92
    and wild rice casserole, 89
    wings, little drums, 16
Chicken breasts
    all'Alba, 79
    amadine, 80
    Barcelona, 79
    Ceci, 83
    curried, chafing dish, 82
    fool's, 81
    Kiev, 82
    melting, 83
    and oysters, 80
    sherried, 82
    sweet and sour, 80
    Szechwan, spicy, 81
Children's unbaked apple dessert, 204
Chinese chews, 227
Chocolate
    cups, brandied, 202
    macaroons, 229
    mousse, ice cream, 178
    orange torte, 170
    pudding, icebox, 179
    roll, with sherry whipped cream, 212
    rum Charlotte, 180
    soufflé, Grand Marnier sauce, 183
    torte, 169
Christmas butter crescents, 226
Chutney, almond, spread, 16
Clam(s)
    and blini, 30
    chowder, New Jersey, 38

Clam(s) *(cont'd)*
    dip, curried, 20
    soup, 39
Cocoa torte, 171
Coconut cake, fresh, 190
Coeur à la crème, 199
Coffee
    almond mousse, 177
    flummery, 178
    mousse, intrigue, 174
Cole slaw, with beans, 164
Cookies
    almond kuchen, 225
    apricot bars, Scotch, 224
    bourbon balls, 225
    brownies
        blond, 226
        butterscotch, 224
    butter crescents, Christmas, 226
    Chinese chews, 227
    cones, Scotch, 230
    date nut chews, 227
    dough, sweet, for pies & cheesecake, 228
    honey jumbles, 228
    lemon cheese squares, 228
    macaroons
        chocolate, 229
        cornflake, 227
    meringues, Stay up all night, 229
    molasses, 229
    oatmeal, 229, 230
    pecan strips, Serbian, 230
    rum balls, 225
    shortbread, Scotch, 231
    snucker doodles, 231
    sugar, 225, 230
    walnut wafers, 231
Coq au vin, 88
Coquilles Saint-Jacques, 122
Corn
    bread, spider cake, 221
    cakes, crisp, 221
    pancakes, 215
    pudding, 139
Cornflake
    macaroons, 227
    ring, 199
Cornish game hens
    stuffed, 95
    two little red hens, 95
Crab(s) and crab meat
    bayou, 113

Crab(s) and crab meat *(cont'd)*
    cakes, 114
    canapé rolls, 20
    casserole, 112
    dip, 18
    imperial, 112
    Lorenzo, 18
    meat
        with baked avocados, 114
        and creamed artichokes, 115
        and ham, rolled, 30
        in ramekins, 115
    salad, New Orleans, 113
    soft-shelled, Parmesan, 114
    soufflé, 115
    soup, 35
        Charleston, 36
        Creole, 36
Cranberry shortcake, 205
Crème caramel, 200
Crêpes
    cheese, 160
    crevette et champignon, 107
    ham and mushroom 134
    lobster Newburg, 116
Croquettes, mushroom, 144
Cucumber(s)
    in cream, 141
    marinated, 167
    soup, 39
Curry
    chicken, 59, 82
    dumplings, 91
    eight boy, 109
    lamb, buffet, 59
    shrimp, 59, 109
    soup, cream of, 37
Cupcakes, black bottom, 191
Custard
    crème caramel, 200
    onion, 146
    sauces, 182, 185, 194

D

Dacquaise, 3-layered meringe, 193
Date nut
    chews, 227
    loaf, 219
Doughnuts, rich, 227

Duck
   Barlovento, 95
   pepper, 95
Dumplings
   curry, 91
   sweet, Germknödel, 184

E

Eggplant, 141
   caponata, 17
   casserole, 141
   Ratatouille, 142
   soufflé, 141
Eggs
   in aspic, 127
   baked, supreme, 130
   bubbly, 130
   and caviar mousse, 128
   cold, frou-frou, 127
   frittata, tomato & bacon, 131
   hard-boiled, with green sauce, 128
   omelet, sweet
      emperor's, 187
      Salzburger nockerln, 187
   open sandwich, 129
   scrambled
      brioche filled with, 129
      casserole, 129
   and spinach galette, 133
   with Tapenade sauce, 128
   tarte aux oignons à l'Alsacienne, 132
   see also Quiches; Soufflés
Eight boy curry, 109
Emperor's omelet, sweet, 187
Escabèche, 122

F

Figs royale, 205
Fish
   baked, with salmon stuffing, 104
   bass, rock, with lemon sauce, 100
   bluefish
      in gin, 99
      with sour cream topping, 99
   bouillabaisse, New England, 35

Fish *(cont'd)*
   finnan haddie, 103
   flounder, poached, 105
   gravlaks, pickled salmon, 25
   herring ring, 31
   mousse, with cucumber mustard sauce, 104
   party dish, 120
   salmon mold, with dill sauce, 101
   shad, herbed, 102
   shad roe
      baked, 101
      Florentine, 102
      ring, 102
      in wine, 101
   shark fritters, 103
   sole
      fillet, with oysters, 105
      mousse, 105
   soup, zuppa di pesce, 47
   swordfish, soy, 103
   see also names of fish and other seafood
Flank steak, marinated, 52
Flounder, poached, 105
Fool's chicken breasts, 81
Foxcroft Mulligan stew, 77
Frankfurter polonaise, 68
French silk, 178
Frittata, tomato and bacon, 131
Frostings, *see* Icings
Fruit desserts
   blueberry
      tart, 204
      pudding, 204
   compote, winter, 206
   figs royale, 205
   fresh fruit, with rum sauce, 205
   orange(s)
      fool, Boodle's, 208
      mélange, 208
      in syrup, 208
   peach(es)
      crisp, candied, 207
      with sour cream & strawberries, 208
      stuffed, baked, 207
   pear(s)
      caramelized with marrons glacés, 209
      with chocolate, 210
      with orange, 209
   plums
      with apricots, 207
      and figs, 207
   raspberries frangipane, 181

Fruit desserts *(cont'd)*
    strawberry
        Bavarian cream, blender, 181
        shortcake, 210
        tarts, easy summer, 206
    see also individual names
Fruit salad, Kintail, 205
Fruitcake, white, 191

G

Galette, egg and spinach, 133
Garlic soup, 39
Gazpacho, 40
Germknödel, yeast dumplings, 184
Gingerbread, old-fashioned, 228
Gnocchi, with cheese, 160
Goose
    breasts of, wild, 96
    Joe's, 96
    soup, Canadian, 40
Gougère, with ham & sour cream, 160
Grand Marnier
    mold, frozen, 177
    sauce, 177, 183
    soufflé, cold, 177
Grapefruit
    crystallized, 199
    and meringue ice cream, 176
Grapenut muffin bread, 218
Grasshopper pie, 195
Gravlaks, pickled salmon, 25
Greek stew, Stifado, 50
Guacamole avocado dip, 16

H

Ham
    à la crème, 60
    aspic, blender, 30
    casserole, paysanne, 60
    and crab meat, 30
    in fruit sauce, 61
    and mushroom crêpes, 134
    parslied, in aspic, 60
    peach mousse, filled with, 31
Hamburger(s)
    edible, 49
    Stroganoff, 50

Hawaiian delight, 34
Health bread, Super duper, 214
Herring ring, 31
Holishes, 138
Hominy soufflé, 162
Honey jumbles, 228
Hummus, chick peas, 20
Hungarian pork chops, 64

I

Ice, lemon blender, 175
Icings
    mocha, 190
    orange cake, 189
Ice cream
    grapefruit & meringue, 176
    French vanilla, 176
    vanilla, with macaroons, 176
Indian puffs, 222

J

Jambon
    à la crème, 60
    persillé, 60
Jannson's temptation, 148
Joe's goose, 96

K

Kaiserschmarren, sweet omelet, 187
Kastanien reis, 188
Key lime pie, 196
Kidney(s)
    stew, 70
    veal, sautéed, 70
Knockwurst, in chafing dish, 20
Kulich, and braided Easter loaves, 223

L

Lamb
    chops, 59
    curry, buffet, 59
    glazed, mock duck, 56

Lamb *(cont'd)*
    leg
        butterfly, two ways, 57
        Western Run House, 56
    roast(s)
        with coffee, 57
        individual, 59
    shish kebab, 59
Lasagne, 163
Leeks, Shannon champ, 147
Lemon
    cheese, 200
    cheese squares, 228
    fluff pudding, 172
    ice, blender, 175
    sauce, 100
    sherbet, 175
    soufflé
        cold, 175
        with custard sauce, 182
    sour cream pie, 196
Lentil
    casserole, 162
    salad, 165
Lettuce
    pain de laitue, 32
    Romaine soufflé, 143
Limpa, Swedish rye bread, 216
Liver(s)
    Chicken
        Charleston, 94
        with Cognac, 93
        in cream, with mushrooms, 92
        English pâté, 23
        pâté, 22
        with sherry & cream, 93
    Goose
        English pâté, 23
        pâté in jelly, 23
Lobster(s)
    Bordelaise, 118
    Maine, deviled, 116
    mousse, 118
    Newburg, with crêpes, 116

M

Meringue desserts
    dacquaise, 193
    Vacherin Norma, 193

Mousse
    apricot, 176
    biscuit glacé, 179
    burnt almond, 174
    chocolate, French silk, 178
    chocolate ice cream, 178
    coffee almond, frozen, 177
    coffee flummery, 178
    coffee intrigue, 174
    egg and caviar, 128
    fish with cucumber mustard sauce, 104
    French silk, chocolate, 178
    Grand Marnier, frozen, 177
    lemon, 175
    lobster, 118
    maple, 179
    peach cream, 180
    shrimp, 111
    sole, 105
    U.S. mint, 178
"Muddles Green" green chicken, 84
Mushroom(s)
    casserole, 145
    caviar, 21
    cheese-stuffed, 21
    croquettes, 144
    piroshki, 24
    raw, filled, 21
    roll, 145
    and scallop casserole, 123
    stuffed, 21
    stuffed with spinach, 144
    under glass, 32
Mussels, 99

N

Noodles Parmesan, baked, 158
Nut
    bread, 216
    torte, 171

O

Oatmeal
    bread, 217
    cookies, 229, 230
Oeufs
    en gelée, 127

Oeufs *(cont'd)*
    froids frou-frou, 127
Olive(s)
    cheese puffs, 22
    marinated, 22
Omelet, sweet
    emperor's, 187
    Salzburg, 187
Onion(s)
    custard, 146
    puffs, 146
    soup, Chablis, 42
    stuffed, 145
    sweet and sour, 146
    tarte aux oignons à l'Alsacienne, 132
Open sandwich, 129
Open sandwich, prize, 32
Orange(s)
    cake, 189
    cake icing, 189
    Charlotte, 181
    fool, Boodle's, 208
    mélange, 208
    pudding, baked, 174
    soufflé, candied, 194
    in syrup, 208
Osso bucco, 77
    Milanese, 76
Oyster(s)
    angels on horseback, 22
    baked, Creole, 125
    bisque, 41
    casserole, 126
    in Champagne sauce, 124
    and chicken breasts, 80
    cotton patch, 125
    deviled, 124
    mock terrapin, 123
    pickled, 125
    poached, & cucumber cocktail, 125
    purée of, in soup, 42
    scalloped, 126
    stew, 41

P

Paella, 119
    Chinese, 119
Pain de laitue, lettuce, 32
Painter's salad, 146

Pancakes
    blini, 30
    carrot, 28
    corn, 215
    sour cream, 220
    topfenpalatschinken, 188
    see also Crêpes
Parsnips, Bakerpatch, 152
Paskha, 188
Pasta
    cannelloni, Sardi's Restaurant, 161
    fettucelli, with green sauce, 156
    gnocchi, with cheese, 160
    lasagne, 163
    mock ravioli, 159–60
    noodles Parmesan, baked, 158
    tabboula, 155
    see also Spaghetti
Pastry
    apricot beignets, 185
    Budapest babka, 185
    baklava, 187
    powidltascherl, 184
Pâté
    of cod's roe, Taramasalata, 22
    chicken liver, 22
    English, 23
    in jelly, 23
Pea(s)
    with celery & mushrooms, 146
    soup, cream of
        chilled, 43
        curried, 43
Peach(es)
    cream, 180
    crisp, candied, 207
    filled with ham mousse, 31
    with sour cream & strawberries, 208
    stuffed, baked, 207
Peanut butter, cocktail style, 24
Pears
    caramelized, with marrons glacés, 209
    with chocolate, 210
    with orange, 209
Pecan
    pie, 197
    strips, Serbian, 230
Peperonata, 24
Peppers, Italian stuffed, 147
Pheasant
    cold breast of, 96

Pheasant *(cont'd)*
    two game birds, 98
Pie
    apricot chiffon, 195
    Brandy Alexander, 196
    grasshopper, 195
    Key lime, 196
    lemon sour cream, 196
    mocha chiffon, 195
    pecan, rich, 197
    rhubarb, creamy, 198
    rose hip & raspberry, 197
    rum cream, 198
    sour cream & raisin, 197
    Thanksgiving chess, 198
    transparent, 198
Piroshki, Russian, 24
Pizza, individual, 25
Plums
    with apricot sauce, 207
    and figs, 207
Popovers, cold oven, 220
Pork
    chops
        and apple casserole, 61
        barbecued, 61
        butterfly, 64
        Creole, 64
        Hungarian, 64
        piquant, 65
        sweet and sour, 65
    tenderloin, suprêmes, 65
Potage printanier, 44
Potato(es)
    and carrot casserole, 138
    Jannson's temptation, 148
    Shannon champ, 147
    skin, hors d'oeuvre, 25
Poulet
    aux choux, 84
    sauce moutarde et pernod, 84
Powidltascherl, 184
Prize open sandwich, 32
Prune soufflé, 194
Puddings
    blueberry, 204
    bread and butter, 201
    chocolate ice box, 179
    corn, 139
    English trifle, 201
    lemon fluff, 172

Puddings *(cont'd)*
    mocha mystery, 202
    orange, baked, 174
    riz imperatrice, 202
    Woodford, 172

Q

Quiches
    aux endives, 132
    gougère, with ham & sour cream, 160
    maison, 132
    spinach pie, 133
    tarte aux oignons à l'Alsacienne, 132

R

Raspberry(ies)
    frangipane, 181
    and rose hip pie, 197
Ratatouille, 142
Ravioli, mock, 159–60
Relish, pickled sour cherries, 57
Rhubarb
    in cream, 210
    pie, creamy, 198
Rice
    with chicken livers, 159
    Mexican, 159
    Milanese, 158
    paella, 119
    pudding, Riz imperatrice, 202
    sour cream, 158
Romaine soufflé, 143
Rose hip & raspberry pie, 197
Rum
    balls, 225
    cream pie, 198
    sauce, 204, 212

S

Salad dressing
    apricot, for fruit, 205
    Irish, 165
    tart cream, 168
Salads
    bean, white, 165

Salads *(cont'd)*
    Bermuda, 166
    cauliflower & broccoli, 164
    chicken & sweetbread, 89
    cole slaw, with beans, 164
    crab, New Orleans, 113
    cucumbers, marinated, 167
    fruit, Kintail, 205
    lentil, 165
    sauerkraut, 167
    shrimp
        and artichoke, 111
        and grapefruit combination, 108
        with macaroni, 110
        and rice, 110, 111
    spinach mold, with tart cream dressing, 168
    tomato(es)
        aspic, 166
        marinated, 164
        and pepper, 166
Sally Lunn, quick, 222
Salmon
    mold, with dill sauce, 101
    pickled, Gravlaks, 25
Salzburger nockerln, 187
Sardine paste, 33
Sauce(s)
    apricot, for pheasant, 98
    apricot and orange, 212
    for baked fish, 104
    berry, 177
    beurre blanc cottage, 116
    brandy, 194, 212
    brown sugar, 172
    cherry dance, thick, 212
    for cold fish, 116
    cucumber mustard, 105
    custard, 185
        brandy, 194
        vanilla, 182
    dill, 101
    Grand Marnier, 183
        strawberry, 177
    green, 128
    lemon, 100
    mock ravioli, 159
    mushroom & truffle, 56
    mustard, 26
    rum, 204, 212
    spaghetti, *see* Spaghetti
    sunshine, 172

Sauce(s) *(cont'd)*
    tuna, 78
Sauerkraut
    with gin, 147
    salad, 167
Scallop(s)
    broiled, 26
    coquilles Saint-Jacques, 122
    and mushroom casserole, 123
Scaloppine al' Marsala, 74
Scotch cones, 230
Scotch shortbread, 231
Seafood
    bouillabaisse, New England, 35
    combination, 120
    escabêche, 122
    paella, Chinese, 119
    vol-au-vent, 123
    see also Fish; and individual names
Seviche in avocados, 27
Shad, herbed, 102
Shad roe
    baked, 101
    Florentine, 102
    ring, 102
    in wine, 101
Shannon champ, 147
Shark fritters, 103
Shellfish, *See individual names*
Sherbet, lemon, 175
Shish kebab, 59
Shrimp
    and artichoke bake, 110
    and artichoke salad, 111
    broiled with garlic butter, 106
    consommé, 45
    and cucumbers with mushrooms, 109
    crevette et champignon, 107
    and egg European, 106
    curry, 59, 109
    Elizabeth, 112
    and grapefruit combination, 108
    gumbo, Louisiana & variations, 108
    happily married, 108
    marinated, 107
    and melon with crème fraîche, 31
    Memphis jambalaya, 119
    mousse, 111
    and mushrooms, 107
    Polynesian, 106
    and rice salad, 110, 111

INDEX *251*

Shrimp *(cont'd)*
    salad with macaroni, 110
    soup, 44
    tequilla, 111
    and wild rice casserole, 108
Snucker doodles, 231
Sole
    fillet, with oysters, 105
    mousse, 105
Sopa con gambas, 44
Soufflé
    apricot, 195
    carrot, 139
    cheese
        impressive, 131
        using bread, 131
    chocolate, with Grand Marnier sauce, 183
    crab, 115
    eggplant, 141
    Grand Marnier, frozen, 177
    hominy, 162
    lemon
        cold, 175
        with custard sauce, 182
    orange, candied, 194
    prune, 194
    Romaine, 143
    spaghetti, 156
    tangerine, cold, 183
Soup
    Andaluçian, 46
    Aspen, cold, 42
    bean, New Jersey, 37
    borscht, 37
    bouillabaisse, New England, 35
    broccoli, cream of, 36
    brown flour, 37
    cantaloupe, chilled, 38
    carrot Vichyssoise, 39
    clam, 39
    clam chowder, New Jersey, 38
    crab, 35
        Charleston, 36
        Creole, 36
    cucumber, 39
    curry, cream of, 37
    fish, Zuppa di pesce, 47
    garlic, 39
    gazpacho, 40
    goose, Canadian, 40
    minestrone, blender, 40

Soup *(cont'd)*
    onion, Chablis, 42
    oyster
        bisque, 41
        purée, 42
        stew, 41
    pea, cream of
        chilled, 43
        curried, 43
    potage printanier, 44
    shrimp, 44
        consommé, 45
    spinach, 44
    squash, butternut, 45
    tomato dill, 45
    turkey, 46
Sour rye bread, 218
Sour cream
    pancakes, 220
    raisin pie, 197
Spaghetti
    alla Carbonara, 157
    with clam sauce, 157
    with meatless sauce, 157
    with Pesto Genovese, 158
    sauce
        Ascanni Italian, 155
        of three meats, 155
    soufflé, 156
    see also Pasta
Spanish roast beef, 54
Spider cake, corn bread, 221
Spinach
    chopped, savory, 149
    holiday ring, 149
    Italian, 147
    mold, with tart cream dressing, 168
    pie, 133
    and rice hors d'oeuvre, 25
    with rich cheese sauce, 149
    and ricotta balls, 148
    soup, 44
    stuffed in mushrooms, 144
    with sour cream topping, 148
Spoon bread, southern puffy, 221
Squash
    acorn, baked, 150
    butternut, soup, 45
    summer, with onions, 150
    winter, baked, 150
Stay up all night meringues, 229

Strawberry
    Bavarian cream, blender, 181
    Grand Marnier Sauce, 177
    shortcake, 210
Steak, *see beef*
Stew
    Foxcroft Mulligan, 76
    kidney, 70
    stifado, Greek, 50
Sweet and sour
    chicken breasts, 80
    onions, 146
    pork, 65
Sweetbreads
    Joseph, 69
    molded, 68
    and mushrooms, creamed, 68
    terrine, 69
Swordfish, soy, 103
Szechwan spicy chicken, 81

T

Tabboula, 155
Tajin of chicken with prunes & almonds, 87
Tandoori chicken, American Embassy, 92
Tangerine soufflé, 183
Taramasalata, pâté of cod's roe, 23
Tarragon chicken, 86, 90
Tart(s)
    blueberry, 204
    carrot, 139
    fruit, easy summer, 206
    onion, 132
Thanksgiving chess pie, 198
Thick cherry dance, sauce, 212
Toffee bread, 199
Tomato(es)
    aspic, 166
    Bessarabian nightmare, 151
    dill soup, 45
    fried and baked, 151
    marinated, 164
    and pepper salad, 166
    with smoked salmon & cucumber, 34
    stuffed, 150
    surprise, 34
Tongue
    and asparagus in aspic, 67
    braised, fresh, 66

Tongue *(cont'd)*
    piquant beef, 66
Topfenpalatschinken, 188
Torte
    almond, 169
    chocolate, 169
    chocolate orange, 170
    cocoa, 171
    mocha, 170
    nut, 171
    walnut, 171
Tournedos
    Maria Pia, 55
    Rossini, 55
Trifle, English, 201
Turkey
    breast, scallops of, 97
    soup, 46
Turnips
    Bakerpatch, 152
    and onions, 153
Two game birds, 98
Two little red hens, 95

U

U.S. mint mousse, 178

V

Vacherin Norma, 193
Veal
    with artichoke bottoms, 71
    birds, with rice, 74
    casserole, 73
    chops, with eggplant, 72
    kidneys, sautéed, 70
    knuckles, braised, 77
        Milanese, 76
    Oscar, 72
    provençal, 71
    scallops
        with cream, 72
        al' Marsala, scaloppine, 74
        with rice, 74
        Richelieu, 73
    in sour cream, 72
    stew, Foxcroft Mulligan, 76
    tenderloin Oscar, 72

Veal *(cont'd)*
    with tuna sauce, Vitello tonnato, 78
Vegetables
    antipasto, marinated, 17
    artichoke(s)
        à la Constantinople, 136
        bottoms, with asparagus tips, 135
        first courses, 26
        hearts, 135
        hearts in aspic, 27
        hearts, sautéed, 135
    asparagus, Syrian, 136
    bean(s)
        green, casserole, 142
        green, in cream, 143
        green, dilled, 16
        green, piquant, 142
        lima, casserole, 143
        lima, lima, 143
    beets
        with cheese, 137
        in orange sauce, 137
    broccoli
        soup, cream of, 36
        spirited, 136
        whipped, 136
    Brussels sprouts
        appetizer, 16
        in onion cream, 137
    cabbage
        and noodles, Holishes, 138
        red, Danish, 137
    carrot(s)
        brandied, 138
        glazed, 138
        and potato casserole, 138
        soufflé, 139
        tart, 139
    celery root, mashed, 139
    corn pudding, 139
    cucumbers in cream, 141
    eggplant, 141
        casserole, 141
        soufflé, 141
    leeks, Shannon champ, 147
    lettuce casserole, 32
    mushroom(s)
        casserole, 145
        croquettes, 144
        roll, 145
        and scallop casserole, 123

Vegetables *(cont'd)*
    mushroom(s)
        stuffed with spinach, 144
    onion(s)
        custard, 146
        puffs, 146
        stuffed, 145
        sweet and sour, 146
    painter's salad, 146
    parsnips, Bakerpatch, 152
    peas, with celery & mushrooms, 146
    peppers, Italian stuffed, 147
    potato(es)
        and carrot casserole, 138
        Jannson's temptation, 148
        Shannon champ, 147
    Ratatouille, 142
    Romaine soufflé, 143
    sauerkraut, with gin, 147
    spinach
        with cheese sauce, 149
        chopped, savory, 149
        holiday ring, 149
        Italian, 147
        and ricotta balls, 148
        with sour cream topping, 148
    squash
        acorn, baked, 150
        summer, with onions, 150
        winter, baked, 150
    tomato(es)
        Bessarabian nightmare, 151
        fried and baked, 151
        stuffed, 150
    turnips
        Bakerpatch, 152
        and onions, 153
    zucchini
        gondolas, stuffed, 152
        Italian, 151
        in sour cream, 151
        stuffed, 152
    see also individual names
Vichyssoise, carrot, 39
Violets and rose petals, candied, 200
Vitello tonnato, 78

W

Waffles, buttermilk, 220

Walnut
    torte, 171
    wafers, 231
Waschermadeln, 185
Western Run House leg of lamb, 56
Wild goose breasts, 96
Wine jelly, 200
Woodford pudding, 172

Z

Zucchini
    gondolas, stuffed, 152
    Italian, 151
    in sour cream, 151
    stuffed, 152
Zuppa di pesce, 47

Approximate Metric Equivalents for the Kitchen

Capacity

1 teaspoon	=	5 milliliters
1 tablespoon	=	15 milliliters
1 cup	=	240 milliliters (0.24 liter)

Weight

1 ounce	=	28 grams
16 ounces	=	454 grams
1 pound	=	0.45 kilograms

Temperature

Fahrenheit	Celsius (Centigrade)
275	135
325	163
350	177
400	204
450	232

To convert Fahrenheit to Celsius, subtract 32 from the Fahrenheit degrees and multiply by 5/9.

The sale of *Private Collections: A Culinary Treasure* is a fund-raising project of the Women's Committee for the benefit of The Walters Art Gallery.

To order additional books, write to:

Private Collections
Women's Committee
The Walters Art Gallery
Baltimore, Maryland 21201